Church in the Round

Other Books by Letty M. Russell

Household of Freedom: Authority in Feminist Theology

The Future of Partnership

Human Liberation in a Feminist Perspective—A Theology

Edited by Letty M. Russell

Dictionary of Feminist Theologies
(with J. Shannon Clarkson)

Inheriting Our Mothers' Gardens: Feminist Theology in Third World Perspective
(with Kwok Pui-lan, Ada María Isasi-Díaz, and Katie Geneva Cannon)

Feminist Interpretation of the Bible

Church in the Round

Feminist Interpretation of the Church

Letty M. Russell

Westminster/John Knox Press
Louisville, Kentucky

Unless otherwise marked, scripture quotations are from the New Revised Standard Version of the Bible, copyright © 1989 by the Division of Christian Education of the National Council of the Churches of Christ in the U.S. A., and are used by permission.

Scripture quotations marked NIV are from *The Holy Bible, New International Version.* Copyright © 1973, 1978, 1984 International Bible Society. Used by permission of Zondervan Bible Publishers.

The excerpts on pp. 17, 75, and 149 are from Chuck Lathrop, "In Search of a Roundtable," in *A Gentle Presence,* copyright © 1977 Chuck Lathrop. Reprinted by permission of The Crossroad Publishing Company.

The excerpts on pp. 58 and 235 are from Bernice Johnson Reagon, "Ella's Song," Songtalk Publishing Company. Reprinted by permission.

The excerpt on p. 71 is from Doris Ellzey Blesoff, "We Are Gathered," in *Everflowing Streams,* ed. Ruth C. Duck and Michael G. Bausch. Reprinted by permission of The Pilgrim Press.

The excerpt on p. 111 is from *Grave of God* by Robert Adolfs. Copyright © 1967 by Robert Adolfs. Reprinted by permission of HarperCollins Publishers.

The excerpt on p. 196 is from Carolyn McDade, "Trouble and Beauty," in *This Tough Spun Web: Songs of Global Struggle and Solidarity, Songs of Carolyn McDade.* Reprinted by permission of Womancenter at Plainville, 76 Everett Skinner Road, Plainville, MA 02762.

Book design by Peggy Claire Calhoun

First edition

Published by Westminster/John Knox Press
Louisville, Kentucky

This book is printed on acid-free paper that meets the American National Standards Institute Z39.48 standard. ∞

PRINTED IN THE UNITED STATES OF AMERICA

9 8 7 6 5

Library of Congress Cataloging-in-Publication Data

Russell, Letty M.
  Church in the round : feminist interpretation of the church /
Letty M. Russell. — 1st ed.
      p.   cm.
  Includes bibliographical references and index.
  ISBN 0-664-25070-X (pbk. : recycled, alk. paper)

  1. Church.   2. Women in Christianity.   3. Feminist theology.
I. Title.
BV600.2.R867 1993   93-9306
262'.0082—dc20

The Presbyterian Church of the Ascension

Contents

Preface

I have always found it difficult to walk away from the church, but I have also found it difficult to walk with it. This sort of love/hate relationship with the church was established at an early age. I was baptized and raised in the Presbyterian Church of Westfield, New Jersey. From the time I was in kindergarten until I went to college I was expected to be at church school or church every Sunday. However, there were times when I found it rather unexciting. When I was in kindergarten, for instance, I ran away from church school and walked home to announce to my astonished and horrified mother that my class was boring! Some sixty years later I still find that attending church is often boring, but now I find it is also alienating. It is this alienation that I face as I begin a journey to seek out what church might mean from a feminist perspective.

The alienation is shared with many other women and men whose pain and anger at the contradictions and oppression of church life lead them to challenge the very idea of talking about a feminist interpretation of the church. It is also increased by knowledge of the disdain and anger of those theologians and church officials who consider women like me to be the problem rather than the church itself. It is impossible for me and for many other alienated women and men to walk away from the church, however, for it has been the bearer of the story of Jesus Christ and the good news of God's love. It seems rather that we have to sit back and ask ourselves about what is happening among us when two or three gather in Christ's name and begin to think through possible ways of being church that will affirm the full humanity of *all* women and men.

I have been engaged in such an action/reflection project for some time and in many places, and this book represents not an account of all of the communities of faith and struggle with whom I have shared this search but rather a reflection on the nature of the church in the light of the questions and insights of such groups. I have been particularly helped in this preparation by participating in the Faith and Order study on the Unity of the Church and the Renewal of Human Community of the World Council of Churches (WCC). In this study, which was initiated in 1982 at the Lima, Peru, meeting of the Faith and Order Commission, one of our tasks was to discover how our understanding of church shifts when we look at it through the eyes of oppressed communities struggling for justice.[1]

Since writing *Household of Freedom: Authority in Feminist Theology*, I have been reflecting on the question of what kind of church could in some way become a household of freedom.[2] What might a church that struggled to practice a sharing of authority in community look like? If this household of freedom is to be a sign of the eschatological household of God, it must have some concrete description that could help us to understand how it would function. I began by asking metaphorically about the furniture in a household of freedom.

A glance at the contents page will make it immediately clear that so far I have come up with only one type of furniture—tables! A lot of community takes place at table, and the Christian heritage already has a long tradition related to table community, table sharing, table talk, and the like. Whether the table is high or low, requiring chairs or only pillows or spread out on the ground itself, the place where the feast is spread is a key metaphor for God's hospitality. At this table there is no permanent seating, and whatever chairs of authority that exist are shared. Christ is the host and bids everyone to come.

This book is called *Church in the Round* because a metaphor is needed to speak about a vision of Christian community of faith and struggle that practices God's hospitality. A metaphor is an imaginative way of describing what is still unknown by using an example from present concrete reality. To speak of "church in the round" is to provide a metaphorical description of a church struggling to become a household of freedom, a community where walls have been broken down so that God's welcome to those who hunger and thirst for justice is made clear. This unknown reality is described in terms that we have all experienced: gathering in the round, with or without tables, and experiencing the welcome of others.

Church in the Round describes a community of faith and struggle working to anticipate God's New Creation by becoming partners with those who are at the margins of church and society. The metaphor in this book speaks of people gathered around the table and in the world in order to connect faith and life in action/reflection (the round table), work for justice in solidarity with those at the margins of society (the kitchen table), and to welcome everyone as partners in God's world house (the welcome table). The concrete reality out of which this metaphor was born for me was my experience of ministry for seventeen years in the East Harlem Protestant Parish in New York City. Thus I have dedicated this book to the Presbyterian Church of the Ascension, where I served as pastor from 1958 to 1968.

Church of the Ascension was the mother church for my ecclesiology. In that congregation I learned about gathering around table and world as a community of faith in Christ and the struggle for justice. It was there I caught my first glimpses of what it might mean to be a church in the round and worked in a shared team ministry to create "a piece of the round." My first book, *Christian Education in Mission,* was a description of what I learned together with the people in East Harlem.[3] This book also comes out of a process of mutual learning and dialogue with many persons and church communities. I am grateful to those communities of support and to those who shared in the dialogue and preparation of this book. I extend my special thanks to Barbara Blodgett and Shannon Clarkson for preparation of the indexes and to Cynthia Thompson and all the editorial staff of Westminster/John Knox Press. Conversations with Henna Han, Serene Jones, Joan Martin, Gladys Moore, and Mary Marple Thies also helped to shape my understanding of "church in the round."

There is an abundance of metaphors and images for the church, both in the scriptures and in Christian theology. Many of these metaphors have deep roots in Hebrew and Christian tradition. Four major clusters of images of the church in the New Testament have been identified by Paul Minear.[4] Some of these, such as "people of God" and "body of Christ," need to be reinterpreted in terms of the metaphor of church in the round. Others, such as sign of God's "New Creation" and "partnership in faith," are helpful in clarifying the already/not yet character of the new metaphor.[5] Though the metaphors of church in the round and its various kinds of tables also refer to the abundant use of table metaphors in the Bible, it is not intended to replace all the others but rather to focus their meaning in a way that makes it more accessible to feminist interpretation.

The need for a feminist interpretation of the church has been recognized by Christian feminists for some time. Whenever one's paradigm or perspective on reality shifts, everything has to be thought through from this new perspective. Using a prism of feminist advocacy of the full humanity of *all* women together with men leads to critique, reconstruction, and reinterpretation of all the Christian traditions.

Much work has been done in the areas of critique and reconstruction related to the church. Most important are *Women-Church* by Rosemary Radford Ruether and *Bread Not Stone* by Elisabeth Schüssler Fiorenza.[6] Most books on feminist theology include at least some sections on doctrines related to the church, with a particular focus of feminist contributions to ecclesiology on ordination of women and on inclusive language and liturgy. It would seem that no matter how alienated women have become with their particular church tradition and structure, there is a need to build on this work by asking how the doctrine of the church would look from a feminist perspective.

The church is a sign of the coming fulfillment of God's promise for New Creation. As a sign, it is always provisional and is in constant need of renewal in order to make an authentic witness to God's love and justice in changing historical, political, economic, and social contexts. Indeed, it sometimes is in need of revolution: of building a new house of freedom where people's hopes for human dignity are incorporated both in social structures and in expressions of faith and service. It is my contention, and that of many other alienated people who refuse to walk away from the church, that we live in such a time. One of the many serious liberation challenges to the churches being raised from different parts of the world is the challenge of the women's movement to the patriarchal interpretation of ecclesiology. Not only critique but alternative ways of reconstructing tradition and church structures are being proposed.

Just as continued work on feminist interpretation of the Bible is needed, so too is historical and constructive work on feminist interpretation of the church needed to express the meaning of feminist advocacy in terms of the nature and mission of the church.[7] Based on the experience of faith and struggle of women working with men to change the church, feminist interpretation of the church is a constructive formulation of some of the changes needed in *ecclesiology,* the theological interpretation of the meaning of church. Whether or not we can show the formulations to be in widespread use is not the issue here. The issue is whether we can use feminist theology to create an understanding of church that would make sense to those who share the perspective of women struggling for the full humanity of all women together with men. My goal is to talk about the church in such a way that those who read this book from a Christian feminist perspective can say, "Yes, I recognize this as the church for which I long, and for which I struggle."

In presenting this particular feminist interpretation of the church, I describe the church as a community of Christ, bought with a price, where everyone is welcome. It is a *community of Christ* because Christ's presence, through the power of the Spirit, constitutes people as a community gathered in Christ's name (Matt. 18:20; 1 Cor. 12:4–6). This community is *bought with a price* because the struggle of Jesus to overcome the structures of sin and death constitutes both the source of new life in the community and its own mandate to continue the same struggle for life on behalf of others (1 Cor. 6:20; Phil. 2:1–11). It is a community *where everyone is welcome* because it gathers around the table of God's hospitality. Its welcome table is a sign of the coming feast of God's mended creation, with the guest list derived from the announcements of the Jubilee year in ancient Israel (Luke 14:12–14).[8]

Part One describes the community of Christ using the metaphor of round table connection. Chapter 1, "Round Table Talk," presents a method of feminist ecclesiology, or interpretation of the church. The spiral methodology of action and reflection is connected to those who have been marginalized in church and society, as well as to biblical and church tradition. Chapter 2, "Leadership in the Round," discusses the nature of leadership needed to do feminist ecclesiology. Ordinarily such a chapter would be at the end of a book on the church, but here it stands as a sort of altar call for those who would like to become leaders in the struggle to re-create the church according to a feminist paradigm of authority in community.

Part Two shifts to the metaphor of kitchen table solidarity and the concrete ways a community, bought with a price, lives out that gift of grace in the solidarity it shares with those who suffer injustice and exclusion. Chapter 3, "Communities of Faith and Struggle," shares the stories of communities where solidarity with the oppressed is a daily reality of ministry. Not only feminist Christian communities but also basic Christian communities and communities of renewal are examined, in order to discern clues that are already emerging concerning feminist and liberation ecclesiology. Chapter 4, "Justice and the Church," begins to look at these clues by asking how solidarity with the oppressed changes the way we understand the marks of the church and its claim to be the mediator of God's salvation.

The final section, Part Three, uses the metaphor of welcome table partnership to discuss the shifts needed in ecclesiology if everyone is to be welcome at God's table, both now and at the final feast of God. Chapter 5, "Community of Hospitality," looks at the doctrine of election and the chosen people of God from the perspective of those who have been excluded from the church. It tries to clarify the way in which election has reinforced racism and other forms of oppression and seeks alternative ways of celebrating God's hospitality. Chapter 6, "Spirituality of Connection," explores ways of nurturing feminist and liberation ecclesiology for persons choosing to be connected to those at the margins of life, as well as to the sisters and brothers in their midst and to the life-giving gifts of tradition. In the context of communities of faith and struggle, feminist spirituality is the practice of bodily, social/political, and personal connectedness so that life comes together in a way that both transcends and includes the bits and pieces that make up our search for wholeness, freedom, and full human dignity.

Perhaps out of these few clues we will catch a vision of church in the round that will more truly speak about the vision of communities of faith and struggle around the world. In this way it may be that some of us will find it a little easier to walk *with* the church as it struggles to become a sign of the presence of God's household!

Part One
Round Table Connection

In his poem "In Search of a Roundtable," Chuck Lathrop has written:

> Concerning the why and how and what and who of ministry,
> one image keeps surfacing:
> A table that is round.[1]

"A table that is round" is a familiar piece of furniture used by people in many cultures and many places for family-style eating. My most recent memory of the round table is the many and various tables prepared for twenty of us when we attended a two-week China Dialogue as theologically trained women of Asia, the United States, and Sweden.[2] We traveled to visit women in China in six different cities. Everywhere we went we gathered at round tables, both for banquets of Peking duck and for daily fare of chicken with bean sprouts. According to C. S. Song, this symbol of Chinese culture and hospitality has even influenced Chinese paintings of Jesus and the disciples sharing a "last supper at round table."[3]

Not only in China but in many other nations, the round table has become a symbol of hospitality and a metaphor for gathering for sharing and dialogue. It speaks concretely of our experiences in coming together and connecting at home, at work, and at worship; it also points to the reality that often persons are excluded from the tables of life, both through denial of shared food and resources and through denial of shared naming and decision making for their community, nation, or world. At God's final eschatological banquet, all will be invited and able to feast together. Like the eucharist and like the church that gathers at Christ's table, the round table is a sign of the coming unity of humanity. It achieves its power as a metaphor only as the *already* of welcome, sharing, talk, and partnership opposes the *not yet* of our divided and dominated world.

The round table, like the other tables that furnish the church in the round, helps to remind us that the church that gathers at the eucharistic table as an expression of its commitment to Jesus Christ is also called to welcome all those whom Christ has welcomed. Like all the other images of church in the Bible, the image of table is "defined by Christology," by the story of Messiah, who came to welcome all those who were marginal, excluded from society and from the religious practices of Jesus' time.[4] Although Paul Minear classifies the table as a "minor" image, which appears infrequently in the New (Greek) Testament and does not reflect a broad spectrum of imagery like that of, for example, "body of Christ," I would say that the table is one of the most important metaphors for church in the Gospels, especially in Luke.[5] Minear includes no less than six images of table in the Greek Testament: loaf, cup, wine, feast, altar, table. They all present "various snapshots of the church as a world-wide company sitting at this one table."[6]

In 1 Corinthians 10:16–21 Paul speaks of partnership together and in Christ through the sharing of the cup and bread. At the Last Supper there is emphasis on betrayal at the table as well as on the promise of the future feast (Luke 22:21–30). The table itself recalls the altar of the Hebrew Testament, both as a symbol of covenant and of sacrifice. "There the Lord of the table constituted this community as a people bound together in his death."[7] The table is always one that is spread as a gift of God and hosted by Christ. When this is added to the abundant reference to feasting and to God's banquet in the Hebrew Testament, it would seem that table community is a major image of church that links the community of Christ to the breaking of bread as well as to sharing with the poor.

If the table is spread by God and hosted by Christ, it must be a table with many connections. The primary connection for people gathering around is the connection to Christ. The church is the community of faith in Jesus Christ. All ways of describing the church are indications of ways that God in Christ has shaped the lives of Christians through the power of the Spirit. Doctrine of the church in this sense is an interpretation of the experience of gathering in Christ's name and then the experience of life in Christ's service. Because Christ is present in the world, especially among those who are neglected, oppressed, and marginalized, the round table is also connected to the margins of both church and society, always welcoming the stranger to the feast or sharing the feast where the "others" gather. Christ's presence also connects us to one another as we share in a partnership of service.

The round table in itself emphasizes connection, for when we gather around we are connected, in an association or relationship with one another. Feminist ecclesiology is also about relationship. It continually asks questions about how things are connected to one another, to their context, and to justice for the oppressed. It asks critical questions about the relationship of the experience of those struggling for the full humanity of all women together with men, to the experience of those struggling for liberation and new life in biblical and church tradition.

And it asks how to make connections across dividing lines of religion, culture, race, class, gender, and sexual orientation so that church and world become connected as a circle of friends.[8]

In Part One: Round Table Connection, we will begin our search for the meaning of the church in the round by developing some of these connections that are so foundational to feminist interpretation of the church. Chapter 1, "Round Table Talk," will discuss how we reflect on our actions as a feminist community of Christ, with particular emphasis on ways of thinking theologically and connectedly about the church. Chapter 2, "Leadership in the Round," will focus on the connections we make with one another in the community of Christ. It will ask, How can we organize our church communities so that they more closely resemble church in the round, and so that "a table that is round" becomes an image for "the why and how and what and who of ministry"?

1 | *Round Table Talk*

T he Presbyterian Church of the Ascension in East Harlem is an old "brick Gothic" structure built with arches of stucco and brick in a style that is supposed to be similar to some Waldensian churches in Italy. Its many floors provide spaces for persons of all ages to gather so that it can serve as a center for many community activities. One year in the early 1970s we decided to create a sanctuary that in itself symbolized our connection to one another as a family that gathered across racial lines. The opportunity came for this move when we decided to refinish the floor and took up the pews in time for a special Pentecost celebration that would begin in the basement and then move in procession to the "upper room" as we waited for the Spirit. For this occasion we placed all the benches in a square, with a large space in the center around the table where we could crowd together for the breaking of bread.

That summer we decided to leave the benches "in the round" and enjoyed the chance to worship while sitting only a few feet from one another. Having eliminated both the back pews and the "high altar and pulpit," we created a huge round table by cutting the largest piece of plywood we could find and placing this circle on the old rectangular table base. When fall arrived, people remembered their old tradition and wanted to move back to the customary separation of chancel, pews, and people. But I didn't forget how wonderful it was to divide the word and bread in the midst of the people, and I managed to talk the elders into moving around the table again the next summer. By the time the second fall had arrived, the new tradition stuck and was considerably reinforced when no one wanted to help move the pews back! Thus was born a round table that symbolized our table talk and table sharing as we gathered in community.

This idea of table talk and sharing was part of the fabric of our lives together wherever we gathered in our community, and it linked us to the images of table gathering in the Greek Testament. Although communal meals are important to many of the writers, according to Paul Minear, the writer of Luke/Acts thought of "table fellowship as interpreted by the table talk" as constituting the gospel. For instance:

The supper shared by the Risen Lord and his "slow of heart" disciples at Emmaus was narrated in such a way as to suggest the potential power of every common meal: "Their eyes were opened and they recognized him; and he vanished out of their sight" (Luke 24:31).[1]

Pentecost reaches its climax in the breaking of bread and the sharing of the apostles' teaching and prayers (Acts 2:42). Round table talk is connected to those who need the sharing of "glad and generous hearts," as well as to the experience and the tradition out of which the community gathers as church in the round (Acts 2:46).

This discussion of round table talk begins with an examination of the "table principle" and asks how our action and reflection are connected to those at the margin. It explores the shifts that come in ecclesiology out of a rereading of tradition from the margin, and this leads to a discussion of feminist ecclesiology that is contextual but makes connections as part of a spiral methodology. A feminist exploration of what it means to "talk back" to tradition takes up the issue of how contextual theologies are connected to biblical and ecclesial tradition.

Connecting to the Margin

There is a lot of talk about connectional churches in Protestant circles, and especially in Methodist churches. Following the references of John Wesley to the Methodist classes, bands, and societies in eighteenth-century England as "the connexion," Methodists understand their life together as one of interdependence. Stressing the network of relationships among persons and groups in a whole denomination, *The Book of Discipline of the United Methodist Church* speaks of the "connectional principle" as the basic form of Methodist polity, in which there is "a sharing of resources and resource persons for mission and ministry—pastors and lay people in local settings and beyond local settings."[2] Another way of describing this principle is to use Jon Sobrino's term "ecclesial solidarity," defined as "the spirit of bearing one another's burdens, of giving and receiving, of mutual teaching and learning, among the various churches and the diverse strata of church structure."[3]

In feminist interpretation of the church, the connectional principle is also a crucial aspect of action and reflection in communities of faith and struggle. Here, however, the principle of connection is worked out in terms of the way in which faith, feminism, church, and world come together. How do we develop a feminist theory about the church that makes sense of women's reality and experiences of oppression and yet continues to affirm Jesus Christ as the source of life and connection in the Christian community?

Faith, feminism, and the church

Several years ago, when I was lecturing on feminist theologies in Japan, a woman stood up and asked me whether it is possible to be a Christian and a feminist. I was not surprised, for many women and men discuss this question in the United States as well as in Japan and around the world. Sometimes their conclusion is that it is not possible for the Christian faith, feminism, and the church to go together.

I, of course, took the opposite position at the lecture and responded that it *must* be possible because I myself am committed to Christ, and I am also committed to working in the church for the full human liberation of women together with men! I believe in the importance of treating women as full human beings because I understand that this is the message that was lived out in the life of Jesus Christ. I believe God desires the growth toward full humanity of all God's children, and this includes men, women, and children of all ages, races, and nationalities in all their very specific differences.

The reason that some think you must be Christian *or* feminist, pro-woman *or* pro-man, pro-nature *or* pro-human, pro–United States *or* pro–other nations is that they have come to believe in the myth of dualism. It is both possible and necessary to be an advocate of more than one thing at a time. The world is not made up of either/or's. If we stopped assuming that it was, we would discover a world full of both/and's and maybe/also's.

Whenever we can arrive at a simple answer by picking one side of a dualism, we can be fairly sure that we have missed the other wonderful and messy ways that things can be both/and. It is possible to be both a feminist and a faithful Christian. It is possible for the two to become one, and I want to explore this possibility by discussing, first, the meaning of feminism and faith and then the way faith and feminism become one in feminist theologies and feminist interpretation of the church.

Like other English words ending in "-ism," feminism is an advocacy word. Just as capitalism advocates a system of economics built around accumulation of capital or profit, and nationalism is advocacy of your nation, feminism is advocacy of women. It is not, therefore, *against* men, but only *for* the needs of women, needs that cannot be met without changes in the lives of both men *and* women. Feminism has many different forms and is expressed in many different ways, but from my point of view as a feminist theologian it represents a search for liberation from all forms of dehumanization on the part of those who advocate full human personhood for all of every race, class, sex, sexual orientation, ability, and age. This means that men can also be feminists if they are willing to advocate for women. Feminists are not necessarily biologically female and do not exhibit any particular gender-stereotyped form of behavior that we usually call "feminine."

The classic text that indicates the attitude of Jesus displaying what we would call feminist attitudes is the short piece written by Dorothy Sayers in 1947 called *Are Women Human?*

> Perhaps it is no wonder that the women were first at the Cradle and last at the Cross. They had never known a man like this Man—there never has been such another . . . ; nobody could possibly guess from the words and deeds of Jesus that there was anything "funny" about woman's nature.[4]

Most certainly, "feminism" is a modern word, an ideology in the sense of a set of ideas used to bring about social change, yet the concern to include those marginal persons who have been considered less than human is not new. Jesus' concern always was to make it clear that all persons are welcome in the reign or household of God. Persons on the margin are not to be excluded because they are poor, sick, or deficient in any way. In this sense, Jesus' inclusion of women as disciples, followers, and witnesses stands as a constant correction of the patriarchal biases of religious leaders in his time and in ours.

Those of us who "fall in faith" with this man and his story of God's welcome experience cognitive dissonance, a contradiction between ideas and actual experience, when we turn from reading the Gospels to looking at the way this message has been interpreted in the church through the ages. Nevertheless, many of us, including myself, continue to find that this is a life-giving story that points us to God's intention for New Creation, in our lives, in society, and in nature as well. And we find ourselves seeking out communities of faith and struggle that speak of life in the midst of all forms of death-dealing oppression.

What is the faith that compels our commitment to live out the story of the life, death, and resurrection of Jesus of Nazareth with our lives? Faith itself is a gift of God, and there is no way to know fully how God's Spirit is at work to turn us around or convert us. It is possible, however, to distinguish the various dimensions of faith described in the Bible. Classical Reformation theology recognized these dimensions as knowing, acting, and trusting (*notitia, assensus,* and *fiducia*).[5] *Faith as knowing* is taking notice of the actions of God in Jesus Christ: getting to know the story of the person in whom we believe, through study, worship, and sharing the story with others. *Faith as acting* is assent to active participation in this story: trying it out by joining others in actions of service and justice. The third dimension, *faith as trusting,* is confidence or complete trust in God's love in Jesus Christ. It is this coming to love and trust God through the work of the Spirit in community that makes the story and actions so important to us in our lives. Together, these dimensions form the happening of faith which is the gift of God.

Our life of faith has many twists and turns. We may have faith as trust and confidence in the promise of God's love in Jesus Christ at one time, yet at another we may find that only action on behalf of those most marginal to society can express our willingness to trust in God. At still another period of our life we may find that only learning all about the story itself satisfies our desire to be close to the life that inspires our own.

We who are feminists also include these dimensions of faith in our Christian commitment. Although there is great stress on authenticity that comes with action on behalf of those who are marginal to church and society, neither the dimension of informed belief nor the trust that God loves us can be ignored. Informed belief is what has led women scholars to assist us to hear more of the story, especially women like Miriam, Hagar, and Sarah, whose stories that have been suppressed or interpreted from a patriarchal perspective. Nor is trust in God such an easy matter, for we need to clarify how we understand God beyond the traditional imperial and paternalistic roles. In the struggle to understand and interpret the meaning of our faith and our feminism, many of us discover that the two become one.

Table principle

Our ways of making connections between faith and feminism may have many names, and most certainly they look very different to women of different cultures, languages, races, and religious backgrounds. But our presuppositions are usually generated out of a critical look at what it might mean to be feminists engaged together in table talk as theological action and reflection. Along with liberation theologians in many parts of the world, feminist theologians of all colors have been asking themselves about the critical principle of this talk. What makes their theologies distinctive? What contribution do they make to the beautiful rainbow spectrum of responses to God's presence in our lives?

The idea of a critical principle as a focus in contextual theologies seems to have come from its use by theologians in Asia seeking to develop an authentic, living theology in the Asian context. For instance, Emerito Nacpil wrote an article in 1976 entitled "The Critical Asian Principle," outlining a method of theological contextualization.[6] By 1990, Asian women had also joined in the discussion of an Asian principle of interpretation as they gathered at a meeting of the Ecumenical Association of Third World Theologians (EATWOT) on Asian Feminist Theology, in Madras, India. From the perspective of theology of struggle in the Philippines, the Filipino women at the meeting reported that the principle of interpretation included promoting the authentic personhood of women, fostering inclusive communities based on just relationships, contributing to national autonomy, and developing respect and care for human beings and the rest of creation.[7] Because feminist theologies are advocacy theologies, what makes them distinctive is articulation of the experience of women struggling for full liberation in community. The presupposition is that the experience of communities of struggle against patriarchy and injustice are the prism for understanding and reinterpreting scripture and tradition, as well as the test of whether a particular methodology makes sense or is "seriously imaginable."

This feminist critical principle of interpretation needs to be applied to interpretation of the church as well as of scripture. *The critical principle of feminist ecclesiology is a table principle.* It looks for ways that God reaches out to include all those whom society and religion have declared outsiders and invites them to gather round God's table of hospitality. The measure of the adequacy of the life of a church is how it is connected to those on the margin, whether those the NRSV calls "the least of these who are members of my family" are receiving the attention to their needs for justice and hope (Matt. 25:40).[8]

The authority for the table principle is the gospel understanding of the household or commonwealth of God. Jesus' preaching is constantly directed toward the invitation of those who are the rejected ones of society, those on the margin, to share the feast of God's new household (Luke 19:1–10). Jesus' message is that all persons are created by God and are welcome in God's household. As Luise Schottroff points out in her informative article, "Women as Followers of Jesus,"

> Above all in the healing miracles we can see that in the *familia dei* sick beggars become healthy people. We should not understand this as a metaphysical miracle to prove Jesus' divine qualities, but rather as a consequence, which we too can imagine, of the solidarity and love which was practiced in this movement of the poor.[9]

Faithfulness to Christ calls us to be constantly open to those who are marginal in our own church communities and in the wider community and to ask critical questions of faith and practice from the perspective of the margin. This perspective was emphasized by Dietrich Bonhoeffer in his well-known statement in *Letters and Papers from Prison*:

> There remains an experience of incomparable value. We have for once learnt to see the great events of world history from below, from the perspective of the outcast, the suspects, the maltreated, the powerless, the oppressed, the reviled—in short, from the perspective of those who suffer.[10]

This theme of the "view from below" has been important to Latin American theologians such as Gustavo Gutiérrez, who develops the theme in *The Power of the Poor in History* as "theology from the underside of history." In his interpretation, modern male Eurocentric theology has been concerned with addressing the questions of the nonbeliever: "The bourgeois unbeliever, atheist, and skeptic have become the principal interpreters of modern history."[11] But the view from below presses liberation theology to take up the questions of the nonperson: "Our question is how to tell the nonperson, the nonhuman, that God is love, and that this love makes us all brothers and sisters."[12]

Feminist theologians join this liberation tradition in moving from the questions of those at the center of society to those considered less than human because they are powerless and unimportant. The imagery of margin is to be preferred, however, over that of above and below because one of the ways persons are marginalized is by hierarchical thinking. In societies and churches where they have been considered of no importance, women not only speak out for themselves and all those on the margin but also move from margin to center so that their voices may be heard. Thus, in her book *Feminist Theory: From Margin to Center*, bell hooks argues that the marginality of black women gives them a critical perspective from which to "criticize the dominant racist, classist, sexist hegemony as well as to envision and create a counter-hegemony."[13]

From the point of view of those who are marginalized, it is an important form of empowerment to choose the margin as a place to stand and work or to move to the center in order to gain the ability to talk back.[14] On the other hand, those who find themselves at the center of power and influence in any organization need to choose the margin as a way of standing in solidarity with those who are oppressed and working for justice. In *Talking Back*, her book on thinking feminist and thinking black, bell hooks calls for placing the struggles and insights of women of color at the center of feminist theory. She is reminding white, educated, middle-class women like myself that our connection to the margin comes as we move from center to margin.

> My placement of black women at the center was not an action to exclude others but rather an invitation, a challenge to those who would hear us speak, to shift paradigms rather than appropriate, to have all readers listen to the voice of a black woman speaking as a subject and not as underprivileged other.[15]

It would be possible to say that in Christ there is neither margin nor center, but this inclusiveness then needs to be put into practice in the churches. In the same way, Paul preached that in Christ neither circumcision nor uncircumcision was a requirement for salvation. "For in Christ Jesus neither circumcision nor uncircumcision counts for anything; the only thing that counts is faith working through love" (Gal. 5:6; see also Acts 10:34–48). Paul advocated the inclusion of the Greeks with the Jews in the churches without any requirement of circumcision. As with other forms of distinction and difference that carry a valuation of superiority and inferiority, power and powerlessness, we are called to act out and make our commitment to inclusion of the marginalized as a sign of God's intention for humanity.

The movement from center to margin and margin to center is a constant motion in both directions as we ask why anyone ought to be on the margin. The margin of churches is constantly changing as persons are made welcome at the center and, in turn, welcome others; as members struggle to remain on the margin with oppressed persons whether or not they have any interest at all in the church.[16] The ultimate goal of God's household is to do away with the margin and the center by joining the one who is at the center of life in the church but dwells on the margin where he lived and died.

Rereading from the margin

One way to move ourselves to the margin or to claim the margin as a base of insight into the meaning of faith and struggle is to reread scripture and tradition from the margin. A good example of this is found in the work of Delores Williams, Elsa Tamez, and Phyllis Trible on the stories of Hagar and Sarah. Each time the story is reread from the perspective of the margin, new insights for the entire faith community are discovered. For instance, the work of Phyllis Trible in *Texts of Terror* has underlined the difference of perspective that comes when the focus is on Sarah rather than Abraham, especially in regard to the failed partnership between Sarah and Hagar, while Elsa Tamez emphasizes the importance of God's promise of blessing to Hagar, and not only to the patriarchs, in "The Woman Who Complicated the History of Salvation."[17] Delores Williams will soon publish a revision of her doctoral thesis on "The Analogous Relation Between Hagar's Experience and African-American Women's Experience," in which she lifts up the wilderness tradition of Hagar as a paradigm for womanist theology, especially emphasizing the importance of Hagar's story as a paradigm of survival and quality of life amid oppression.[18]

According to Delores Williams, womanist theology makes use of Alice Walker's description of "womanist," as a black feminist whose origins are in black folk culture, as a means of characterizing theology that rereads the Christian faith from the margin. Walker derives womanist from the word "womanish," used by mothers to tell daughters that they are "wanting to know more and in greater depth than is good for one . . . outrageous, audacious, courageous and willful behavior." A womanist is "responsible, in charge, serious." Walker includes in her description a fourth definition: "Womanist is to feminist as purple to lavender."[19]

Although white women and women of color share in the oppression of patriarchal structures, the double or triple layer of oppression experienced by women of color who are often also poor means that their experience is as different from that of white feminists as "purple to lavender" or as Hagar to Sarah. Therefore, rereading from the margin requires critical analysis of the nature of marginality and of the power relationships involved in their story as well as in our stories as women and men of different colors, classes, cultures, and sexual orientations. The method for engaging in this analysis and rereading from the margin is that of a spiral of action and reflection.

Before moving on to look at the method of round table talk, let us look at a rereading of the story of Hagar and Sarah in Genesis 16:1–16 and 21:9–21 from the margin, so that we can be more clear about their difference and connection in the story.[20]

From the perspective of the oppressed and marginal, this story is truly what Phyllis Trible calls a "text of terror." In chapter 16, Sarah tries to overcome her barrenness and failure to produce male progeny for the patriarchal family by giving her slave, Hagar, as a wife to Abraham. Hagar, oppressed by her nationality, class, and sex, awakens to the possibility of new status as a mother but is treated so harshly by Sarah that she flees toward her original homeland, Egypt, until God sends her back into slavery after appearing to her in an annunciation of Ishmael's birth. The two women are caught in a downward spiral of patriarchal oppression. On the pedestal or in slavery they are linked by the process of male succession, yet they are not able to see this or resist the barriers it places between them. Sarah, depressed, suppressed, and repressed, takes out her terror on her slave. Hagar, in her own desperate bid for survival, flees to the wilderness only to meet a God who promises to care for her family but sends her back into slavery.

From the perspective of the oppressed and marginal, this is also a story of survival. In chapter 16, Hagar is struggling to gain her own freedom and to survive in her exodus journey. Then in chapter 21 she is exiled in a wilderness that holds no water and no life for her or her fatherless child. While Abraham and God hold all the resources, the two women vie with each other for their own survival and that of their children. Sarah is also struggling for survival, first to overcome her barrenness and do her duty to produce progeny as part of God's promise to Abraham, and then to prevent the loss of her own status and means of support should Ishmael be the firstborn. As Delores Williams has pointed out, if anything happened to Abraham and Ishmael was firstborn, Sarah, always dependent on the males, would have been sent back to her parents' family or simply eliminated.[21]

Yet from the perspective of the oppressed and marginal, this story can also be one of promise. As we know, the story of Hagar and Sarah is part of the entire patriarchal story of promise of God's blessing to Abraham and to Israel. In the narrative, Sarah is part of that promise because God always intervenes to save her so that Isaac may be saved. But the story seems to reflect an idolatry of Isaac as Abraham's heir in that nothing is too great a sacrifice, if it is necessary for the story of the promise to Abraham to be fulfilled. According to Trible, the sacrifice of Isaac in Genesis 22 seems to indicate that Abraham is willing to offer his child and therefore to receive him back, but Sarah has no chance to relinquish her fierce attachment to the child or her oppression of Hagar and her child.[22] Hagar's story also contains a promise. She receives the first theophany in the Bible and is the only person to give God a name: "You are El-roi [God of seeing]" (Gen. 16:13).[23] God promises to multiply her descendants as well, so that the child of injustice and the child of promise are both blessed by God (Gen. 21:12–13). The patriarchal narrative understood this as a confirmation of Abraham's blessing, but we can also see it as an alternative exodus motif for those who are marginalized.

Rereading from the margin, we see what African American slaves saw long ago: Hagar is a model for survival and resistance in slavery. In spite of being oppressed by her mistress, she not only survives but cares for a family that lives and achieves quality of life. No wonder, as Delores Williams points out, Hagar and the wilderness experience became a model for freedom in the African American churches, during slavery and up to the present. Her life is a paradigm for womanist concerns as she shows herself "responsible, in charge, serious."[24] Her discovery of God in the wilderness experience continues to call to those in the African American tradition in their journey toward freedom as they celebrate their own wilderness conversion experiences by singing,

> Tell me, how did you feel when you come out de wilderness? . . .
> Well, my soul was so happy when I come out de wilderness . . .
> I'm a leaning on de Lord, Who died on Calvary.[25]

We will never know Sarah's final agonies for the narrator pronounces her dead right after the sacrifice story and is only interested in describing Abraham's purchase of land for the burial (Gen. 23). We do know, however, that rereading her story from the margin shows the toll of patriarchal oppression that connects the two women but also points to the class and national differences that drive them apart.

The Spiral Connection

Just this short rereading of Hagar and Sarah from the margin helps us to see the complex web of oppression that covers over the way in which we might see, write, or tell a particular story or doctrine of the community of faith. It is very important to recognize that what you see depends on where you are standing. To read the story by identifying with either of the two women in the light of critical analysis of patriarchal social structures yields a rereading from the margin of women's oppression, in contrast to joining the narrator in identifying with Abraham and the unquestioned acceptance of patriarchal reality and the rights of firstborn males. Identifying with Hagar in the light of a critical analysis of racism and classism leads to a devastating view of the actions of Sarah and Abraham and an affirmation of

Hagar's survival struggles. Identifying with Ishmael or Isaac leads to a radical questioning of the rights of parents and divine sanction for child abuse.

Feminist methodology

The complexity introduced by particular attention to the social contexts of original texts and of their interpreters, as well as to the contexts out of which persons interpret their faith, has led both feminist and liberation theologians to develop a spiral method of action and reflection that makes connections between context and tradition as a means of theological table talk. This method assumes that we each view our theology, our understanding of how God is at work in our lives, through a particular lens of language, thought, and action. Its purpose is to help us all make the connections that enable us to think and act our way into faithfulness in the midst of struggles of justice and human wholeness that are so much a part of a world full of persons longing to be free. It draws on our own social and ecclesial context and experience but subjects it to critical analysis and connects it to the tradition and to actions with others who are struggling for life.

The methodologies used in feminist theologies vary with the training, the task, and the religious and cultural tradition of the participants. Yet, in one way or another, these methods have to take into account the struggle to move beyond the competitive and hierarchical forms of patriarchal methods, which seek a truth that is made secure through the vanquishing of all other truths. Recognizing that a theology connected to the margin must include the experience of those women who are "the oppressed of the oppressed," feminist theologies work contextually out of communities of faith and struggle. They search for ways of working and learning together with women suffering from social structures of racism, classism, heterosexism, ageism, and other forms of exclusion and who often suffer multiple disadvantages in an oppressive world. Speaking at an EATWOT Conference on Irruption of the Third World, Mercy Amba Oduyoye highlighted the necessity of hearing the voices of Third World women.

> It sounded like a joke to some when Marianne Katoppo of Indonesia . . . called the attention of the session to the necessity to watch our language about God and before God. It was not intended as comic relief; it was the irruption within the irruption, trumpeting the existence of some other hurts, spotlighting women's marginalization from the theological enterprise and indeed from decision-making in the churches.[26]

Out of a starting point connected to those who are marginalized comes the theological spiral that Beverly Harrison has called a "liberation social ethics methodology" and Katie Cannon calls "emancipatory praxis."[27] This style of theologizing in a continuing spiral of engagement and reflection begins with *commitment* to the task of raising up signs of

God's new household with those who are struggling for justice and full humanity. It continues by *sharing experiences* of commitment and struggle in a concrete context of engagement. Third, the theological spiral leads to a *critical analysis* of the context of the experiences, seeking to understand the social and historical factors that affect the community of struggle. Out of this commitment to action in solidarity with the marginalized, and out of sharing of experiences and social analysis, arise *questions about biblical and church tradition* that help us gain new insight into the meaning of the gospel as good news for the oppressed and marginalized. This new understanding of tradition flows from and leads to *action, celebration, and further reflection* in the continuing theological spiral.[28]

You have seen something of this spiral, which connects biblical faith with participation in God's action for justice and wholeness, in the discussion of Hagar and Sarah in Genesis 16 and 21. Recently I had an opportunity to test out the use of this spiral connection at a conference on Global Women of Faith in Dialogue that was held at the Stony Point Center in New York.[29] In a session with Katie Cannon called Ourselves and Our Experience, I had the responsibility of teaching how we relate experience to theology, and of course I used the theological spiral. I had small groups discuss their own stories or one of the stories from the book *Inheriting Our Mothers' Gardens* in order to see how the stories of women raise questions for the Christian tradition. Just to make clear what the basic outlines of that tradition were, I asked everyone to connect their question or issue with one of the parts of the Apostles' Creed.

Several of the Asian women made connections between the apostolic faith and the life story of Chung Hyun Kyung, a Professor at Ewha University who gave one of the plenary addresses at the 1991 WCC Assembly in Canberra.[30] According to her story in the book *Inheriting Our Mothers' Gardens*, Dr. Chung was more than thirty years old when she discovered that she had a birth or surrogate mother as well as the mother who had raised her. The story tells of her two mothers who, like Hagar and Sarah, competed over her father and his children, as well as of their search for ways to overcome their deep sorrow and pain, or *han*.[31]

The women discussing Chung Hyun Kyung's story saw that a lot of work would need to be done to discuss the meaning of "I believe in God," to understand in what way God can be the God of Dr. Chung's mothers' combined search for life through Korean traditions of Christianity, Buddhism, and Shamanism. They suggested that we make God "too small" as our own private "Christian God" when we are not willing to recognize that God can work in and through the whole world and through all religions and ideologies. The Asian women theological students also connected Dr. Chung's story, and the animosity of the two mothers, to the question of sin. Here they asked whether sin was to be discovered in the actions of the two women, or of her father, who had two "wives," or of the patriarchal society that values male heirs above all else. Looking at these many dimensions of sin, they began to examine what it means to say, "I believe in the forgiveness of sin." One clue they discussed was that forgiveness includes repentance and change; until that happens, sinful patriarchal social structures must be opposed because they are death-dealing to women and to so many others. The creedal affirmation of resurrection, however, gave us hope that these structures will not have the last word, because the power of God's love has overcome sin and evil in the world. A lot more social analysis was needed, as well as research into biblical and church tradition, but at least the connection between faith and experience was made so the spiral of reflection and action could continue as part of their development of Asian feminist theology.

Rereading from the context

To pay attention to context is to make connections. The word "context" indicates the surroundings to which something is connected or related. This surrounding might be textual material, or circumstances that influence the formulation of a text or doctrine, or the contemporary circumstances that influence the angle of interpretation.[32] One way of describing context is to talk about connections. Things are viewed and interpreted differently according to how and to whom they are connected. The emphasis on context in liberation and feminist theologies stems from recognition of the bias in the tradition itself as well as in the view of the small group of largely white Western males who have interpreted that tradition out of their clerical and academic contexts.

Context provides a critical gaze for looking at the connections between ways things are read and the experience and social location of text and reader, but context does not stay isolated in the spiral methodology. Although the method tends to be inductive because it moves from experience to a theological interpretation of that experience, the content of feminist theology is still concerned with the way Christian tradition shapes life for women of faith and struggle. It no longer separates doctrinal interpretation from action or application. Rather, it asks about the social location and the actions of those asking the questions and searches for clues for continuing actions of faith and struggle. In this sense we can speak of "doing theology," or of "doing table talk," because the theology itself is a spiral that connects action and reflection in a continuing process of discovery.

One of the criticisms of contextual theology is that it no longer allows for universal principles that can be held in common by all the churches, and thus it impedes ecumenical work for doctrinal agreement and church unity. It is true that contextual theologies are suspicious of any theology which proposes abstract statements that can be expected to hold true in every circumstance. Experience has shown those who have had little voice in shaping the tradition that such universal statements reflect the understanding of reality experienced by those with the power and knowledge to name that reality. In Spanish *real* means "royal," and in English "real" stems from a word which meant "regal." In pointing this out in her book *The Politics of Reality*, Marilyn Frye says, "Reality is that which pertains to the one in power, is that over which he has power, is his domain, his estate, is proper to him."[33]

Feminist and liberation theologians are concerned, nevertheless, about ways in which to further dialogue, doctrinal agreement, and unity among the churches and within the world. They search for unity in ways that allow for diversity of social, cultural, political, and economic contexts out of which the faith of the church is articulated. Context is not understood as the opposite of universal. The focus on context is intended to bring together both the universal and the particular in a way that respects unity in diversity. As Michael Kinnamon has pointed out, there are limits to acceptable diversity in the modern ecumenical movement, but these have to do with absence of love and idolatrous allegiance, not with "racial, cultural, theological, liturgical diversity."[34]

Paying attention to context does not detract from either faith or action. Rather, it emphasizes the connection between the context in which a community stands (and its understanding and interpretation of shared tradition) and shared struggles for justice in all parts of the globe. It refuses to prioritize one particular ingredient in the theological spiral over the others. Instead, it asks about the way in which all aspects of doing theology are being honored in going around the spiral. In this manner the contextual perspective is asked to give an account of the ways tradition is interpreted and to share that account in dialogue with those who seek doctrinal convergence. Those seeking convergence are asked how those doctrines function in the contexts of those who have been the "outsiders" or "outsiders of the outsiders" in church and society.

This need for contextual as well as doctrinal approaches to the questions of church unity was recognized in the World Council of Churches' Faith and Order study of the unity of the church and the renewal of human community. This study included those who were developing methods of liberation and feminist theologies as well as more traditional theological methods.[35] In an unpublished paper for this study L. A. Hoedemaker has written that

> it is probably more productive to interpret the tension as implying a permanent mutual call to give account of the "contextual" substance of the tradition and of the "traditional" substance of the various contextual positions. In that way, the classical unity-discourse and the "historical struggle"-discourse should prevent each other from hypostasizing themselves as the central point of reference.[36]

Dealing with contexts and connections appears to create a web of confusion and disorder, but that very web provides a strong pattern that can address a multifaceted web of oppression. When the reality in which we live is so complex and so often painful, we need a means of table talk that can respond to that complexity and pain by going more deeply into our own situations before moving toward dialogue. According to J. Deotis Roberts, each theology has to work around the passion of its people in their own contexts. It has to work around the point of "visceral engagement" of the theology in order to gain insight or understanding into the affinity with the passion of others and enter into dialogue. In his view, the way forward in theology is to connect with the passion so that we finally connect with others.[37]

Going around the spiral

The reason that table talk is described as a spiral rather than a circle is that the movement of action and reflection does not simply go around the same circle. Rather, it moves to discover new clues and new questions in a continuing spiral that never comes out in exactly the same place. This is because our experience and contexts are always changing, and each time we see from a slightly different point of view or with a new set of questions. Each time, we look at our experience and context in solidarity with those on the margin; do critical analysis of the social, political, economic, historical, and ecclesial reality; raise questions for interpretation of scripture and tradition; and search for clues to action and continuing reflection. The order of doing table talk is not the same each time. It depends on the particular context of those doing the theology and the point of entry that is most helpful in that circumstance.

The continuing spiral is evident in the writing of this book as a whole because it is concerned to discover clues to thought and action about the church from a feminist perspective. Each time a new angle is examined it is necessary to ask ourselves how the feminist perspective shapes our understanding of scripture and tradition. For instance, the Introduction touched base with the four major movements of the spiral at least twice in an attempt to explain what the book was about and to raise questions about feminist interpretation of the church. A glance at the Introduction shows that I began with my own experience of alienation and marginality as a woman in the church and moved to a series of questions in response to this experience that require analysis and research. I then moved to a tentative description of the metaphor "church in the round" as "a community of faith and struggle working to anticipate God's New Creation by becoming partners with those who are at the margins of church and society." I had multiple questions and descriptions because I had been around the spiral many times and in many different contexts, so no one single entry point seemed to reflect enough of the ongoing table talk.

I then moved to my own actions in a marginal context as a clue to the emphasis in this book on the round table metaphor and on the connection of our table talk to solidarity in listening and acting with those at the margin. This metaphor was linked to the images of the church in the Greek Testament to indicate the point at which a connection to tradition could be made. The Introduction then begins to spiral around a second time as I move from questions about the image or metaphor to questions about the task of feminist interpretation, a brief analysis of others who have contributed to this enterprise, and an expression of its importance and hoped-for result.

The move around the spiral a second time then leads to a more general description of the meaning of church as "a community of Christ, bought with a price, where everyone is welcome." This points to the action that concerns this particular spiral, that of the projected work in the chapters of the book.

It is obvious that this introduction touches many things superficially and that the critical social analysis and research into tradition lie ahead. Yet going around the spiral helps to focus our thinking for the continuing process of action/reflection, in this book, in our lives, and in the church. It is hoped that, in the words of the Shaker hymn "Simple Gifts,"

> To turn, turn will be our delight
> Till by turning, turning we come round right.[38]

Talking Back to Tradition

We have already seen that table talk as both action and reflection is not disconnected from scripture and tradition. Rather, round table talk is designed to *talk back* to tradition. It is often "talking back" in the sense used by bell hooks, of claiming a voice at the center of the church as interpreter of what it means to followers of Christ in contemporary society. "It should be understood that the liberatory voice will necessarily confront, disturb, demand that listeners even alter ways of hearing and being."[39]

Table talk is also talking back in the sense that feminist interpreters are no longer willing to allow talk about God, about themselves, or about the church to continue in its patriarchal framework of understanding and interpretation. The patriarchal paradigm of reality places everything in a hierarchy of domination and subordination, accepting the marginalization of the powerless as a given. This paradigm is a manifestation of a social system that changes form but continues to define women as marginal to the male center, so that each woman is assigned her social, economic, racial, and political status according to the man to whom she "belongs."[40] This understanding can no longer go unchallenged by those who are willing to join Audre Lorde in her "transformation of silence into language and action."[41]

In a positive sense, talking back is a constant movement around the spiral, bringing scripture and tradition into connection with context, critical analysis, and action by those at the margins of church and society. This dialogue finds its conversation partners among communities of faith and struggle, who in turn become the prism for the feminist self-understanding of what it means to be church.

Feminist understanding of tradition

In an article entitled "Sexism as Ideology and Social System: Can Christianity Be Liberated from Patriarchy?" Rosemary Radford Ruether has asserted that "Christianity, for the first time in its history, is faced with a large-scale challenge to the patriarchal interpretation of religion and an increasingly coherent vision of an alternative way of constructing the tradition from its roots."[42]

This challenge is coming from both men and women, but it is the feminist theologians who are providing most of the research necessary for this ever-increasing volume of "back talk." There certainly is no lack of interest in biblical and church tradition, but there is a great deal of interest in "theology in a different voice." Thus Christian and Jewish feminists work with their own traditions but begin to reinterpret those traditions according to a critique of patriarchy and a constructive attempt to write theology out of a paradigm of community or shared partnership.

A recent example of this round table talk is found in *Weaving the Visions: New Patterns in Feminist Spirituality.* The editors represent two streams of feminist religious scholarship. Carol Christ is working with others in developing *thealogy* as the expression of creative thinking and writing about Goddesses, and Judith Plaskow is working with others to transform Jewish and Christian theology from within the communities of faith. Yet they both agree that the anthology presents theology in a different voice by reinterpreting "traditional theological categories of history, God, man, and world" in the light of very diverse experiences of women. "We began with an initial section called 'Our Heritage Is Our Power' (history), followed by 'Naming the Sacred' ('God'), 'Self in Relation' ('Man'), and 'Transforming the World' (world)."[43]

From within the discussion of Christian theology, tradition has a range of meanings, all of which need to be reinterpreted from a feminist perspective. Since the middle of the twentieth century there has been an ever-increasing rate of historical change in the world, and at the same time an increasing interest in understanding how tradition continues to connect the church to the sources of its faith and life and yet also allows it to change and evolve. Protestant, Roman Catholic, and Orthodox scholars have been attempting to clarify their own understanding of tradition and to come to some common understanding of tradition. Recognizing that both scripture and tradition are forms of the traditioning of the gospel of

Jesus Christ, they have begun to emphasize distinctions within the meaning of tradition rather than between scripture and tradition.[44]

In historical and theological investigations, distinctions are made between *Tradition (paradosis*, the "handing over" of Jesus Christ [Matt. 17:22; Rom. 8:31–32]) and *traditions* (particular confessional patterns of faithfulness). The 1963 Faith and Order study of the World Council of Churches on Tradition and Traditions summarizes an ecumenical consensus that distinguishes between tradition, traditions, and *the* Tradition (or Tradition). The Faith and Order study makes three distinctions in order to clarify the various aspects of tradition as a general category that includes both the process of transmission and the content of what is transmitted.[45] "*The* Tradition" refers to Christ as the content of the traditioning process by which God hands over Christ to coming generations and nations and the scriptural witness to God's action. The total traditioning process that operates in human history and society is called "tradition," and "traditions" is used for patterns of church life such as confessions, liturgies, and polities.

These three distinctions are helpful in making clear what we mean when we talk of connecting to the tradition. However, the Faith and Order categories are sometimes confusing because they do not sufficiently emphasize the importance of church tradition, especially for the Roman Catholic and Orthodox churches. Thus Yves Congar, in his book on *Tradition and Traditions,* includes additional categories of tradition interpreted by the teaching authority of the church through the ages.[46] The Faith and Order categories are also dissimilar in importance and use. To speak of Christ and God handing over Christ as the basic action of Tradition is not the same as speaking of tradition as a category of human existence. The former refers to the act and content of the tradition, and the latter refers to the human traditioning process by which persons and communities continue to create the future out of a "usable past."[47]

It would seem to me that it is important to work with at least four categories of tradition as both process and content by dividing the first category of the Faith and Order study in two. The first category recognizes that all the distinctions are seeking to make clear the ways the church continues to stay connected to "the Tradition" as the action of God's Mission in sending or handing over Jesus Christ to the world. A "new" second category, the "deposit of faith" in the witness of scripture and church doctrine, could be called "tradition" because this is one of the most frequent ways of referring to the Christian tradition. This category seems to be included in the first one in the Faith and Order distinctions. A third category would be the process of handing over that is part of the human way of shaping history and could be called "traditioning." By changing the Faith and Order category of "tradition" to a gerund, the continuing process would be emphasized. The fourth and final category would be the confessional patterns of church life, which could be called "traditions" because of the emphasis on their variety in the different confessional groups.

In this book I will be following this four-part usage, as I examine it from a feminist perspective. From this perspective, perhaps the most important category is traditioning: the still living and evolving past by which we create the future. For as we seek to reread from the margin and to reinterpret both biblical and church tradition, it is this recognition of the way our understanding of the meaning of God's action in the world changes that forms the rationale for the spiral connection. Tradition witnesses to the presence of God in Jesus Christ and in our lives, but its meaning changes as the context of the message and the messengers change. Although many feminists would question that the story of Christ has special privilege as a witness to God's intention to create a new household, I myself consider that the biblical witness to this action still makes sense of my existence and that the witness of the church continues to be what Rita Nakashima Brock has called a "transforming memory" of the future.[48]

To say that the witness of the church is important as a bearer of transforming memory is not to ignore the reality that it is also the bearer of the seeds of patriarchal domination and a supporter of the status quo in most areas of the world. Rather, it is to affirm the importance of the "communion of saints," both past and present in our lives, as we search out ways that traditioning can become a transforming and liberating process for women and other marginal peoples. The way in which feminist theologians have discussed the question of how the tradition functions in feminist theology has been by discussing the authority of all forms of tradition. Without rehearsing the entire discussion of this in *Feminist Interpretation of the Bible* and other related books by Elisabeth Fiorenza, Rosemary Ruether, myself, and many others, it is important to make clear the role that tradition plays in feminist interpretation of the church as I understand it.[49]

Authority, like all forms of power, is a description of relationship in which one party is able to accomplish certain ends in regard to another. Authority is a form of legitimated power. Persons give assent to a tradition, or to a person, institution, or law, because they consider that whatever is being asserted is a legitimate assertion or request. Thus, those who consider that God's Spirit is able to enliven scripture and church tradition, so that they speak of God's intention, also are likely to wrestle with whether to give assent to what these teach. For a person not believing in God, or not brought up in such a tradition, the teachings or request might have some interest but they would not have authority to evoke consent.

Christian tradition has authority in the lives of those who trust in God's love in Jesus Christ because the first category, *the Tradition*, of God handing over Jesus Christ is understood as assisting in the knowledge of that love and what it means in the life of the Christian community. The fourth category also is important to the way authority functions as a bond of relationship that gives persons a sense of security, identity, and direction in their lives; human beings are constantly *traditioning* a body of past knowledge that makes it possible to act with confidence in making their way into the future. In order to make these choices more simple they develop habits of action and thinking, or the third category—*traditions*—that keep them in touch with their cultural and religious commitments.

A particular community of people have a shared way of understanding and interpreting reality, and within that particular community there is a common paradigm or interpretive framework for what constitutes legitimate authority.[50] The second category, of scriptural and church *tradition*, functions authoritatively in faith communities whose model or paradigm for understanding God's presence includes the claim that God is to be known through them, but different communities stress one aspect of this tradition more than others. There are many ways of construing the meaning of God's presence, as the existence of Roman Catholic sacramental theology, Reformed theology of the word, Quaker theology of the Spirit, and many more theological frameworks will attest. Nevertheless, according to David Kelsey in *The Uses of Scripture in Recent Theology*, the construction of a Christian theological framework or paradigm has three limits if it is to be recognized as in touch with Christian tradition. It must be a reasoned and intelligible form of discourse, it must make use of the structure of Christian tradition and biblical interpretation, and it must speak of what is "seriously imaginable" in a particular time and place.[51]

Community of faith and struggle

Each community of faith has its own paradigm of what constitutes authoritative tradition for that community, but insofar as that community is in touch with the wider Christian community, it has formed its theological understanding about scripture, tradition, reason, and experience of the community. Feminist theologies are also formed out of communities of faith and vary in their understanding of what constitutes authoritative tradition. Many find not only that Christian tradition does not have authority for them but also that worship of the Goddess or another form of spirituality is more liberating and freeing for them as women.[52] Many others, however, struggle to make the connections with the various forms of tradition, while at the same time asking what would be not only seriously imaginable but also life-affirming for them as women of faith.

For those who are Christian feminists the emphasis is on the discernment of the community of faith and struggle, those who understand their calling as Christians in the light of the struggle for justice and full humanity for all women together with men. This community does not exclude men from participation, but its focus is on those who have been the outsiders, the marginal ones who are able to articulate their hope for new life and dignity. Men can be feminist advocates of justice for women in the community of struggle, but the discernment of what oppression and liberation mean for women has to be rooted in the experience of women.

As I have already indicated, it is the community of faith and struggle that is the prism for understanding feminist ecclesiology. The experience out of which the ecclesiology is shaped is that of those struggling for full human personhood and dignity and reflecting critically upon their struggle. Out of communities of struggle that are acting for justice, freedom, and full human dignity for women come critical analysis and new insight that provide a lens of experience through which to interpret tradition in all its forms. In feminist ecclesiology the appeal to women's experience is not just to the experience of white women or poor women or Hispanic women. Rather, it is to the experience of each particular group of women as it is reflected upon critically by those who are struggling for the full participation of women together with men in all the structures of church and society.

The community of faith and struggle, then, is the community that makes use of its critically reflected experience of struggle in the process of traditioning by which it selects from the still living and evolving past of scriptural and church tradition as a means of shaping an alternative future. Its appeal to Tradition in no way is a denial of its own process and experience but rather a faith affirmation that God is present in and through their struggle for justice and discernment of the meaning of the gospel message. Nor is it a denial of the need for careful critical thought as the community uses the theological spiral to make connections between its ongoing life and its continuing work of advocacy and welcome for those on the margins of church and society.

As we shall see in chapter 3, the measure of its faithfulness is not the particular structure or confessional tradition that is the basis of its gathering, but whether indeed it is able to raise up signs of God's intended new household in which even "the least of these" are welcome. Feminist Christian communities take many forms and are important in creating an imaginative construal of what might constitute signs of feminist ecclesiology. They are not the only place where communities of faith and struggle exist, however, for the communities can be part of many other forms and styles of churches, including mainstream Protestant and Roman Catholic churches in the United States.

It is communities of faith and struggle that put together the imaginative construal of what has authority for feminist ecclesiology and theology, but these communities are still connected to the worldwide Christian community and to all those who are engaged in the same liberation struggles. One way of explaining how it is possible to develop local theologies and ecclesiologies but at the same time to be part of the whole Christian church is suggested by Robert Schreiter in *Constructing Local Theologies*. Making use of a proposal of American linguistics scholar Noam Chomsky for a model for language acquisition, Schreiter builds up a theory of how tradition functions in local contexts yet is connected to the universal church and to all the forms of tradition we have discussed.[53] Schreiter is writing out of his experience of missions in Africa and is particularly interested in showing the way indigenous theologies develop in connection with Roman Catholic tradition, but his model is helpful as an example of one way in which communities of faith and struggle can be connected to tradition as well as to the margin in their own particular context.

In his model, Chomsky distinguishes between competence and performance in language systems. *Competence* is something that human beings all have in their native language, and out of which we are able to generate language from a very early age. We do not have direct access to this competence but can only recognize its presence because of observation of *performance*, in which persons talk and use language with immense variety and creativity. In order to explain how the language works, *grammar* is developed and takes on a normative function of describing which performances are considered properly to reflect competence in a given language.

Schreiter makes use of this model of a language system as an analogy to the system of Christian tradition.

> Faith is analogous to language competence. Theology and the expressive tradition (liturgy, wider forms of praxis) are analogous to language performance. The loci of orthodoxy (however construed: Scriptures, creeds, councils, confessions, magisterium) represent a grammar, mediating competence and performance.[54]

This model takes the magisterium and orthodox tradition more seriously than most feminist theologies because it seems to be describing the way local communities talk back to tradition but are still subject to the "normative grammar" of church tradition. Nevertheless, if the emphasis is placed on competence or faith, then the Tradition as God handing over Jesus Christ is still part of the mystery of the faith that moves in ways not subject to the grammar—or *table manners*—of tradition.[55] The creeds, scripture, confessions, and teaching of the church have evolved out of what have always been local theologies. Over the centuries certain local theologies have made universal claims, yet these claims continue to be shaped and reshaped as local communities evolve their own theology as performance in lived-out and celebrated faith and struggle.

Just how normative the grammar of tradition is for a particular community of faith and struggle depends on its members' configuration of what is authoritative or life-giving in that particular community and in the light of their particular struggle. For many the Bible will have a particularly important place both as a prototype of the way in which faith, tradition, and local theologies interact and as a source of the grammar of tradition.[56] Although the grammar of scripture and church tradition helps each to be responsive and responsible to other Christian communities and communions, a group ultimately finds authority in God's action in Christ as seen in and through the ever-changing forms of proclamation, worship, partnership, and service of the community of faith.

Feminist understanding of the church

Discussion of tradition and ecclesiology from a feminist perspective is most definitely a way of talking back to a community whose self-understanding has been shaped in all its aspects of tradition from a patriarchal paradigm of authority as domination. The shift to the metaphor of church in the round is one way of talking back because it reconfigures the paradigm of what evokes assent from the image of the household ruled by a patriarch to one of a household where everyone gathers around the common table to break bread and to share table talk and hospitality. All are welcome to participate in the table talk because in that way they become participants in their own journey of faith and struggle for the mending and liberation of creation.

Round table ecclesiology reflects the self-understanding of the community of faith and struggle about its life in a changing pattern of faith, justice, and hospitality. According to Paul Hanson in *The People Called*, this tradition is shared in the earliest traditions of the Hebrew and Greek testaments.

> The community of faith in the Bible is the people *called*. It is the people *called* from diverse sorts of bondage to freedom, *called* to a sense of identity founded on a common bond with the God of righteousness and compassion, and *called* to the twin vocations of worship and participation in the creative, redemptive purpose . . . directed to the restoration of the whole creation.[57]

The word "church" or *ekklesia* in the Greek Testament was not the only word used to describe the early Christians. An earlier term seems to have been "people of the Way," and the word *koinonia*, or community, was often used to refer to the gathering of Christians in each place (Acts 24:14; 2:42).[58] Within a few years it seems that the local churches were described as *ekklesia tou theou* (*ekklesia* of God), gathered in the name of Christ (1 Thess. 2:14).[59] *Ekklesia* had been used in the Septuagint to translate the word *qahal*, meaning assembly, meeting, or gathering. The Greek Testament does not use the word "synagogue" except to refer to Jewish congregations (except in James 2:2 in the Greek), so it is often assumed that *ekklesia* was to be understood in terms of *qahal*, with its overtones of a holy set-apart assembly of Israel (Deut. 23:1–14). Yet is more likely that a new meaning had been attached to the Greek word, which conveyed its particular Christian usage to the Greek-speaking world.[60]

Ekklesia is found only three times in the Gospels: once in the Matthew 16:18 declaration about Peter and twice in Matthew 18:17. It appears that in seeking to convey the openness of the new Christian communities in contrast to the restricted Jewish communities, Paul and others working with the Gentiles used a word to describe the gatherings of Christians that was not so much a reference to *qahal* as a reference to the Greek political assemblies and thus to the theo-political assemblies of the people of God (Acts 19:32, 39–41). In the same way the word "Christian" was probably coined as a secular word to refer to the Christians as a political group associated with Christ (Acts 11:26).

The usage of the word *ekklesia* reflects its functional character. It is used as a description of the totality of Christians living in any one place—a city or a house (1 Cor. 1:2; 16:19). It is also used to describe the church universal to which all believers belong as part of the eschatological people of God (1 Cor. 12:28). These communities were defined simply by the presence of Christ in their midst and viewed their task as that of proclamation of the Gospel (Matt. 18:20).

In the Introduction I described the self-interpretation of feminist ecclesiology as reflection on the church as "a community of Christ, bought with a price, where everyone is welcome." The church has always understood itself in the light of Christology, but that understanding of Christ's presence in the church has also shifted over the centuries. As Gutiérrez has pointed out in *The Power of the Poor in History,* the Roman Catholic church in Western Christendom saw Christ as its founder and focused its self-understanding "from within," clinging to its means of salvation in a hostile world and incorporating the "others" into the church as their only hope of salvation.[61] From the time of Vatican Council II (1962–1965), the church came to see Christ as present and active in the world and focused its self-understanding "from without," seeking to be a sign and sacrament of salvation.

Since the time of Vatican II and the second general conference of Latin American bishops held in Medellín, Colombia, in 1968, liberation theologians of the Roman Catholic Church, and of Protestant churches as well, have come to see Christ as identified with the poor and oppressed and have focused on a self-understanding "from underneath" with the poor and despised. The church finds its identity in siding with the poor of the world in witness to God's liberating action. It is this latter identity that feminist ecclesiology shares with the ecclesiology of the Latin American liberation theologians. For although there are many forms of feminist theology, an ecclesiology that is shaped in the round, and committed to the struggle to stand with those on the margin, is both a feminist and a liberation theology at one and the same time. For this reason it is possible to speak of feminist/liberation ecclesiology. In any case it is important to remember that feminist ecclesiology is committed to justice for all marginalized persons and not just women, and liberation ecclesiology is not truly about liberation if it is not committed to liberation of all women together with men.

According to Hans Küng in his book *The Church,* "Ecclesiology is a response and call to constantly changing historical situations." It is "necessarily subject to continual change and must constantly be undertaken anew."[62] Thus it is possible to say that ecclesiology is by its very nature not only talking back to tradition but also talking back and forth between tradition and its historical context. Feminist ecclesiology is no different in this respect from any other expression of the church's self-understanding, but it is different in that the self-understanding includes action/reflection on the way faith shapes life in the struggle for justice on behalf of marginalized people. What makes its back talk so startling is that the voices doing the talking have not been those of the church officials and scholars who are the usual interpreters of meaning in the church.

The church has been discussing its nature for a very long time. The first book on the church was published in 1301, when the struggles with the state led the church to recognize that the nature of the church could not be assumed as given by God.[63] The discussion of what it means to be a faithful church has continued ever since. That we do not fully know the mission and nature of the church, and that the church as we know it never embodies fully what we believe about the church, has never prevented the church from seeking to interpret its calling. In the same way, feminist ecclesiology neither fully knows the meaning of church in this perspective, nor does it expect to find communities that fully embody its vision. Nevertheless, those who write feminist ecclesiology join the ancient tradition of faith, seeking understanding as they risk sharing in the action and reflection of communities of faith and struggle.

In the interpretation of the Apostles' Creed we are called to "believe the holy catholic church." This formulation of the creed seems to indicate that we believe the church and not *in* the church because we believe that no matter what its present failings it is still a community of Christ that offers the possibility of new life and continuing nurture of the faith through the word and sacraments. As Küng says, we believe *in* God, Christ, and the Holy Spirit, but the church is not God. To believe the church is to believe that by its very particular concrete actions, in which we share as a participant, it points beyond itself to God in Christ and to God's grace.[64]

To believe the church is to believe it exists and to risk believing that the particular communities of faith and struggle where we are members partake in some way of the one church of Jesus Christ. Participation in local church is at the same time participation with all who are united to Christ. Churches that are feminist Christian communities or basic Christian communities are also local manifestations of the one church. Those who join them also risk their inadequacy in living up to their calling to be communities of church and struggle. Although the insights of women in struggle for full humanity are key to the interpretation of the gospel among Christian feminists, their insights into ways of being the church of

Jesus Christ may contribute to the self-understanding of the whole church. It may well be that the insights of women into the meaning of faithfulness for all Christians will one day make it no longer necessary for women to gather apart to give an account of the hope that is in them.

There is no perfect church, and our imperfect church is the only one we have as we seek to point beyond ourselves to God's new household. As Dorothee Sölle puts it in her book *Thinking About God*, "Wherever God acts in a liberating way in and through human beings, there is participation in that liberating action of God, involvement, allowing oneself to be drawn into the process of liberation; there 'church' appears in the full sense of the word, related to the kingdom of God."[65]

The same is true for the metaphor of church in the round. There is no perfect expression of this reality of authority shared in community, but at least those of us who take round table talk seriously know that reflection on faith and struggle with those on the margin can at least become a small piece of the round. We move forward with whatever piece we have received in expectation that Christ will be present among us as we crowd together around the table with the one who comes to serve and not to be served (Mark 10:45).

2 | Leadership in the Round

A prominent image of chivalry in Western culture is the description of how King Arthur tried to stop the warfare between feudal lords by inviting one hundred and fifty knights to serve at the round table. In the tales of King Arthur, the round table is an ever-elusive utopian vision of community that is worth every chivalrous man's exploits and every lovely maiden's broken heart. Because of this legacy, leadership and round tables are not considered a contradiction in terms. The king still presided at the table, and the others had to give an accounting of their noble deeds each year at Pentecost.[1]

The vision of the church gathered around God's table is different from the image of King Arthur's table in two respects. First, it is a vision already experienced through the presence of Christ's Spirit in the midst of communities of faith and their struggle for justice and new life. At Pentecost it is not so much the deeds of great men that are celebrated as the great deeds of God, who has reconciled the people of the earth. Second, this vision includes not just knights but courtly advisers, castle help, and peasants from the land, as well as faithful women and men of every tongue, race, and nationality.[2] It is an image that compels us to anticipate the coming Great Feast of God's eschatological household!

But there remains a way in which the church in Western society still remains connected to the style of leadership at the round table. We forget that the white male Eurocentric church is not the only guest at the table and still sing about following the gleam of yesteryear with "banners unfurled o'er all the world."[3] And an image of "knights in the days of old" still plagues the patriarchal leadership of the churches as they move ever so slowly to include women as well as men, poor as well as rich, and people of all colors in the search for a table where all are welcome.

The quest for a table that is truly round continues among those who reject hierarchy and competition and, instead, search for alternative models of partnership in which "moving up the table" is no longer the issue. Leadership, however, is still the issue because human institutions need care in the development of relationships and purpose, whether they are ordered in the round or in a pyramid. The need for alternative models of leadership becomes ever more pressing as women and men seek alternative forms of organization that will assist them in affirming the life of this whole planet rather than in embracing death-dealing domination. The church has a responsibility to join in this quest and to ask in what way its own orders or ministries contribute to church and world in the round.

What would it mean to see real live models of partnership among those women and men who share Christ's ministry? As women move into positions of leadership in church and society, this is a question that presses in on those of us who have a vision of leadership that is liberating and empowering. New styles of ministry, both lay and ordained, are emerging in our time, but we are still in a quest to understand fully what this style of leadership will mean. The clues are barely perceptible on the horizon. Like Paul, who describes creation as waiting "with eager longing for the revealing of the children of God" (Rom. 8:19), we wait eagerly to see signs of real live feminist leaders. The question of new styles of feminist ministry leads not to definition but to a quest for insight.

For me this quest for understanding of feminist styles of ministry is a Christian pilgrimage I undertake as a white Western theologian. But within the larger worldwide feminist community, women of all colors, races, classes, sexual orientations, cultures, religions, and ideologies have to make their own quest for those who will lift up and exemplify the meaning of feminist leadership. In sharing this quest as Christian women we recognize that our calling to ministry is a call to share in Christ's ministry of service. Yet we also ask ourselves in what way the gifts of service to our neighbor can lead us to new styles of leadership in a church in the round.

In chapter 2, this quest for leadership in the round leads to a consideration of the way our current understanding of ordination is shaped by theological doctrines of hierarchical divine order rather than by a gospel understanding of the order of freedom. Women in ministry are questioning not just doctrines and models of ministry but the structures of the churches themselves. Appealing to the experience of the early house churches as well as to the Gospel stories of Jesus' own ministry, feminists are moving on to overturn "the masters' tables" and to challenge the tradition of the patriarchal household. The quest for leadership in the round continues as feminists search out the relationship of leadership to authority and to the gifts of the Spirit in the community. It is at least possible at this moment in the continuing quest to celebrate those who provide us with models of leadership behavior and to lift up their gifts of leadership for church in the round.

Order and Organization

The vision of King Arthur no longer serves us very well as a model for leadership. Neither would any attempt to perpetuate this model through an "order of the round table." In centuries past, such knightly fraternities flourished as a way of uniting men in some common rule or honorary distinction, and these medieval social structures continue in the patterns of religious orders in churches today. This traditional order of a patriarchal hierarchy remains as the predominant form of organization in church life, in spite of the changing patterns of organization in various social and cultural contexts.

Order and change

The word "order" comes from the Latin word *ordo* and has many meanings related to ranking and placing things in a row or line. In church tradition the word came to refer not only to the ranks of clergy and religious, which were parallel to similar orders in Roman patriarchal society and military organization, but also to laws, rules, and procedures. These hierarchical ways of organizing the life of the church were understood as a reflection of God's divine ordering of the universe and of human nature and destiny. Thus in Roman Catholic theology the discussion of natural law was a discussion of the natural ordering of human relationships and the ethics of right living according to this law.

In Protestant theology there was a rejection of the idea that human beings could know or do the good in the natural order, and the order of redemption or of grace and forgiveness was stressed as the beginning point of righteousness. Nevertheless, Protestant theology has often spoken of orders of creation such as family, work, government, and religion that are shared by all humankind as a basis for ordering social relationships. In the various traditions these unchanging patterns of social behavior are like the laws of nature, established in creation and considered part of divine or supernatural order made known through the self-revelation of God.[4] Until the modern era, persons did not expect change and usually tried to live in harmony with these established patterns of relationship.

History as well has been understood as part of God's order, with its own laws and with patterns that are unchanging. In such a view, for instance, "revolution" was understood as going round and round like the stars in their course. However, with the discovery that history can be changed by human actions so that new social structures and ways of life can be created, "revolution" came to mean a radical break or crisis in society, the creation of "a new house of freedom," where social arrangements went beyond the mere revolving of one fixed pattern in which one king or bishop replaced another. The understanding that emerged out of the Western revolutions of the eighteenth century, such as the French Revolution of 1789, questioned the idea that God orders things in unchanging patterns and called forth the development of modern theology to interpret tradition in this changing pattern of history.

In contemporary society, even those theologians who affirm that

God's supernatural order is the basic structure and purpose of all society, and of creation itself, still understand human beings in the light of change. We live in a historicized world in which change does not repeat one pattern but rather is a continuing process of human life. Today we find that humankind is threatened, not primarily by the natural forces of the cosmos but by its own historical power, which threatens the cosmos and drags all reality into history.[5] The challenge for justice, peace, and integrity of creation recognizes that God's design is not static but rather is a changing pattern, created out of human freedom, that is more and more a pattern of human disorder.

If it is the case that order can be understood dynamically as well as statically, then the orders of the church can also be understood as dynamic and changing in their responsibility to build up the community for its ministry in the world. Church historians and theologians no longer hold that a particular pattern of ministry was established by Christ from the beginnings of the church. Rather, they search for ways to show that a particular church tradition represents a continuation of the basic Tradition of Jesus' life and ministry, and continuing presence through the Spirit in the life of the church. Countless books document the church and its changing ministry, some with the purpose of showing how the tradition has *not* changed and others with the purpose of showing how it *must* change.

The traditioning process assists us to draw from the still living and evolving past as we seek to shape the future. But how free we are to move away from the tradition of scripture and church doctrine and the traditions of the church is a matter of much disagreement among different confessions. This is one of the reasons that the convergence document of the Faith and Order Commission of the World Council of Churches titled "Baptism, Eucharist, and Ministry" had a minimum of convergence on ministry, in comparison with baptism and eucharist.[6] After one page on the calling of the whole people of God, the other twelve pages are devoted to clerical ordination, in an attempt to find some convergence on such topics as forms of ordination, apostolic succession, and mutual recognition of ministry. The issue of ordination of women receives one paragraph, with the discussion of its "problems" relegated to the commentary notes. Obviously, ordination is still a "deposit of faith" that has become a stumbling block in the ecumenical movement. In spite of the opinion of many theologians, it is not women who are the problem but the doctrines of ordination that are problematic.

Those confessions which consider ordained ministry or priesthood to be of the *esse* or being of the church tend to suggest the restriction of ordination to the sacramental or pastoral role and limit priesthood to celibate men as a basic church doctrine, whether or not it has scriptural basis or meets the needs of churches with a severe shortage of priests. In

Eastern Orthodox churches, those priests who are married were married before ordination, and they are then not allowed to become bishops. In the Roman Catholic churches a permanent diaconate of married men is permitted, but they are not able to become priests.

Those confessions which consider ministry to be necessary to the fullness of the church, or its *plene esse,* and those which consider it necessary to the well-being of the church, or its *bene esse,* are more willing to broaden the categories of ministry, frequently considering the ordination of married women and men to be part of their traditions, although most continue to reject the ordination of open and affirming gay men and lesbians. More and more, however, feminists who experience the frustrations and problems of the ministry and priesthood in its present form consider it to be part of the *male esse* of the church. They understand that the practice of ordained ministry in its present form is frequently bad for the well-being of the church and are calling for reexamination of ordination and of the ordering of church life.[7]

Organization and ordination

Implicit in this call for new understanding of ministry in the life of the church is the recognition that religious orders of vocation, polity, and church law can no longer be understood as static patterns set out by divine order. They are *gifts* of God rather than *givens* of God: part of the changing patterns of church life that evolve out of the function of the church in its work of service and witness to God's love and justice in the wider society. The ministries of the church are part of the organization of church life as it responds to the Spirit of Christ continually at work in its midst. This Spirit leads to a new order of freedom, in which Christ has set us free to be for others (Gal. 5:1).[8] In this understanding, ministry is the response of each and every Christian to Christ's call to freedom. In their baptism Christians are set free to serve now, in and through many communities and situations. The call to ministry is not an option for some Christians. It is basic to the existence of all Christians as they seek to live together as partners in Christ's service.[9]

Much has been written about ministry as *diakonia,* or service. This word is a basic description of what it means to follow Jesus Christ, whose call to ministry is described in Luke 4:18–19. In 1 Corinthians 12:28, Paul reminds us that there are a variety of gifts recognized in the congregations. "And God has appointed in the church first apostles, second prophets, third teachers; then deeds of power, then gifts of healing, forms of assistance, forms of leadership, various kinds of tongues."

The way in which the church structured the gifts of ministry so that some are set apart by ordination served a need of the church for ordered leadership, but it has had disastrous effects in producing a class division between "upper-class" clergy and "lower-class" laity. No matter how much we all emphasize that there is only one ministry of Jesus Christ and that we all share in this ministry, the clerical structures continue to reinforce structures of hierarchy and domination, whether or not the particular clergyperson is male or female.

These problems are well known in the literature of church renewal and pastoral theology, but they have been pressed with greater urgency by feminist theologians in response to the experience of laywomen as "third class" (below clergy and laymen), and to the experience of women clergy, who are caught in what is called "status inconsistency." They are now "upper-class clergy," but as women they can't measure up to the role of sacred masculinity so they remain "third class" according to gender. Some of these problems and the possibilities for changing patterns have been explored by Lynn Rhodes in her book *Co-Creating: A Feminist Vision of Ministry.* After reviewing feminist writings on ministry over the past twenty years, she interviews white women pastors to find out what vision of the church is emerging from their theory and practice in many and changing contexts.[10]

It is unfortunate that Rhodes limits her interviews to white women Protestants, as many of the visions and alternatives are coming from women of color who pursue their ministry at the margins of society in this country and around the world. Musimbi Kanyoro, a staff member of the Lutheran World Federation, has recently noted that her travels around the world have highlighted the concern of many women in Africa and Asia about the failure of their churches to ordain women.

> Women wish to participate fully in the renewal of their churches. Their spiritual gifts for ministry need to be recognized in all of the life of the church, including ordained ministries. . . . It is no use for churches in Africa and Asia to use cultural excuses to bar women, and at the same time, hope to "minister" and to witness Christ in matters [such as the caste system or polygamy] where cultures are a hindrance.[11]

Women in the Roman Catholic Church were the first to recognize that the root problem was not just women's ordination but the need to transform ordination and the church itself into alternative forms such as those of women-church.[12]

Rhodes maintains that an evolving style of feminist ministry is "organized contextually and defined by its vision." Like other liberation theologies, feminist theologies emphasize a ministry oriented toward the mission of the church as it seeks to address particular contexts "in the light of their analysis of God's intent for the world."[13] This is clearly a form of ministry that is viewed functionally rather than as an ontological order of life, yet women and men who carry out such a ministry are also very much concerned with the development of professional, interpersonal, pastoral, and liturgical skills that assist in their pastoral work.

In seeking to carry out their clerical roles, women clergy frequently confront tensions, not only because of sexism in their denominations and congregations but also because their practice of ministry has moved away from the old patriarchal models. In her helpful survey, "Changing Understandings of Ordination," Barbara Brown Zikmund lists three of these major tensions in current interpretations of ordination that are highlighted in the experience of those women who manage to find pastoral positions.[14]

The first is the tension caused by their need to function as clergy in a particular context while being asked to conform to a universal norm of what a clergyperson will do and be in a denomination. Women emphasize the contextual aspect of their ministry and prefer not to be "set apart" from their congregations, since they develop relationships among the people as those who share their baptism and commitment. This emphasis on relationality is a new style in ministry, which comes in part because of women's enculturation as nurturers and those more concerned with relationships than functions.[15]

This sets up additional tensions between emphasis on sacred rites associated particularly with the sacrament of communion and ministry of the word. Following Schillebeeckx, Zikmund points out that ordination was originally for the purpose of preaching and teaching, while the offering of eucharist by a man or woman who was the local host in a small house church did not seem to present a problem to be discussed.[16] Yet it is the offering of eucharist that has come to signify the privilege of ordination in Protestant, Roman Catholic, and Orthodox churches. Many women would like to see the sacraments return to their communal function, with emphasis on baptism of all members for ministry and the need to equip the saints through teaching and preaching.[17]

A third tension between the office and person of the ordained minister is particularly increased by the presence of women. In a church that has had a dualistic view of sexuality and spirituality, even to have women in leadership confronts the myth that identifies women with sexuality and body and men with spirit and intellect. Women are embodied pastors. They bring their sexuality with them, and they make it clear that sexuality and spirituality go together as both women and men are embodied persons before God and in the world. By office, women who are ordained are granted power to function as clergy, but as female persons they are traditionally denied access to the power of sacred masculinity that resides in clerical ordination. Their very being calls the old ways of thinking into question, and often it is the women themselves who bear the pain of being rejected by those not willing to change.

These tensions are shared by many ordained clergy and are not unique to women. Yet the marginal perspective women bring to ordained ministry, because they "don't fit" the old male roles, leads to new critique and exploration of old theological issues. In the midst of this critique, women begin to ask whether or not they want to be ordained at all and begin to notice that the more basic issue is the need to transform the church structures that divide clergy from people and obscure the meaning of ministry as the work of Christ that is shared by all those who are united with him through baptism.

Those who begin to explore such questions often find themselves involved with alternative forms of Christian community such as Women-Church, where they can continue to carry out the functions of church life but without the hierarchical structures in which they are often trapped as participants in established church institutions. Chapter 3 of this book will be exploring some of these alternative structures further, but here it is important to note that the setting aside of clerical ordination has already happened in feminist Christian communities, some of which call themselves Women-Church. In her book *Women-Church*, Rosemary Radford Ruether calls for "the dismantling of clerical concepts of ministry and church" but makes it clear that forms of ministry or leadership are needed in Women-Churches, where there is no clerical caste but instead a variety of ministries of function, such as liturgists, teachers, administrators, community organizers, and spiritual counselors. She emphasizes as well that the traditional functions of church life, such as study, liturgy, social praxis, and communal life, are important for feminist communities, but that these functions are carried out by various persons in the group and not necessarily by clergy.[18]

I myself am an ordained clergyperson in the Presbyterian Church (U.S.A.). I sought ordination in 1957 because I could only integrate worship, social action, and education in my ministry in East Harlem if I was recognized as a leader of worship as well as an educator and activist. Given the structures of the church, I needed ordination in order to have the power to function in the integrated way that I envisioned for the team ministry of the Presbyterian Church of the Ascension. I was prepared to be ordained and would have left the United Presbyterian Church to be ordained elsewhere if the denomination had not begun to ordain women as well as men just before my last year of seminary.

I must confess, however, that the growing alienation and disillusionment with the church and clerical structures that so many women share are part of my life as well. I am very clear at this point in my life that I would rather not be ordained, as I do not believe that ordination makes one any different than other baptized Christians, and I know that the received traditions and practice of ordination are frequently harmful to the health of many lesbian or heterosexual women, gay men, and laypersons, as well as to the health of the church. The only reason I remain ordained at this point in my life is because, as a woman who has overcome denial of access to ordination and broken the old patriarchal orders of ordination, I stand in solidarity with my many sisters and brothers who are denied the opportunity to be considered for ordination simply because of their sex or sexual orientation. I also have the opportunity of modeling alternative forms of ministry and subverting the clergy line with the women and men I teach in seminary and those with whom I work and worship. I do not view ordination as an indelible order, and whether to remain a clergyperson continues to be an open question for me and for many others.

Quest for feminist leadership

The entire question of ordination and ministry has become more than problematic. From the perspective of feminist experience and the critique of patriarchy, ordination has now become a parasitic reference for ministry, just as Father is a parasitic reference for God.[19] As "kleenex" becomes the generic name for tissue, or "xerox" for a duplication process, Father (one metaphor for God) has become the name of God, and clerical ordination is now the name for ministry. All the rich variety of gifts is lost as ministry ceases to be the way everyone serves in the name of the one who came to serve and becomes a special class or category of people whose privilege is reinforced by religious doctrines.

For this reason it seems best to have a moratorium on the word "ministry" when speaking about the gifts of leadership in the Christian congregation, and to use it sparingly in reference to the many ways Christians are called to exercise these gifts. Leadership is not the idea behind ministry. It specifically is a reference to one who is a servant and who renders humble service to others, in service at the table, with footwashing and all the rest (Mark 1:29–31; Acts 6:1–6). In the Greek Testament the word for ministry, *diakonia,* is coupled with the even stronger word *doulos.* In the Greek, Paul speaks of Jesus as one who "emptied himself as a slave," and of himself as a slave of Christ (Phil. 1:1; 2:6–11). He balances this slave metaphor with the one of lord for Christ and apostle for himself, thus asserting that this slavery is also a form of freedom or empowerment.

The problem here is that this dialectic of empowered service/slavery and servant/slave empowerment is always lost in a dualistic patriarchal paradigm, so that in the church certain persons are assigned the roles of servant and others who may call themselves servant or minister take up the power and status of lord. Over and over the dialectic is lost in dualism, so that from a feminist perspective it becomes important to search for other expressions of our ministry that clearly own both the gifts for service and the empowerment for others that comes through those gifts of the Spirit.

Just how pressing this quest for new language has become is underlined by the New Revised Standard Version of the Bible, which has generally chosen to use the English word "slave" rather than "servant" when *doulos* appears in the text. (Interestingly enough, it translates *doulos* as "servant" in reference to Paul and Timothy in Philippians 1:1.) This use of "slave" makes the whole concept of servant/lord even more problematic in a racist society, where the word "slave" carries with it the lingering history of chattel slavery and the domination of the master. In a similar manner it is problematic for women in Asian cultures, where husbands are called "lord" and women often find themselves in situations of domestic slavery. For women who have been victims of the theology of service that reinforces their personal and social role of inferiority, it does not seem that the patriarchal metaphor of lord and servant/slave conveys a new order of freedom and empowerment to share their gifts.

From the point of view of this aspect of ministry, many feminist theologians do not want to speak of a God who desires others to be slaves, and they do not think of leadership in the church as a form of lordship. They join the many women and men who find themselves on a quest for new forms of leadership as the church reaches out to those who have been marginalized as permanent servants. Moving back into the resources of our faith tradition like many before them, they reread the story of Jesus and the early church for clues that might make sense in this new situation.

From my own perspective it seems that to use the term "leadership" might be a refreshing way to discuss the organization of church life, but this word also has many overtones and problems of domination. It has been so identified with leadership exercised as authority over community that it is difficult to use the word "leadership" with the intention of describing its exercise as authority in community or as partnership. In addition, this word appears only three times in the NRSV: once in Paul's list of God's gifts to the church and twice with patriarchal overtones in reference to Moses and Aaron, in Numbers 33:1 and Hebrews 3:16, but not to Miriam.

The Pauline understanding of leadership is not individualistic but very much related to all the gifts of the Spirit for the community, but it does seem to imply the exercise of authority or power in a community. The word used by Paul in his list of spiritual gifts in 1 Corinthians 12:28 is *kybernesis* and refers to steering, or piloting a ship, and thus to the ability to hold a leading position in the upbuilding of the church community. Although "leadership" is used only three times, the word "leader" is frequently used of persons in authority, and especially for the leaders of the Jewish people. The term is not used in the Gospels to describe the ministry of Jesus because he is presented as one who sought to overturn religious and political leadership as domination and to carry out his ministry through actions of healing, teaching, and preaching. Yet these actions on Jesus' part, as well as the entire list of gifts in 1 Corinthians 12, would in contemporary society be described as forms of leadership.

As an image for what is needed in building up alternative forms of church in the round, leadership has some advantages. It carries much less theological baggage because it is a secular word. It also conveys the need for women and other powerless or oppressed persons to take responsibility in the life of the church as leaders, rather than preferring passive servant roles. In addition, the use of the word "leadership" raises issues of power, conflict, goal setting, and direction without covering them over with the generic form of ministry. Service is the key form of life to any follower of Christ, and one of the many ways to serve is as a leader in the church. Whether one is ordained or not ceases to be the issue; the question becomes one of the style of leadership behavior that is most helpful to congregations in their particular contexts.

The exercise of leadership authority through domination was common in biblical times and remains so in every other time, including our own. Yet leadership still has everything to do with community, because, in basic terms, leadership is the ability to evoke a following. People look for leaders or persons in authority who can evoke their consent because they need a sense of security and direction for their lives.[20] Leadership behavior can come in many forms, according to a particular context or need and according to the particular gifts of the person. In a feminist perspective there are never too many leaders, for power is not understood as a zero sum game that requires competition and hoarding in order to "win." Rather, power and leadership gifts multiply as they are shared and more and more persons become partners in communities of faith and struggle.

The issue for feminists is not whether there should be leaders in church in the round but how to be a feminist leader in a patriarchal world: how to create new styles of feminist leadership that are truly ministry or service without the hierarchical structures of ordination as presently practiced. Therefore, I want to sketch out the difference between the styles of patriarchal and feminist leadership. In using this descriptive topology for analysis, I do not want to imply that there are only two styles or that they are ever only of one type or the other. In the patriarchal world we inhabit, leadership style has to be a mixture in order for it to survive. Different women and men aim at a variety of styles of leadership depending on their context, on their religious and ideological commitments, and upon their access to power and authority.

Patriarchal styles of leadership draw their model of behavior from a patriarchal paradigm of reality. This configuration of attitudes, actions, and theories establishes norms of language, thought, and action in a model of male domination over other subordinate men, women, and all creation. According to Elisabeth Schüssler Fiorenza, this way of seeing, being, and acting assigns women their status according to the class, race, religion, and country of the men to whom they "belong."[21]

In patriarchal styles of leadership, authority is exercised by standing above and is enhanced through a capitalist model of power accumulation at the expense of others. The elites of our country are trained in this form of leadership. For instance, the slogan at Yale in the 1960s was "Each spring one thousand leaders!" An alumnus like President Bush is still valued as a leader, not for his "one thousand points of light" but for his use of the model of power accumulation.

Feminist styles of leadership would draw their model of behavior from a partnership paradigm. This perspective on reality establishes norms of language, thought, and action in a model of shared authority in community. This paradigm has a variety of designations, including partnership, friendship, community, relationship, mutuality, and matriarchy. They indicate an intention, not simply to reverse the paradigm of domination but to search out an alternative way of ordering our reality and world that is less harmful to human beings, to nature, and to all creation.[22] Such a perspective is feminist because it represents a position of advocacy for the full humanity of all women together with men.[23] As Barbara Smith writes,

> Feminism is the political theory and practice that struggles to free *all* women: women of color, working-class women, poor women, disabled women, lesbians, old women—as well as white, economically privileged, heterosexual women. Anything less than this vision of total freedom is not feminism, but merely female self-aggrandizement.[24]

In feminist styles of leadership, authority is exercised by standing with others by seeking to share power and authority. Power is seen as something to be multiplied and shared rather than accumulated at the top. A feminist leader is one who inspires others to be leaders, especially those on the margins of church and society who do not think they are "somebody." Effectiveness is related to how well the leader empowers those who are assigned marginal roles because of systemic racism, heterosexism, classism, sexism, disableism, and the like.

In our quest for feminist leadership we need to be asking ourselves how we know this form of leadership when we see it. The pattern of leadership behavior is not given in advance and so takes on different forms in different contexts. Yet often when women who are leaders are described, we hear that they have made use of some form of circular management structure to replace the hierarchical pyramid. For instance, Frances Hesselbein, the chief executive of the Girl Scouts of the U.S.A., has organized the national and regional Girl Scout staff in a weblike structure in which ever-widening circles of staff and volunteers are woven together by multiple lines of communication, and decision making flows around and across and not up and down a ladder of authority. According to Sally Helgesen, writing about Hesselbein and other women leaders in *The Female Advantage*, the authority of this form of leadership comes from connection rather than from position at the top, and staff people work in teams rather than competing with each other.[25] The circular pattern is recognizable as leadership in the round and evokes other leaders who share this partnering style.

Before moving on to look further for other models and clues, I would say provisionally that we know the style of leadership that is being practiced by the style of leadership practiced by the followers. Many factors of personality, culture, and institutional context affect styles of leadership, yet one important factor is always the modeling that persons have experienced. This is why the predominant model of domination in educational and pastoral leadership is distressing to Christian feminists. We affirm that the purpose of feminist leadership needs to be the sharing of authority in community in ways that empower those at the margin to share in leading their communities. As Sweet Honey in the Rock sing in "Ella's Song,"

> Struggling myself don't mean a whole lot. I've come to realize
> that teaching others to stand there and fight
> is the only way our struggle survives.[26]

Overturning the Masters' Tables

Sharing the vision of the possibility of a table at which not just one hundred and fifty knights are welcome but where the whole world is offered God's hospitality begins with opposing those systems that require "limited seating" at the table. In this sense it requires overturning the tables in the masters' house. Just as Jesus overturned the tables in the temple (Matt. 21:1–17), those who advocate a Christian feminist vision of church in the round must begin with opposing and exposing the social and ecclesial patterns of domination and subordination that have been perpetuated in the ordering of church structures.

All four Gospels portray Jesus as one who challenges the temple establishment of his time. The different versions point ambiguously to future destruction of the temple establishment, but also to the fulfillment of the prophetic expectation that there will be a messianic purification of God's house as part of the final banquet of the coming household of God. We can be fairly sure that both the priestly rulers and the people knew that Jesus was condemning not just the merchants but also their masters, the priestly ruling class, and the temple system of taxation and the Roman rulers who controlled the system.[27] This is why the Gospels report that they sought to destroy Jesus and began to question his authority (Luke 19:47–20:8).

Jesus challenges the "disorder" of the religious establishment in the name of God's new order of freedom in community, and the authorities seek to silence the troublemaker. His action of reversal of "things as they are" continues to inspire the Spirit-filled efforts of persons who search for renewal of the church as institution in every generation. Women who are called to leadership or ministry in the church remember the actions of Jesus in his iconoclasm of patriarchy, as well as those of their sisters, as part of what Elisabeth Fiorenza calls the "discipleship of equals" that emerged around Jesus and in the early house churches.[28] At the same time they work to shift the continuing de-formation of Christian communities into patriarchal households toward communities where the Spirit of Christ creates partnership in leadership and service.

Iconoclasm of patriarchy

It would seem to me that a feminist perspective on leadership has much to commend itself in a world so bent on domination, injustice, and destruction that humanity and the earth itself may not survive. But it is also important to claim our religious roots as well and to declare that these ideas are in no sense new, nor are they just propaganda. There are strong religious roots to these ideas in many religions, and at least the Jewish, Christian, and Muslim faiths honor their embodiment in the story of a prophet such as Jesus. For his story, although told in the language of patriarchy, is the story of a man who stood against patriarchal leadership, modeled a new way of life in God's household, and paid for this stand with his life.

Jesus' example of ministry demonstrates a reversal of expectation about leadership not only among the Jewish and Roman rulers of his own time but also among the Christian leaders who were to follow. Rosemary Ruether calls this iconoclasm the "kenosis of the Father," to emphasize that the self-emptying process of Christ's incarnation as a "slave" in Philippians 2:7 includes a self-emptying of God's power as divine patriarch.[29] Although in the later Greek Testament we see the beginning of rejection of Jesus' iconoclasm of patriarchal leadership, Jesus' own prophetic example of ministry as freely chosen service, of leadership as *diakonia*, demonstrates a reversal of patriarchal expectation and the absurdity of patriarchal privilege in the church institutions of today.

This model of ministry and of leadership is taken up and interpreted in different ways by the Gospel writers, and one way of reminding ourselves of this is to look at their interpretation of vocation, or God's call to freedom and service in community. As Mary Rose D'Angelo points out, "The last pictures of Jesus in the Gospels offer a particularly helpful approach to their understanding of Jesus and the Christian call, as they appear to present Jesus as the author expects the community to encounter him."[30] Together these pictures represent ways in which Jesus' iconoclasm of patriarchy has emptied out the models of leadership so that those who follow the Christ will live out the new reality of God's household.

Let us look for a moment at these Gospel pictures as described by Mary Rose D'Angelo in order to see the possibilities of servant leadership in the work of Christ.[31]

In Luke, Jesus is portrayed as a prophet and hero of spiritual life who has been sent to call God's people to "repentance, liberation, and God's justice." Advocacy for the oppressed and welcome of the poor and marginal into God's household portrays the fulfillment of God's promise by the practice of God's hospitality. John has a very different ending in his Gospel, yet he too models Jesus' ministry and our calling as one of hospitality. Jesus is sent by God not only as prophet, but as "God's life-gift, true and living bread, water, vine, dwelling, light." Jesus shares the power of God as the power of love. We are to abide in Jesus, nourished by the Spirit, and, in turn, become sources of life and nourishment for others.

In Matthew, Jesus is presented as the source of wisdom. In the final scene Jesus appears to his disciples and promises to be with them as they continue to interpret and live out the Law and words of Sophia Jesus.[32] In Mark we discover Jesus as a crucified Messiah and are challenged to follow him to the cross, living against the powers of patriarchy but unwilling to use the "tools of the master" in advocacy for those who have been excluded by religious and secular authorities. His priestly sacrifice is not an end in itself but a demonstration of Jesus' solidarity with us in suffering.

These images of Jesus' ministry so briefly sketched in no way do justice to Mary Rose D'Angelo's careful exposition of the Gospel texts and themes, nor do they establish how we are to interpret their meaning in our lives. Yet study of the Gospels from the perspective of authority in community leads us to a new evaluation of what it means to live out Jesus' ministry of prophet, ruler, priest, and teacher. Jesus becomes a ruler with power to heal and welcome marginal people into God's household. As prophet he preaches God's welcome to the poor and those at the margins, while at the same time standing as priest in solidarity in suffering and cross. At the very least, these images of vocation that come to us from the Gospels seem to indicate a new way of living and discipleship, which calls into question the model of leadership as domination and pushes us toward new models of servant leadership that are open to women as well as men.

Women in leadership

The inclusion of women in the leadership of the early Christian community was a break from the Jewish tradition of the woman's role. In the Hebrew Testament the role of woman as priest was resisted because of its association with the rival religion of Asherah. Women were recognized as prophets through whom God spoke, but their primary role was that of mother (2 Kings 22:14–20; Joel 2:28). In the temple, and later in the synagogue, women were not allowed to provide leadership in worship or in the teaching of scripture.[33]

In the Greek Testament the radical break in patriarchal structures provides a new order of freedom in which women as followers are welcomed by Jesus into a discipleship of equals. They were included in the earliest congregations and also became local leaders and traveling evangelists. Yet by the end of the Greek Testament period, two different and contrary trajectories of women's roles developed. Colossians and Ephesians and the Pastoral Epistles limited women's teaching role, while at the same time Mark and John placed women on an equal level with men as witnesses to Christ (John 4:1–42; 1 Tim. 2:11–13).[34]

We cannot speak of the exclusion of women as priests in the Greek Testament because this model of ministry or leadership does not exist in that period.[35] Rather, the royal priesthood applies to *all* members of the new people, who live by the mercy of God, as signified by baptism in the death of Jesus Christ (1 Peter 2:9). Baptism, not circumcision, is the sign of Christ's calling to service for both women and men. In baptism all put on Christ or are joined to his resurrected body as the firstfruits of the New Creation (Gal. 3:27–28). All receive the same gifts of the one Spirit (1 Cor. 12:13; Col. 3:9–11). Ordination as the laying on of hands was not practiced in the Pauline churches in regard to the role of president and deacon. In the Palestinian churches, ordination was practiced in setting aside the presbyter or elder in a manner similar to Jewish custom.[36]

There is no clear consensus on how many of these functions of ministry were performed by women, but it is possible to discern some of the roles they played in the earliest congregations. In these congregations religious and cultural patriarchal patterns were replaced by a community in which privileged religious, class, and gender roles were abolished. There is no reason to assume that women were excluded from the leadership of the house churches or from presiding at worship, especially when the worship was held in their homes (Col. 4:15). The "household codes" in Ephesians and the Pastoral Epistles seem to reflect a later patriarchal reaction to just such leadership by seeking to reestablish an order of subordination. Paul explicitly mentions women as his missionary co-workers, with the same terms being used for women and men in this regard: Prisca as co-worker; Junia as apostle; Apphia as sister (Rom. 16:3, 7; Philemon 2).

In Romans 16:1, Phoebe is called not only *diakonos* (minister, missionary, servant), but also *prostatis* (leading officer, president, governor, superintendent). In comparison to the ministry of deaconess in the later church, their ministry was not limited to ministry with women or to specific roles or functions. Yet the words of Paul in 1 Corinthians 11:2–16 indicate the continuing tension with the surrounding cultural norms as Paul allows women to prophesy but says they should cover their heads. His appeal to a revealed hierarchy of God-Christ-man-woman opens up the way for further injunctions of subordination for the sake of church order (1 Cor. 14:33–36).

House churches and household codes

In the post-Pauline era much of the appeal to hierarchy as reflection of the patriarchal household and the patriarchal divine order was a response to the conflicting views of such other Spirit-filled Christian communities as the Gnostics and the Montanists. In addition the early churches, which had been formed as new families or households without a patriarch, came under increasing pressure to conform to Roman patriarchal social and political structures. Women and slaves were no longer equal members of the house communities as they began to follow the prevailing household codes for the relationships among members of a patriarchal household (Eph. 5:21–6:9; Col. 3:18–4:1; 1 Tim.5:1–6:2; Titus; 1 Peter 2:18–3:7). The "disorderly" Christian communities led by Spirit-filled prophets gave way to "orderly" structures of domination and subordination that conformed to the surrounding social structures.

Prophets had played a prominent role in the early Christian community, and Paul took for granted that women would act as prophets, communicating divine oracles in the Christian assembly. He only insisted that they not overstep the gender differences between women and men (1 Cor. 12:2–16).[37] In the second century the Montanists continued this prophetic ministry and appealed to Galatians 3:28 as the basis for their inclusion of women as leading prophets who converted, baptized, and celebrated eucharist.[38] Some of the Gnostic groups were open to women's participation because of their inclusion of male and female cosmic principles or archetypes.

In the second and third centuries the leadership of women within the Christian community was a very lively and controversial issue in which both sides appealed to apostolic tradition to make their point. The development of church orders during that period reflects the continuing patriarchal reaction against female leadership. Women are acknowledged as disciples, but not as those appointed by Jesus to teach and proclaim Christ. The early, more charismatic role of widow is suppressed, and the Eastern Church begins to develop the role of deaconess as a ministry of women with women.[39]

Gradually the Christian ministry replaced the old Roman priesthood as the clergy of the established religion of the empire, and a hierarchy of order emerged. By the fourth century a new priestly caste had reassimilated the Hebrew image of temple priesthood, with taboos against women in the sanctuary. In the medieval period canon law forbade women the priesthood on grounds of the unfit nature of the female to represent Christ. At the same time women were forbidden to exercise authority as preachers, although both queens and abbesses were invested with the juridical authority of bishops.[40]

The Protestant Reformers continued to exclude women from preaching and teaching and from ordination. In fact, they took away the only other option besides marriage that had been open to women with spiritual gifts for ministry, that of monastic orders. Only in left-wing movements and churches were women allowed to preach, in recognition of the charisma of ordination as a gift of the Spirit for prophecy. Although subsequent church history made many changes in the understanding and function of ordination, few of these changes have succeeded in carrying out the iconoclasm of patriarchy and the overturning of the masters' tables.

The trajectory of the patriarchal household with its household codes or rules of domination and subordination is still very much with us. And yet, at the same time, the other tradition of freedom and of welcome of all humanity at the Lord's Supper continues Jesus' reversal of all that is high and low and moves us toward a new form of leadership in the round.

This leadership begins as women once more take up their ancient heritage as Spirit-filled leaders in Christian community. The impetus for this reversal of "things as they are" is the recognition of the need for forms of organization that connect us to those at the margin of society. One such leader is a Korean woman named Henna Yogumhyun Han, an ordained United Methodist pastor who has found her own way in Korean-American ministry by founding the Rainbow Church. This church is a faith community of Korean-American women in international marriages affiliated with the Seaford (New York) United Methodist Church. The Rainbow Church invites the whole family to attend church at the same time so that the fathers and children can attend English-language worship and Sunday school and the women can attend their Women-Church in the Korean language. Following the services the families share a meal and discussion.

These women, many of them G.I. brides, have great difficulty in the United States and often run into misunderstanding and abuse from husbands who do not speak the same language or share the same culture. They are lonely and isolated, often rejected by Korean congregations because the women were formerly bar women and entertainers who lived outside U.S. bases in Korea. They and their children face discrimination in the United States because of racism. Henna Han has a crisis hot line for the women and is planning to establish a shelter for battered women and children. As part of her ministry of partnership with those considered to be nobodies, and who themselves have very low self-esteem, she has created a worship service in the round. The women gather around a low round table, where they look down on a cross. Here they learn that Christ came to share life with them, that he welcomes those who are the lowest in society and inspires them by the Spirit of his love to lift them up for new life and service. The women gather as a community of the Spirit, and through Henna Han's leadership in solidarity with the margin they discover that the tables have been overturned and that Christ has made them welcome![41]

Round Table Leadership

Henna Han is not the only woman of Spirit who dares to take up the challenge of round table leadership. This search for new styles of partnership in the church has become a worldwide movement dedicated to changing Jacob's-ladder leadership to leadership in the form of Sarah's circle.[42] In fact, women are well on their way to making sure their circle includes not only all the Sarahs of the world but also all the Hagars. In Africa, women have formed a five-year project called "The Circle of Concerned African Women in Theology."[43] The Asian Women's Resource Centre for Culture and Theology promotes the work of women through programs and through the journal *In God's Image*.[44] The women's commissions of the Ecumenical Association of Third World Theologians carry on regional and international conferences.[45]

The women have been joined by the World Council of Churches in its Ecumenical Decade of Churches in Solidarity with Women. In her book on the decade entitled *Who Will Roll the Stone Away?* Mercy Amba Oduyoye says, "In the Decade 1988–98 we seek justice for women, to dream 'bold dreams' for a new community, and to act both locally and globally for the conversion of church and society towards the recognition of the full humanity of women."[46]

This decade is for men as well as women. The whole church is asked to be in solidarity with women by making it clear that it no longer considers them less than human. If the churches cannot find some way to bring unity and justice within their communities, their integrity as communities of Christ is in question.[47] The search for inclusive solidarity among different nationalities, classes, races, gender, and so much more is under way, and part of that search is for leadership that contributes to the building up of churches by literally "going in circles."

Feminist interpretation of the church calls into question the contradictions between the theological interpretations of ministry as service and the practices of clerical privilege and exclusion. In my opinion, the overcoming of the contradictions points us not only back, to the origins of Spirit-filled communities among the first Christians, but forward to a time when the gifts of the Spirit for leadership are recognized among all those who share new life in Christ. Meanwhile, one step I would advocate is a moratorium wherever possible on language reflecting distinctions between laity and clergy. Instead, it might be helpful to speak of the gifts of the Spirit *charismata* that are given by Christ for the leadership of the church. In the same way we need to move away from emphasis on orders and divine unchanging patterns of church life and toward an emphasis on an organization that seeks to be faithful to the work of Christ in ever-changing contexts.

Community of the Spirit

The appeal to the authority of the Spirit is not new in a church that was born of Spirit and continued to be renewed by Spirit-filled movements through the ages (Acts 2:17). The Greek Testament witness to the primacy of the Spirit in the creation and upbuilding of Christian community is underlined by the Apostles' Creed, whose third article begins, "I believe in the Holy Spirit." All the subsequent phrases, including the "holy, catholic church, the communion of saints," are derivative from this affirmation of the third person of the Trinity.[48] There is according to Ernst Käsemann, "a concept in Pauline and sub-Pauline theology which describes in a theologically exact and comprehensive way the essence and scope of every ecclesiastical ministry and function—namely, the concept of charisma.[49]

This Spirit Christology and ecclesiology were not created by Paul but came out of the earlier Antiochene-Christian, Jewish-Christian missionary movement and its theology. In this ecclesiology, baptism by the Spirit was the foundation of all church life.[50] Paul shares this emphasis on the importance of the Spirit in the life of the church. Thus, for instance, in Romans 6:23 he declares that "the free gift [charisma] of God is eternal life in Christ Jesus our Lord." Using earlier Christian hymns, Paul seeks both to affirm this Spirit ecclesiology and to correct the tradition by making clear that we do not already live in the New Creation. In the not-yet of the present, we receive both the divine gift and the task that goes with it. For Paul the test of genuine charisma is not displayed through supernatural power but rather in the service it renders. It is a free gift of the community and its purpose is to strengthen that community in its service (1 Cor. 14).[51] All who have been baptized into the risen and glorified body of Christ are empowered to offer their bodies in the service of God as their spiritual worship (Rom. 12:1).

Paul often uses hymns as he seeks both to honor and to order this Hellenistic-Jewish received tradition. One of these is the early baptismal hymn of Galatians 3:26–28, which celebrates the new life of freedom in Christ received through baptism. Through the new life as a member of Christ, the Christian is no longer bound by the old patriarchal forms. In the new order of freedom the community lives beyond the division of Jew and Greek, slave and free, male and female. As Elisabeth Fiorenza puts it:

> As such, Gal. 3:28a does not assert that there are no longer men and women in Christ, but that patriarchal marriage—and sexual relationships between male and female—is no longer constitutive of the new community in Christ. Irrespective of their procreative capacities and of the social roles connected with them, persons will be full members of the Christian movement in and through baptism.[52]

In this beginning of the New Creation, distinctions of religion, race, class, nationality, and gender are no longer significant: "So if anyone is in Christ, there is a new creation: everything old has passed away; see, everything has become new!" (2 Cor. 5:17). The forms of organization are dependent on the Spirit and the service of Christ, but these forms are created by those who receive the gifts of leadership in the congregations.

Authority in community

By the time of Paul there were still no definite forms of leadership, but he does supply us with three lists of the gifts of Christ's Spirit that are to be found among those who are responsible for leadership in congregations (1 Cor. 12:8–10, 18–30; Rom. 12:6–8). A later list from about 90 C.E. is also to be found in Ephesians 4:11. As we have already seen, the gift of leadership, administration, or cybernetics (*kybernesis*) appears only in 1 Corinthians 12:28, but all the gifts listed are what today would be considered gifts to be used in the leadership or building up of the church for service in the world. To avoid the use of "ministry" and "service" because of their difficulty, Jürgen Moltmann has chosen to speak of these gifts of leadership as "assignments." The entire community is assigned through baptism to become a sign of God's coming reign and to carry out this assignment in various ways.[53] Some of the gifts are kerygmatic and have to do with making known the word of the gospel (apostles, prophets, evangelists, teachers, and admonishers). Other gifts are related to diakonic leadership of service (deacons and deaconesses, widows, healers, exorcists). A third variety of gifts are cybernetic, or gifts of rule.[54]

Whatever name we give the gifts of the Spirit, it is important to recognize that they are still Christ's gifts of wisdom and power, granted to the congregation through the Spirit (2 Cor. 1:22). According to Ernst Käsemann, Paul basically understood *charis* as the power of the resurrected Christ at work in those who are joined to Christ through baptism (1 Cor. 12:6, 11). All of the baptized are "office-bearers," and each has a charism or power and the responsibility to exercise that gift for the good of others (1 Cor. 14).[55]

These manifestations of the gift of new life received in baptism receive their authority from Christ, who is at work in them. The assent of the congregation to the gifts and to their practice is also a sign of authority, but the gifts belong to Christ and do not in themselves convey any permanent power. Leadership in the church has what the Downtown Presbyterian Church in Rochester, New York, has called "*an authority of purpose,* as distinguished from *authority of position* or office." This church encourages all members to discover their gifts of leadership as they form groups to carry out projects on behalf of the community as well as projects needed in the life of the church.[56]

Power understood as the ability to accomplish desired ends is present in human relationships no matter how particular communities or societies are organized. Nevertheless, Christian communities recognize that the source of power in their life is the love of Christ which inspires and directs them. This is a style of power not of coercion but of empowerment of others. Those who exercise legitimated power or authority are those who assist members of the congregation in making use of their gifts in the service of Christ's love in the world. This authority is one of leadership in the round as it connects to what was described as the first category of Christian tradition in chapter 1, the Tradition of Christ, and to the fourth category, traditions of the church. It also connects to those at the margins of society who search for word of God's love and justice.[57]

Without denying the importance of empowerment for service in the life of the church, we can still recognize that there is a need for new naming and new actions that spring from an authority of purpose, not from authority of clerical privilege. In a sense we can say that we need at least for the moment to get rid of the chairs at the table, so there is no limited seating. At the Last Supper there were probably no chairs, for people reclined at table while eating a feast. Nevertheless the "seating" is traditionally rumored to have been limited to twelve Jewish males. Now that the Spirit and the seating are unlimited, we need to look for clues in the tradition and in our own lives about what feminist leadership gifts at that table might look like. We will most certainly not expect any one model or task to emerge, but it seems we could expect a particular style of leadership behavior, with clues or indications that the empowerment of authority in community is already beginning to happen.

Clues to feminist leadership

We can learn a lot as Christians in a quest for feminist leadership from the understanding of Jesus' call to freely chosen service and from the gifts of the Spirit discovered in the early church and in every age. Yet it seems to me that in this liminal period when we are searching for "real live feminist leaders" we need also to look for models of women who have exercised leadership and shown a style of leadership behavior. One way to do this is to think of women who have been role models for us and what they have taught us. Another is to point to examples of leadership in which authority is exercised by standing with the community in solidarity with those who are most marginal. A third way is to speak of characteristics of women's leadership and their contribution to new styles of leadership in the church. This last approach is well developed by Joan Campbell in a new ecumenical volume on *Women and Church.* She describes the style of women's leadership as relational, connectional, flexible, intimate, and passionate.[58] These are some of the styles noted earlier in this chapter in reference to the research of Lynn Rhodes and Barbara Brown Zikmund.

These are all helpful, although the third option has its dangers in terms of assigning certain biological or cultural stereotypes to women. Here, however, I would like to emphasize the first two options by lifting up four clues as they emerge in the life of Miriam. In this use of Miriam as a model I am greatly helped by Phyllis Trible's article, "Bringing Miriam Out of the Shadows," as she works with the texts of Exodus 1, 2, and 15 and Numbers 12 and 20.[59] Having honored the liminal or provisional status of our quest by using a biblical model that all can examine, I will end by suggesting a few contemporary examples. These are intended to serve only as an invitation for examples and clues from everyone who shares this quest for feminist/liberation leadership.

My first clue is that *leaders are made for people and not people for leaders.*

Echoing Jesus' words in Mark 2:27, we remember that "the sabbath was made for humankind, and not humankind for the sabbath." Institutional structures that provide images of strength and direction for institutions are matters of organization, not of order. Leadership is a matter to be arranged as a way of expressing the calling and mission of the people. Thus it is situation-variable and changes in different contexts, but as a gift of the Spirit to the church communities in their service of the world, it is exercised in *diakonia* with the communities. This is a conviction shared by many persons who are working to "reinvent the church" as a community of faith and struggle for liberation. Thus Leonardo Boff describes *ecclesiogenesis* as the church being reborn so that "first comes the flock, and then, for the sake of the flock, the shepherd."[60] Although Boff still considers the hierarchy important for the church, he is clear that its purpose is to share in the service of the faith community. As Hans Küng puts it, ecclesiology is in error when it turns out to be "hierarchology."[61]

Miriam's leadership in exile seems to indicate a similar concern for inclusion of the people. In Numbers 12:2 we read one of the fragments left from her suppressed story of leadership as the priestly writers do their best to dismiss the authority of this uppity woman. Thus with Aaron she confronts Moses for marrying a non-Israelite woman and for refusing to share the prophetic role, saying, "Has the Lord spoken only through Moses? Has [God] not spoken through us also?" Whether or not Miriam is jealous of Moses' Cushite wife because she is African and of higher status, as is argued by Randall Bailey, or prejudiced against her as a non-Hebrew we do not know for sure, but we do know that she is not afraid to confront patriarchal authority.[62] Miriam appears to claim her own prophetic role and to advocate for a more inclusive form of leadership that more adequately serves the needs of the community.

Those of us who have been reading the reports of the World Council of Churches Assembly in Canberra in February 1991 are aware of a modern Miriam named Chung Hyun Kyung. In her plenary address on the Holy Spirit, Professor Chung evoked the voices of martyred spirits and used Korean shaman ritual to express the Spirit's presence among us.[63] Cries of heresy were in the air when she declared that as a postcolonial theologian she is developing a theology that is life-giving for the poor and suffering women of Korea. The controversy over her theological presentation was most certainly in part a controversy over whom theology will serve and whether or not the Lord has spoken only through white Western male theologians.

The second clue is that *where leadership is present, community happens.* If feminist leadership is supportive of authority in community, then the exercise of this leadership concentrates on ways to evoke partnership or community. The *koinonia*-creating presence of Christ transforms the exercise of power into that of power for healing and the assertion of authority as a claim that God is present among the least of our sisters and brothers. A Greek Testament understanding of *koinonia* as a new focus of relationship in the common history of Jesus Christ that sets us free for others helps us to understand that the actual exercise of leadership in Christian perspective is an exercise of partnership. It is this gift of the Spirit that shapes leadership as partnership in Christ.

In continuing to examine the story of Miriam in Numbers 12:2–14 and 20:1–2, we discover that her leadership also seems to create community. In spite of the worst the patriarchal writers and God can do to this uppity woman, the community of Israel does not abandon her. Even though she is shut up outside the camp for seven days, they wait until she is "brought in again." Miriam is stricken with leprosy and continues to suffer this living death, but they journey and wait with her and she with them until, like Moses and Aaron, she dies before seeing the promised land. In sickness and suffering the community remains with this leader who helped to create their community.

Recently, in my own small town of Guilford, Connecticut, similar patriarchal condemnation was visited on a man named Jay Bowes for his ministry in the Peace and Justice Center of St. George Roman Catholic Church. Fired from his job as director because he attended the wedding of a former priest of the church, Jay and two women were actually "fired" because they were too uppity as lay leaders. Where Jay and the others were at work, community happened and people were empowered. This one small center has a large local program for youth and adults that includes a resource and education center, social action projects, and social advocacy groups for peace and justice. Already, in part because of Jay's work, the Guilford community had been blessed by the spin-off of Guilford Interfaith Housing, the Women and Family Life Center of Guilford, Meals on Wheels, and a Friendly Visitor program. Where this man is at work, community happens both inside and outside the church, and many in this community refuse to abandon Jay in his wilderness time.[64]

My third clue is that *leadership makes new naming possible*. It is not surprising that Jesus is identified with divine Wisdom, or Sophia, in the Gospels, and especially in Matthew. He renames and refocuses God's intention for all people and makes it possible for many to hear that intention as good news! Those who have been excluded by the old law are given a new opportunity for discipleship. Those who have been named as nobodies, distant from God, are now welcomed into God's household. The poor and lowly become the instruments for understanding the meaning of justice and love and the shape of Jesus' ministry (Matt. 25:31–46). Those who hear this new naming of their reality begin the long spiral of conversion/conscientization as they learn to recognize the contradictions in their lives between what they have been taught and what they experience as liberating and life-giving. As leaders enable them to value their own language, culture, history, and personal gifts as gifts of God, people learn to pray, sing, act, and dance out the *kerygma* of God's justice and love.

Most certainly this is part of Miriam's role with her people. Along with Jubal, Miriam is associated with the invention of music. In one of the earliest fragments of poetry in the Bible, we can still hear Miriam praise God for liberation after the crossing of the Red Sea (Ex. 15:21).

> "Sing to the LORD, for [God] has
> triumphed gloriously;
> horse and rider [God] has thrown
> into the sea."[65]

Of course, we know who stole all her stuff! As the patriarchal text now reads, the rest of the psalm is placed on Moses' lips. Phyllis Trible argues, however, that "the very retention of a Miriamic ending, in the presence of a Mosaic avalanche," is evidence of its antiquity.[66] Miriam continued with her people as one who gave voice to their prayers and praise in "timbrel and dance."

In 1991 at Yale Divinity School I co-taught a course with M. Shawn Copeland titled Feminist Theology in Third World Perspective. Just the opportunity to try to work out a way to be partners together across white and African American racial divisions was exciting, not to mention the possibility of global dialogue among women of many colors and cultures.[67] But one of the most striking aspects of this course was the way students began to do their own naming in response to the readings. For instance, one woman from Peru who cross-registered from another part of the university is finding the language of feminism both liberating and risky. In her first reflection paper she said:

> It was scary to get these things out on paper; but it was very useful. Facing the way I see the world is the best way to cause any change in me that will collaborate to make this world a better place. But at the same time, change is scary: first, because I have to challenge the status quo and this is hard especially in Latin America; but also because I feel that the God I was taught to believe in will get upset with me if I break the status quo.[68]

The final clue is that *leadership in a patriarchal world is at best multicultural and at worst leads to martyrdom.* The liturgy or work of the people (*leitourgia*) includes their culture and their way of expressing faith and struggle. Those in leadership positions are called to include the cultures of the people with whom they are serving, but they need also to include their own culture so that they are authentic to their own story. This bicultural or multicultural expression and leadership must also include one additional culture if it is to be heard and be helpful in interpreting the journey of liberation. It must include the culture of the dominant group so that people understand the tradition that is controlling their lives.

This means in theological studies, for instance, that we cannot do theology without a spiral of critical action/reflection that includes experience, critical social reflection, tradition, and action. Multicultural leadership makes possible the journey in a patriarchal world; it resists standing above while at the same time makes a way for new alternatives that can endure in the face of patriarchy. Sometimes this difficult mix leads to burnout. It is often the case that people do not want to recognize gifts among them that may disturb and challenge in new ways. At other times, being willing to stand with those who are oppressed, excluded, or ignored may lead to solidarity in suffering for those who speak out for justice.

Miriam learned about the cost of such leadership when leprosy was the punishment for speaking the truth about the needs of the people. She knew the people, and she also knew her own self-identity as a prophet, but the text tells us that patriarchy tried to have the last word with her. Not quite finished off, she nevertheless was condemned to a life of leprosy for opposing the will of Moses and of God. This same patriarchal image of God continues to be upset when we as uppity women seek to be part of a new feminist culture that advocates for the oppressed, while at the same time "serving in Pharaoh's court." Yet it is just this willingness to work in at least three directions, and sometimes pay the cost, that may make possible the small anticipations of church in the round.

An African American woman in the Feminist Theology in Third World Perspective course helped me to express this tension in the light of her own story. Pat Boozer learned to be bicultural from her grandmother, who taught her that she was equal to everyone else. As a child it was very clear to Pat that she was not treated as an equal in white-dominant society. She puzzled about this, because her grandmother could not be wrong. Finally she realized that her grandmother did not tell her that she would be *treated* equally, but only that she was indeed equal. Having learned this, Pat went on to live as one who is equal and to learn about the culture of the oppressors so that she could make a stand for justice in our society.[69]

These clues are not rules for what feminist/liberation leadership might look like. In regard to this particular quest we do not have all the answers by any means. As Doris Ellzey Blesoff says in her song, "We Are Gathered,"

> Well, we don't have all the answers,
> but we sure do have the questions;
> we know that to create is to survive.[70]

These clues need to be tested out in our own experience to see if they are in touch with the feminist quest for new styles of ministry as we understand it.[71] This form of leadership behavior still has no name. Words like "service," "ministry," and "lordship" are all so tied to paradigms of patriarchy it is difficult to spring them loose to new meanings. Yet other words, like "enablement," "mentorship," and "partnership," don't have a very broad usage. We can call it a gift and a power from God for the community of faith and struggle, but we also need to discuss what words will help to name this quest for new styles of leadership. Meanwhile, even if we don't have a name, we do have a foremother! So when words fail, we can at least say, "Be a Miriam!"

Even though a full understanding of what feminist leadership and service might look like in church and society is still in its liminal stage, there is no doubt that there are many, many Miriams in all parts of history and all cultures: women who have created their own way as leaders in spite of patriarchal denial, suppression, and attempted erasure of their gifts. One of the tasks that women face in our time is to rediscover, re-cover, reread, and retell the stories of these women leaders so that all may know that women and men together share these gifts. Out of this may come new models and images of what leadership behavior would mean in the midst of a community of shared authority.

Judy Chicago's *The Dinner Party* is one attempt of a white woman feminist to invite white Western women to enter into their own heritage by sharing a table with Goddesses and women of all the centuries of the development of Western civilization. Using thirty-nine place settings, she honors thirteen women on each of the three sides of a triangular table. The women are in turn supported by 999 other women contemporaries whose names are inscribed on the tiles of the "Heritage Floor." The images of the women are contained by their plates yet are developed out of a butterfly motif as a symbol of liberation in the midst of containment, and this in turn is most often represented by various patterns of a woman's vagina. In her journal entry of June 2, 1974, Judy Chicago writes:

> I want to make butterfly images that are hard, strong, soft, passive, opaque, transparent—all different states—and I want them all to have vaginas so they'll be female butterflies and at the same time be shells, flowers, flesh, forest—all kinds of things simultaneously.[72]

Working with nearly four hundred artisans for five years, Judy Chicago set out to gather the gifts of women as potters, painters, and needleworkers and to offer them up for honor and for sharing by those who would come to share in the dinner party. The presentation of women and their gifts of inspired leadership represents a recovery and sharing of women's heritage not only in the history told but in the style of the art itself. Alice Walker has pointed out her disappointment in the treatment of Sojourner Truth in the "Third Wing," where she represents the African American woman's contribution to history in the period between the American Revolution and the Women's Revolution. Sojourner Truth is presented with three faces rather than the more predominant motif of the vagina pattern, and Alice Walker wonders if this is because it is difficult for white women to admit that black women are fully embodied women with vaginas.[73]

This serves to warn us that the dinner table, like the round table of King Arthur, is a "moveable feast." It catches an image of women in leadership, yet there is a great deal it does not catch, and it needs, in turn, to be replaced with a more global and inclusive table. Chicago herself recognizes this and writes that the table is not only limited by its representative number but also because most of the women we know about in history are from the ruling classes.

> History has been written from the point of view of those who have been in power. It is not an objective record of the human race—we do not know the history of humankind. A true history would allow us to see the mingled efforts of peoples of all colors and sexes, all countries and races, all seeing the universe in their own diverse ways.[74]

The table does catch a good deal of the imagery intended in the round table metaphor for feminist ecclesiology, for it brings together the sacred and the ordinary, the altar and the dinner table, the Last Supper and the shared meal of all participants. The corners of the table are designed as altar cloths, embroidered with Goddess symbols in triangles. The cloths are called "millennium runners," because this points to a future vision of inclusion for those who have been rendered invisible.

> The Millennium is a symbolic reference to that moment in the future when the double standard—which defines men's rituals as not only significant but sacred, while rendering women's invisible—will end, and all human effort will be honored for its part in the richness of human experience.[75]

The cloths are also called millennium runners because M is the thirteenth letter of the alphabet. There are thirteen guests seated along each wing of the triangular table, representing a women's version of the thirteen guests at the Last Supper. According to Chicago, *The Dinner Party* on one level "is a reinterpretation of the Last Supper from the point of view of those who have done the cooking and serving throughout history."[76] The table is not round, but its intention is to lift up women's gifts and invite us all so we may begin to share in the search for new patterns of creativity, leadership, and service among women. Like the round table talk and leadership, it makes connections not only to tradition but also to those who live at the margins of society.

Leadership in the round seeks to move away from the traditions of ordination and orders as authority of domination and to emphasize instead authority exercised in community. This does not deny the need for organization in the life of the church or for rituals of recognition of the gifts of the Spirit. The powers or gifts that God has given a local, regional, national, or international church body need to be recognized and organized for the work of God's new household of justice and freedom. But these spiritual powers are not permanently indelible orders that create a superior clerical caste in the churches. In the same way that the structures of apartheid have to be dismantled if racism is to be addressed, the structures of patriarchal clericalism have to be dismantled if sexism is to be addressed in the church. Leadership will only truly be in the round when it functions to carry out the calling of Jesus Christ to make all persons welcome as they gather around God's table of New Creation.

Part Two
Kitchen Table Solidarity

"**I**f you can't stand the heat, get out of the kitchen!" This familiar saying reminds us of something important about kitchens: a lot of work goes on in them, and they can get very messy, hot, and difficult.[1] Our solidarity work begins in kitchens because it is there, rather than at a formal dinner table or a mythical knightly round table, that the daily activities and lives of persons are shaped and molded. Sometimes this kitchen table is in the house of the master, and those who are cooking and serving are poor women and women of color. These women have shown over the centuries that they can stand the heat and withstand the domination of the rich white mistresses and masters. In other homes the kitchen table may be a scene of conflict and abuse as it reflects the lived reality of many families in crisis. In still others the kitchen table is a source of identity and solidarity for the family, which gathers up the bits and pieces of its life as its members prepare and share whatever food they have.

A lot of people who use this expression never spent much time in a kitchen, but at least, if they were to think about it, they might recognize that Martha probably had every right to complain to Jesus because she knew Mary needed to be in the place where the work gets done (Luke 10:38–42). Or they might even want to enrich the dialogue a little and have Jesus say to Martha, "If you can't stand the heat, get out of the kitchen!"[2]

At any rate, none of us should be surprised when the church in the round calls for kitchen tables, where we get down to the sweaty tasks of daily living, as well as for round tables that draw us into a partnership of sharing and reflection. We need kitchen tables in the church for, as Chuck Lathrop says, it is not "magic bread" we are baking but dough that takes its "dying-in-order-to-rise-again-time."

> And it is we in the present
> who are mixing and kneading
> the dough for the future.[3]

The image of the kitchen table is far removed from the "tables" that are lists of church order, in which persons are ranked according to position. Instead, its emphasis is on the daily work of women who care for homes and families, preparing the dough for the future of their children and sometimes breaking the bread not only at home but in the assembled church community.

For most women, and probably for Mary and Martha as well, there is no question of the artificial distinction between "serving at table" and "listening to the word of Jesus."[4] Even Luke's construction of what may have been a tradition about a famous missionary couple seems to be open to the idea that they both shared in the learning. According to Mary Rose D'Angelo's article "Women Partners in the New Testament," there is an ancient and widespread reading of 10:39 that says Martha "had a sister named Mary *who also* sat at the feet of Jesus" as a disciple of the rabbi.[5] Both discipleship and service are essential, and both take place in women's lives as they join with others in communities of solidarity with those who yearn for liberation and wholeness in their lives.

The story of Mary and Martha both conceals and reveals the possibility of kitchen table solidarity for a church in the round. It conceals it because Luke and John recast it and inserted it in their Gospel accounts to serve their own purposes. Elisabeth Fiorenza has shown that not only here but elsewhere Luke intends to show women in subordinate roles in church ministry to fit his image of an ordered, patriarchal form of church life, as well as to emphasize the separation of the ministries of word and table.[6] To do this he turns the two partners who served together at the Lord's Table into competing kitchen helpers. John's account of Mary and Martha in 12:1–8 presents the women in a more positive light but overshadows Mary's anointing of Jesus with the story of Lazarus. Patriarchal tradition downplayed her role even further by mixing up her story with that of Mary Magdalene and the sinful woman of Luke 7:36–50.

The story may also reflect some memory that goes back to the lifetime of Jesus, but its use in Luke and John reveals what appears to be an early tradition about a famous missionary couple engaged in kitchen table ministry: Martha, the *diakonos* or minister at the Lord's Table; Mary, the *adelphe* or sister.[7] The two probably served together in a house church and were not necessarily sisters from the same family. These titles, along with others like co-worker and apostle, were very fluid designations of leadership in the early church and were applied by Paul to women as well as men. For instance, Paul speaks of another female missionary couple, Euodia and Syntyche, as those who have contended or "struggled" side by side with him in the work of the gospel (Phil. 4:2–3).[8]

In Part Two: Kitchen Table Solidarity, we will continue our reflection on the meaning of church in the round by listening to the voices of women and men who recognize that their own lives have been "bought with a price" and make a commitment to struggle side by side in solidarity with those who are oppressed (1 Cor. 6:20). Chapter 3, "Communities of Faith and Struggle," shares the experience of these communities in their everyday, kitchen table existence in order to reflect on the structures that shape communities of faith that are struggling to become church in the round. Chapter 4, "Justice and the Church," reexamines theological discussions of the role of the church in God's saving and liberating action and asks about the nature of the church and its identifying characteristics in the light of struggles for justice.

3 | *Communities of Faith and Struggle*

The Presbyterian Church of the Ascension in East Harlem is built of brick and sandwiched between two brick apartment buildings near the corner gas station on 106th Street and First Avenue in New York City. The homes of that community are also built of brick, whether they are early twentieth-century walk-up apartments or mid-century housing projects. Yet small kitchens, not brick buildings, are the center of a great deal of the activity of that community and church. In all seasons of the year, the center of life in each crowded apartment is the kitchen table. Not only are meals prepared and eaten there, but every other activity, from unpacking groceries and doing homework to partying and card playing, takes place there, for it is usually the only table. The kitchen table is the scene of arguments, reprimands, and fighting as well as the scene of counting up the small cash supply or filling out forms for court or the welfare office. As the center of daily life it reflects the basic activities of the families, both good and bad.

The older buildings sometimes had a metal top placed over the bathtub, to create a kitchen table next to the sink and stove. In the sixth-floor walk-up apartment where I lived the tub and its tabletop were gone, but the added shower left no room for a table and the kitchen sink did duty for brushing teeth as well as washing dishes. But in the ministry I shared in East Harlem, the kitchen was unmistakably a center of activity and almost always the place where visitors sat for coffee or conversation. In order to make clear the connection between the life of the church and the community, many gatherings for home Bible study or liturgy were held around the table. Each Sunday the congregation recited "The Parish Purpose" from Luke 4:18–19, declaring that the Spirit of the Lord was upon them to bring good news to the poor and preach deliverance to the captives. Through the week, many of the members lived out that calling in their own apartments and around their kitchen tables, as connections were made between faith and the struggle for life and between neighbors driven apart by alienation and fear. The kitchen table became a place of struggle for liberation and was every bit as much a part of the church as the large round table in the brick sanctuary a few blocks away.

Communities of faith and struggle provide us with an opportunity to glimpse the many ways church in the round happens in small grass-roots communities in their daily struggles for justice and new life. Whether or not they have kitchen tables, the communities are built up from the bottom in the struggles of everyday life. In her book *Against Machismo*, Elsa Tamez underlines the fact that the struggle to transform relationships between women and men in the church begins at this daily "kitchen table" level where most women spend their lives.

> This struggle has always been "natural" for poor women, for indigenous women, for black women, for *mestizo* women [of mixed European and American Indian ancestry], for peasant women, for working women, for middle-class women. For there is a truth here that we cannot overlook and that we who seek a new order of life must embrace: the foretastes of utopia are experienced in everyday life, and it is in everyday life that we begin to build this utopia (Vidales). There is no place else.[1]

As we saw in chapter 1, a community of faith and struggle makes use of its critically reflected experience of struggle for justice and life as it selects from the still living and evolving past of scriptural and church traditions as a means of shaping an alternative future. It lives out of a faith that God is present, in and through the struggle for justice in solidarity with those at the margins of the church and society and in the discernment of the meaning of the gospel message. In *Ecclesiogenesis: The Base Communities Reinvent the Church*, Leonardo Boff tells us, "Community must be understood as a spirit to be created, as an inspiration to bend one's constant efforts to overcome barriers between persons and to generate a relationship of solidarity and reciprocity."[2]

Although the measure of its faithfulness is not a particular organizational structure or confessional tradition, the particular structures that shape the life of the community are crucial to its witness as a sign of God's new household where persons share life together as partners. For instance, it is seldom possible to sustain new styles of egalitarian leadership in the Spirit if the structural patterns of the church continue to be hierarchical. Attention must be paid not only to the communities but to the institutions of which they are a part. The communities provide leaven and critique for the larger institutions, but these institutions are often capable of disbanding and discouraging such communities unless their structures resist this move to centralize power.

In this chapter, "Communities of Faith and Struggle," I will describe some of the social structures of these communities that have emerged in response to particular contexts of struggle against oppression. In order to see more clearly what these structures look like and how they become a prism for the understanding of feminist and liberation ecclesiology, we will look briefly at a variety of types of communities that have arisen in the later part of the twentieth century. The chapter concludes with a suggestion of some clues to feminist liberation ecclesiology that can be tested out in the last three chapters of this book. These small signs may help us catch the vision of new life that might be possible in the life of the church.

A Time of Kairos

Kairos is a very particular type of time. Unlike *chronos,* or time that can be counted and counted upon with watches and calendars, *kairos* is a special time of crisis or particular opportunity. Thus at the beginning of Jesus' ministry, Mark 1:15 says, "The time [*kairos*] is fulfilled, and the kingdom of God has come near; repent, and believe in the good news." In Jesus' preaching the promises of the prophets are fulfilled and the year of Jubilee is at hand. This special moment presents a crisis of discernment and decision to accept the good news of the advent of God's new household.[3] As Paul puts it in 2 Corinthians 6:2, "Now is the acceptable time [*kairos*]; see, now is the day of salvation!"

This appointed time of decision making has always been a part of the biblical message and of theological interpretation of the meaning of eschatology, or the end or purpose of life and history. It also comes to the fore as a description of contemporary events whenever there is a great crisis in which a decision must be made. In our time the *kairos* appears in the worsening crises of oppression, poverty, injustice, and ecological disaster that confront us on every side. How are we to interpret these signs of the times and how are we to respond? In Europe a time of crisis and a call for decision came at the time of Hitler's rise to power, leading to the Barmen Declaration of the Confessing Church. In the Third World today the decision comes in a crisis of white Eurocentric domination, leading to "The Kairos Document" and two related documents called "Kairos Central America" and "The Road to Damascus." The first document is a Christian, biblical, and theological response to the crisis of apartheid in South Africa, written in 1985. It declares, in part:

> For very many Christians in South Africa this is the KAIROS, the moment of grace and opportunity, the favourable time in which God issues a challenge to decisive action. It is a dangerous time because, if this opportunity is missed, and allowed to pass by, the loss for the Church, for the Gospel and for all the people of South Africa will be immeasurable.[4]

The later two documents are responses from other groups, joining the first in speaking a prophetic word to the church out of situations of turmoil and oppression. All three have been published together in *Kairos: Three Prophetic Challenges to the Church,* edited by Robert McAfee Brown, as a call to the churches in North America to respond to the crisis of groaning around them by identifying themselves with struggles for liberation and justice around the world.

Signs of Jubilee

In a sense these statements are signs of God's Jubilee, when the people and the land are set free. It is the challenge that Luke has Jesus present as he begins his ministry. The good news of God's Jubilee is being fulfilled; all accumulated inequities will be wiped out, and all God's people can begin at the same point. Other kings, like Herod, had sent out good news proclamations of their reign, but Jesus makes good news for the poor the keynote of his proclamation of God's reign. No wonder he becomes a prophet without welcome in his hometown when he makes the announcement that the rules of the power game are changing (Mark 6:4).[5]

The legislation of Leviticus 25:1–34 makes provision for a jubilee year of liberation every fifty years, in which everything that came from God is returned so that it can be redistributed. Even if the legislation was mainly "Zion's fiction," what seems to have been a social proposal becomes what Sharon Ringe calls a liberated metaphor that continues to be "read forward."[6] Isaiah 58:6 and 61:1–2 use the imagery of release from captivity and good news for the poor to announce that memory of God's future is already happening as the oppressed are set at liberty and the jubilee year arrives.

People often resent the use of a so-called political slogan like "oppression" in theological discussion, but, as Elsa Tamez has reminded us, the word itself is embedded in the biblical tradition.[7] The oppressed that Jesus has come to set free are the crushed ones: the bruised of society, the nonpersons who have no room to breathe or to live as human beings. God is specially concerned for such people because they have been denied their created humanity by the way the social system in which they live is functioning. They in turn are those who know what good news is all about, as they long for a time when they will be economically, politically, personally, and physically free to live and work in justice and peace.

The messianic word of comfort for the oppressed is also a word of judgment for the oppressor, for, if the rules of the social/economic/political game change, the benefits of belonging to the dominant group will be distributed in a new way. Often Christian congregations don't hear this word of judgment because they identify with the wrong persons in the biblical story. In Luke 4 they hear only the comforting words about Jesus' call to ministry of service and identify with Jesus. This identity is then interpreted as a call to serve those "less fortunate" rather than as a call to solidarity in the struggle for justice. Yet it is possible that the message might come home more sharply if we were to identify with the townspeople of Nazareth. When they saw that the message of freedom was not going to benefit them, they sought to destroy the messenger.

In contrast to Mark's account, in which the people are hostile from the beginning, Luke presents the people of Nazareth as responding favorably to

Jesus' prophetic proclamation until they remember that this is only "Joseph's son." In the face of their growing doubt and hostility, Jesus indicates that he will carry his ministry to the Gentiles if he is rejected by his own people. Having heard Jesus preach, the people expect him to perform miracles and healings to confirm his message, but it appears that since his words were not met with faith, he cannot and will not perform signs.

In this moment of decision, or *kairos*, Jesus' words produce rage among his audience, and they seek to kill him by throwing him off a cliff or possibly by stoning him as a false prophet (Luke 13:34–35). Jesus escapes, but the shadow of rejection and cross hangs over his ministry from the very beginning. Using modern terminology, we might say that Jesus confronted their classism, in claiming that an ordinary townsperson could be the Messiah, and their racism, in declaring that the Jubilee would be for all people. It is no wonder that those whose social location is not among those longing for the Jubilee prefer to identify with Jesus rather than the people who rejected his good news!

It is also no wonder that those in the East Harlem Protestant Parish called this text their "Parish Purpose" or that "The Kairos Document" invoked this prophetic tradition as the basis of its call for prophetic theology and the basis of its hope.[8] In a setting of poverty, racism, and oppression these words from Isaiah are good news. Jesus had come to set the oppressed at liberty and welcome the nobodies of society, and the church is challenged to carry out this ministry. As far as I can remember, no one in East Harlem ever paid much attention to the other side of the year of Jubilee or wondered why Luke dropped the second half of verse 2 in Isaiah 61, which speaks of "the day of vengeance." Our agenda was clear. We sang, "This is the year of Jubilee . . . My Lord has set the people free . . ." and tried as best we knew how to live out that freedom.[9] Those of us who know ourselves to be on the other side of this tradition need to search out our own forms of imaginative and constructive repentance in order to make the prophet welcome in our own country!

Confessing churches

Communities of faith and struggle in situations of oppression in Africa, Central America, and Asia are responding to the moment of *kairos* and calling churches around the world to become confessing churches that say no to oppression even when that leads to martyrdom. According to Robert McAfee Brown, these documents have much in common besides their roots in the biblical liberation tradition.[10] They share the characteristics of urgency about the life-and-death situation of the people in their contexts of poverty, oppression, and war. They are all a result of group process and discussion and came out of many kitchen table communities of faith and struggle who shared in the discussion and repeated redrafting. They are contextual theologies: shaped out of commitment to act in solidarity with the poor and oppressed, making use of social analysis of their situations of pain, and continuing the theological spiral with serious rereading of the Gospel and church tradition. They conclude with a call to themselves and the churches to confess their sins of worshiping the false gods of imperialism, money, and racism and to move to action in the struggle for justice.

The documents represent a collective confession of the inadequacy of most ecclesiology and church practice for the crisis of suffering that people face in our groaning world. This is particularly clear as we recognize that the three types of theology described and critiqued in "The Kairos Document" represent theologies present not only in Third World contexts but also in North American contexts.

State theology is the theological justification of the status quo with its racism, capitalism, and totalitarianism. It misuses theological and biblical concepts for its own political purposes and worships a God who blesses and upholds the state [2.1–2.4].

Church theology is a liberal theology that is cautiously critical of apartheid but seeks reconciliation and nonviolence without critical social analysis of the source of the division and of the violence in unjust structures of oppression. Its call for peace when there is no peace is made possible by a dualistic way of thinking that separates faith and spirituality from the public and political realm and assigns only the spiritual realm to the ministry of the church [3.1–3.4].

Prophetic theology is a biblical theology that focuses on the liberating message of the Bible in the critical situation of oppression faced by the people in South Africa. By use of the theological spiral of contextual theology, prophetic theology seeks to analyze the situation so that it can discern the signs of the times and name the sins and evils as well as lifting up a hope of salvation. Such a theology will continue to evolve as the situation changes, seeking to discern ways to confess the faith in a rapidly changing time of crisis [4.1–4.6]. For instance, in South Africa today the prophetic theology is seeking out an understanding of what postexilic theology will mean beyond liberation from apartheid.[11]

Confessional churches

Those of us in the United States are more likely to be part of confessional churches than confessing churches. These churches are rooted in their traditions and, more often than not, if they are what are called "mainline churches," they are likely to practice some form of state or church theology rather than a prophetic theology. But they too are faced with a crisis, that of growing irrelevance in contemporary society. In their book *American Mainline Religion*, Wade Clark Roof and William McKinney document what this means for churches which have made up the religious and cultural center. They describe mainline or mainstream religion as "the dominant, culturally established faiths held by the majority of Americans."[12] Although for much of American history mainline churches were white and Protestant, this gradually changed with the inclusion of Roman Catholics and Jews.

Since the 1960s, black churches have begun to become part of the mainline, and now conservative churches are beginning to move toward the religious and cultural center as white liberal churches move to the "sideline."[13] Nevertheless, most talk of mainline churches is focused around their decline in influence and usually assumes that the churches are predominantly white, even though this misnaming is not an accurate description of the religious and cultural center of our pluralistic and changing nation. Saying "mainline" when we mean "white mainline" or "white, liberal, Protestant mainline" perpetuates the assumption of white privilege and affluence, by ignoring the actual mainline presence of Roman Catholics and of persons of all colors and classes, and allows this "old mainline group" to continue preaching a gospel of inclusion and welcome while practicing white advantage and dominance.

The crisis in white mainline confessional churches today is one of nondecision. As the nation and world have changed and grown ever more pluralistic, fragmented, and alienated, the churches have followed the lead of dominant American politics of the last twenty years and tried to move away from the social vision of justice that was shared in the struggles of the sixties. As Rosemary Radford Ruether put it in 1989:

> The last 16 years have been marked by a concerted effort to retreat from the dread 1960s and re-establish an "innocent," unself-critical Americanism. . . . [The] reaction has included efforts to delegitimate liberation theology—both its challenge to American power in Latin America and its capacity to draw conscientious North American Christians into solidarity with Latin American liberation movements.[14]

Although the American churches have long followed a tradition of emphasis on private and public morality rather than on doctrine and worship, they no longer know how to speak with any form of consensus in the face of moral and ideological pluralism and, instead, are faced with a struggle between what Roof and McKinney call "religious moralists" and "secular humanists."[15] The latter group is heavily represented by people who have been leaving the churches in the search for communities of social justice ever since white mainline churches began retreating from their public moral commitments, but they are often on a deeply religious quest for a community that connects faith and struggle. In fact, this seems to be one of the reasons for the decline of white liberal churches. The membership of these churches is very individualistic and thus tolerant of many types of theological interpretation. Yet they are largely controlled by upper-middle-class males who are conservative in politics and economics.

The loss is to the "left"; not to the religious right, as is usually supposed, but to the more progressive positions of political and social morality possible outside most institutional churches. As Roof and McKinney put it, the mainline church is losing members to "the secularists it has spawned," not to "the conservatives it has scorned."[16]

An example of this split is the current debate in the churches over issues of sexuality. The response in 1991 to the human sexuality study of the Presbyterian Church, "Keeping Body and Soul Together: Sexuality, Spirituality, and Social Justice," reflects the growing split in that church, not just between liberals and conservatives but between two interpretations or paradigms of the way the world ought to function. Those advocates of a feminist liberation paradigm or interpretation of reality and what counts as authoritative in the Christian tradition call for a change in the traditional patriarchal paradigm of social hierarchy and authority as domination that continues to underlie both liberal and conservative theology.[17]

The paradigm of partnership emphasizes the social sin of patriarchal domination that underlies the fear of human sexuality and the practice of homosexuality and restricts women's control of their own bodies. The language of this appeal for new structures of partnership and equality in human relationships is heard as radical rhetoric and secular ideology by the majority of those who control the church establishment and perceive reality through the lens of the patriarchal paradigm. Thus the latter group rejected the statement of the sexuality report that

> the problem of sexuality has been misnamed in the church as the problem of homosexuality or of non-marital sex. It is time to clarify our moral vision and speak clearly and candidly. . . . We must not shy away from declaring, in the church and throughout this society: our problem is conformity to the unjust norm of compulsory heterosexuality and gender inequality.[18]

Whether liberal or conservative in theology, the liberal patriarchal paradigm draws attention to those moral sins that appear to threaten the male privilege of the nuclear family system but conceals the suffering and pain of those who do not benefit from this system because they are single parents, women and children caught in situations of family violence, or same-sex couples who find that their long-term committed relationships of love are to be condemned by God. The report points out that those representing the paradigm to "justice love" are considered advocates of moral license, rather than persons struggling to find a path toward moral institutional and personal responsibility.

> The church can exercise creative moral leadership only by marking a path between moral conformity and moral license. To do so, it is incumbent upon us to acknowledge how significant a gap now exists between

official church teachings and the sexual practices of most people, including many church members.

This gap is occurring . . . because the conventional moral code is inadequate for large numbers of people today—young and old, male and female, gay and straight, married and unmarried.[19]

Like the *kairos* documents, this human sexuality report arose out of a need to minister to the pain and oppression of people who are crying out for love with justice in the churches. They call the churches to choose "the things that make for peace," rather than rejecting the prophets (Luke 19:41).[20] Like the *kairos* documents the report is not the last word on the truth of the gospel, or of what some persons would call "politically correct jargon." But they are all signs of the *kairos* facing the churches today in the northern as well as in the southern half of our globe. They speak of danger and out-of-control oppressive situations, but they also speak of hope: the hope for conversion in the churches and for the coming of a new society. According to Audrey Chapman, in her book *Faith, Power, and Politics: Political Ministry in Mainline Churches*, to allow the moment to pass will result in

immeasurable loss for the churches and the gospel. There are still grounds for hope at least, if not for optimism, that some within the mainline churches, perhaps a smaller and more coherent group, will respond to the opportunity of this moment.[21]

According to Tex Sample in *U.S. Lifestyles and Mainline Churches*, the churches that are theologically and morally conservative share the patriarchal perspective on personal morality but are not necessarily politically right-wing, for they draw from many working-class groups who are supporters of policies such as those endorsed by the Democratic Party. They continue to grow because they provide a sense of community and a strong standard of patriarchal personal morality. This is often a source of identity for people lost in the social changes of our time, and it is particularly important to many women, who see this standard as a means of protecting themselves and their families in situations of economic dependency and potential abandonment or mistreatment.[22] They also grow because they have continued to recruit the conservative group within the mushrooming population of "baby boomers." At the same time the liberal baby boomers are staying away from white mainline churches to search for self-fulfillment in other cultural, religious, and social movements, including those for social change.[23]

The fastest-growing churches today are conservative churches that are using modern promotion and marketing techniques to reach out to the baby-boomer population and their children. This population began to be born in 1946 after World War II and numbers 76.4 million persons, nearly one person in three in our society. Megachurches of more than 2,000 worshipers have increased from 10 to 300 in the last twenty years, and the market economy and many other institutions are busy responding to the interests of this group as it moves toward middle age.[24] Market research says that people like convenience, accessibility, private worship experience, programs for all ages, and a sense of community and belonging. This is what they get at the Willow Creek Church in South Barrington, Illinois, where 15,000 people worship each week, and at the Second Baptist Church in Houston, where 1.1 percent of the population of Houston worships and 18,126 are members.[25]

Roof and McKinney quote a spoof of the megachurch from *The Wall Street Journal* that calls for a marketing plan to revitalize major religious faiths and includes a middle-American Christian church called "Mac-Church." It also recommends a new denominational branch in Judaism for baby boomers, and a "market-segmentation approach" for Roman Catholicism: RC Light for liberals, RC Classic for traditionalists, and RC Free for those interested in liberation theology.[26] But this is no spoof. The megachurch concept is responding to perceived needs of a large population in contemporary American society. The problem is that its response to cultural crisis is not a call to decision for engagement in the struggle for peace, justice, and integrity of creation but rather a call to withdraw further into a passive, self-centered, privatized experience of TV-style religion. The challenge of a *kairos* document or of the Jubilee is as difficult to hear in such an environment of personal self-fulfillment as that of old-line liberal churches. Yet this cultural response is also part of the social change and ferment in society today, which calls for new understanding and commitment and new structures that are adapted to the way the churches move to meet the crises of our time.

God's Mission and the Church

The paradigm shift that is part of the emergence of feminist and liberation theologies has been developing in history since the Enlightenment, when the impact of modern science led to the need for modern theologies. Peter Hodgson describes this time as follows:

> The Enlightenment was a period of revolutionary intellectual and cultural transformation . . . during the eighteenth and early nineteenth centuries, inaugurating the "modern era." It was precipitated by sweeping accomplishments in the natural sciences . . . and by emerging acceptance of the scientific world view.[27]

This view questioned the authority of the church and called for claims to be supported by reason and evidence. In turn, it led to the use of modern scientific thinking in the way that theologies were developed, either to accommodate to this world view or to counter it with traditional church teaching. Hodgson's thesis is that we have reached a new period of postmodern enlightenment and are moving to a new paradigm, or way of thinking, about reality and also about theology and ecclesiology, where "stress will fall more upon the public than the private, the social than the individual, liberation than liberty, equality than hierarchy, inquiry than authority, praxis than theory, the ecumenical than the provincial, the plural than the monolithic, the global than the national, the ecological than the anthropological."[28] His book sketches out how the new cultural paradigm leads to the response of a new model of ecclesial freedom.

We can also see the roots of this shift in theology and ecclesiology from the perspective of the shifts in understanding of the meaning of mission, as many churches have moved out of the nineteenth-century understanding of mission as what the churches did to convert nonbelievers in foreign lands. Gradually they have come to understand that the work of mission is the sending, traditioning, and liberating work of God in Christ, who is active in every land both within and outside the church. In the twentieth century, missiologists speak of the church as a participant in God's Mission rather than of the church's mission.[29]

Mission of God

As early as 1932, Karl Barth related his thinking to missiology by asserting the theocentric nature of mission, and in 1931 Emil Brunner had already pointed out that "the church exists by mission, just as fire exists by burning."[30] The understanding that all missionary activity was a participation in God's Mission, or the *missio Dei*, was already part of the traditional doctrine of the economic Trinity, which described the way God is known in and through the stewardship of the world. This doctrine understood God's action on behalf of the world as an action divine, "self-sending" through Christ and the Holy Spirit into the world. In this sense the church does not have a mission; rather, it participates in God's Mission in the redemption of humanity and the restoration of all creation. God's economic activity continues in the work of housekeeping and invites us all to take part through acts of justice and peace. This theocentric interpretation of mission had been largely forgotten in the development of the Western missionary movements until it began to be developed as a way of speaking about God's action and involvement in the world in the light of the crisis of World War II.[31] This gradually became a motif of ecumenical world missionary conferences and moved into various documents of the World Council of Churches.

After the New Delhi Assembly of the WCC in 1961, the concept of the *missio Dei* became the underlying presupposition of the study Missionary Structures of the Congregation. Two of the main perspectives of that study are reported in the final report as a shift in thinking to "God-world-church" rather than "God-church-world," and to "participation in God's Mission."[32] The same concern is to be seen in the Vatican II document *De Ecclesia,* where the theology of the church is understood in terms of participating in God's Mission to the world.[33]

Although systematic theologians have not paid much attention to the *missio Dei* concept, they have also become involved in the theme because of the growing interest in the historical or changing nature of the world and humanity and the biblical themes of history as a series of meaningful events moving toward fulfillment through God's action. The shift toward the recognition of the importance of eschatology and of the focus of Jesus' ministry on the Jubilee, and the fulfillment of God's household, also provides a focus on the events of world history of which the church is a small part rather than a major actor: a postscript on God's love affair with the world. Thus Leonardo Boff says:

> These three elements—Kingdom, world, and Church—must be spelled out in their proper order. First is the Kingdom as the primary reality that gives rise to the others. Second is the world as the place where the Kingdom is concretized and the Church is realized. Finally, the Church is the anticipatory and sacramental realization of the Kingdom in the world, as well as the means whereby the Kingdom is anticipated most concretely in the world.[34]

The shift from an *ecclesiocentric* to a *theocentric* and, for some, to an *oikocentric* perspective means that the church becomes more modest in its claims to be the medium of God's action and instead sees itself as a sign or instrument of that action, which is taking place in and through all parts of the groaning universe. As we shall see in chapter 4, this has implications as well for the way the traditional doctrine of the church as the locus, or place of salvation, is interpreted.

In the same period of time, liberation theologies were beginning to develop in Latin America. As early as 1956, basic church communities were being formed in Brazil through the community evangelization movement in Rio de Janeiro. In response to the encouragement of the Medellín Bishops' Conference in 1961, the basic Christian communities became a means for participation with God in the suffering of the people and for the rebirth of the church.[35] Stimulated by the theology of Vatican II and acknowledging the influence of political theologies in Europe, Latin American theologians such as Gustavo Gutiérrez nevertheless began to develop their own style of theology "from the underside of history," beginning with what was happening in the crises of poverty and tyranny in their part of the groaning world.[36] The understanding of God's liberating action shares with the understanding of God's Mission a common root in the commitment to join God in the midst of those who long for Jubilee.

I myself have always recognized the links in my feminist liberation theology to the theological understanding of God's Mission. It is no accident that I wrote my doctoral thesis on the understanding of Tradition as Mission, nor that the person who pioneered this understanding reinterpretation of Mission in the World Council of Churches was my late husband, the Dutch missiologist Hans Hoekendijk.[37] In a recent conversation with Barbara Anne Keely, a doctoral student who had written her thesis on my work, I noted with surprise that she had not picked God's Mission out as one of the themes of my theology. Her comment that this theme was not mentioned very frequently in my books led me to realize that although I have understood my theology this way, and have made it clear in a number of my books, I think of God's Mission or action in the world as equivalent to God's liberating action or liberation. I tend to avoid the use of the word "mission" because it has been so frequently used to mean proselytism, or drawing people into membership, and propaganda that convinces persons to "become as we are" that it is likely to be misunderstood.[38]

Yet as soon as I began to look for liberation structures for the church, I also realized that a lot of my earlier work with the World Council of Churches' study on Missionary Structures of the Congregation is important to the way I look for alternative forms of Christian community that are structured for the work of carrying out Jesus' ministry of setting free those who are oppressed. For this reason I want to set the discussion of liberation church structures of communities of faith and struggle in the context of that earlier study of the way the structures of the church change when the form of the church follows God's Mission of mending the creation.

Missionary structures

The report of the missionary structures study identifies at least four types of structures suited to participation in God's Mission in a pluralistic society that were identified through participant action study of church renewal efforts in the 1960s in North America: family type, permanent availability, permanent community, and task force.[39] Evolving such forms was not a capitulation to secularism, but rather a recognition that God's Trinitarian activity on behalf of the whole world calls the church to structure its life for participation in God's Mission and especially for those who are marginalized, oppressed, and denied their human dignity in that world. The life of the church is derivative from God's Mission and is shaped by the needs of those who are marginalized and oppressed in the world and by the gifts it can bring to the particular challenges of its own context.

The forms of renewal that were described in the study are familiar both as present realities in some of our church ministries and as nostalgic reminders of the optimism about justice and freedom that was a part of the 1960s. One form was named the *family type* because it was seen as a residential congregation of not more than a hundred persons, small enough so that people of all ages, races, classes, and life styles could learn to become a family. It was not necessarily to be made up of family units, but rather to focus on the major task of nurture as it formed alternative extended-family congregations in a situation where there might be many single persons and many dislocated and broken families. By creating churches small enough for this type of face-to-face nurture, the churches could specialize in developing partners in ministry to the community where the family church was located. An example of this type of congregation might be a small house church in a residential area, but such congregations will have continuing financial difficulties unless they are linked together in a shared network or organization that assists in coordinating their efforts. The formation of basic Christian communities in the North American context has led to development of some of these structures, which are often linked to a large church institution.

The *permanent community structures* also continue to be developed as Protestant as well as Roman Catholic communities seek to provide regular programs of residential retreat, spiritual renewal, or community service. These communities are made up of groups of people who have agreed to live together under a common discipline as an expression of their commitment to Jesus Christ. Sometimes people live together, and at other times they share common meals and spiritual disciplines as part of intentional living and ministry in their community.

The *permanent availability structures* continue to enable churches to serve long-term needs, making services available to people whenever and however they need them without necessarily involving them in the life of that church community. The work of counseling, emergency help, shelter, and food has always been part of the ministry of the churches, but here it is organized by a particular congregation, who see their ministry as, for example, that of running an ecumenical shelter for homeless persons, battered women, or persons with AIDS. The emphasis here is one way a community works together to be permanently or regularly available to those who need its services.

Probably the missionary structure identified by the study as a *task force* is the one that has developed a great deal as groups have seen a need for social change and organized to reach a specific goal. This structure is particularly well suited to a pluralistic and changing society that calls for flexible organization. Groups are formed in response to particular issues or tasks and go out of existence when the task is completed or taken up by another group or government agency. Of course, groups often go out of existence for other reasons as well, such as lack of money or volunteers.

Such groups can also gather for worship as well as service, and when the task force congregation ends the members can return to other continuing structures or turn to a new issue. Often permanent availability groups begin as task forces and take on a different form to accommodate an ongoing ministry for some group in particular need. An advantage for ecclesial groups that stay focused on one task is that the commitment to the task allows community to develop around that "third thing," and their flexibility allows them to take new forms as necessary. In East Harlem where I was a pastor we had task forces working in education, in housing, and in narcotics. The last two task forces went out of existence when the work was taken up by larger community-based groups, but the education task force became a permanent availability structure as it evolved into a self-supporting reading and tutorial program.

Perhaps such a listing of alternative organizational structures for congregations raises more questions than anything else. If that is so, at least it makes clear that the emerging liberation structures of the 1980s and 1990s are not so different from other eras, both in their problems and in the willingness of some persons to risk change in the life of the church. One question it raises is that of the relationship of these congregations to existing church institutions. A major point made in the 1967 study was that the needs of the world do not run along confessional lines, and organizing around those needs would require an ecumenical sharing of resources so that congregations would meet where needs arise and not just in traditional church buildings.

Another point made was that there is no reason in a pluralistic society that persons need to be members of only one church. It might well be that a person could have a primary membership—for instance, in a permanent availability structure for battered women—and at the same time be part of a family-type church. The study focused on congregations in an attempt to claim to avoid debate on whether these groups were truly "church," but it discovered that most of the congregations structured for mission had a fully developed church life, including worship, study, service, and shared community.

Liberation structures

When we look back at the design for such structures from the point of view of liberation communities today we immediately notice a major shift in structure. Although both types of communities are committed to participation in God's action for justice in the world, the missionary structure groups came out of the context of the Protestant ecumenical movement and, in North America, were renewal groups associated with liberal white mainline denominations. By and large the renewal was initiated by middle-class educated men.

On the other hand the liberation structures emerge out of liberation movements in their societies and are associated in some way with both Protestant and Roman Catholic churches. They too are not always accepted by larger church institutions, but they lay claim to be fully church and even to be working to "reinvent the church."[40] Because their members come from groups struggling to break free from racist, sexist, homophobic, classist, imperialistic, and other oppressions, they place far greater emphasis on critical social analysis of power in political, social, and economic relationships and first priority on commitment to act in solidarity with the poor and oppressed. The presence of large numbers of women in all these communities of faith and struggle sometimes also leads to a focus on the full humanity of women together with men, as well as to a sense of openness and connection with many religious faiths and with movements for peace and renewal of the earth.

Liberation structures emerge out of their contexts of struggle and are not of any one uniform type. In analyzing the social structures around them, people might very well decide to use one of the missionary structures, especially those of task force or family or community style. Their concern, however, is not with one type of "correct" structure or church form but with the many types needed for communities of faith as they gather with those who seek to work for justice and wholeness in their lives and in the society. In a pluralistic world they do not have only one form, nor are they just one common blend; they are many particular forms of organization that share in a common commitment to Christ and to sharing Christ's ministry on behalf of God's Jubilee.

Those working in basic Christian communities particularly reject the old sociological division of the church as community and the church as society or institution. According to Leonardo Boff there is always a power structure in every community, not just in institutional churches. "Historically, social formations are mixed; they have some societal and some communitarian characteristics."[41] Both institution and community need structure, and both need the charisms of God's participation in God's Mission. Basic Christian communities and feminist Christian communities are not opposed to institutionalization and organization. In fact, they are often part of well-organized networks of groups. What they are opposed to is inflexible and dominating institutional forms that exercise power for the benefit of those who control these institutions. To these groups they communicate a word of *kairos* calling for an end to domination and for institutionalization of structures of shared authority in community and of partnership in church and society.

In the next section of this chapter we will be looking at renewed Christian congregations (RCCs), who retain their more traditional church buildings and denominational structures but move to stand in solidarity with oppressed groups, either as advocates or as members of the groups themselves, organized in denominational church structures. We will then turn to look at a variety of basic Christian communities (BCCs) in different parts of the world to see how these communities form both a movement and a structure for social change. Finally, we look at feminist Christian communities (FCCs) and how these communities are part of the paradigm shift away from patriarchal oppression toward the full partnership of women together with men.

In looking at these particular examples of churches of faith and struggle I am in no way trying to duplicate the many excellent studies of these groups by other authors or the first-hand accounts by church members of their experiences in very concrete, kitchen table contexts. Rather, I will be looking at the characteristics of these groups in order to search out clues for feminist liberation ecclesiology, because the development of this ecclesiology comes out of and is accountable back to the communities of faith who are acting out the vision of God's new household.

In discussing the various liberation communities I will be asking a series of questions about their connections both to the faith traditions of the church and the struggles for justice and life of which they are a part. Just as Robert Schreiter has asked how local theologies retain their Christian identity when they emerge out of the local situation and articulate the gospel in a cultural context different from those out of which Christian doctrine was shaped, I want to ask about the connection of these communities to both faith and tradition. Schreiter indicates that Christian identity in local theologies depends upon being connected to the tradition and its witness to Jesus Christ as the bearer of salvation (one), sharing in word, sacrament, and the praxis of community and Christian performance (holy), as well as in communication with other churches for mutual judgment and correction of Christian performance (catholic and apostolic).[42]

My questions addressed to these communities of struggle are similar, but they focus more on the question of how the groups relate to liberation struggles than on the question of their Christian identity. The groups being described are practicing the presence of Christ's Spirit in many different ways, yet all of them continue through various structures to share in the word, in liturgy, service, and a community of sharing and struggle. With Boff, I assume that these groups *are* church when they gather as church and ask about how they are seeking to show this faithfulness in their structures and mission. What makes them distinctive is not their traditional church life but their willingness to be connected to the struggle of particular groups for freedom and full humanity. Thus these communities become liberation and/or feminist churches of faith *and* struggle.

There are five questions to ask about the structures of these liberation communities.

First, what is the liberation movement that shapes their life and perspective on the meaning of their participation in God's Mission or liberating action? It may well be that more than one movement is involved, but at least one connection to a liberation struggle is needed if the group is to see itself as participating in that struggle. A movement is a network of organizations and people who all share one particular goal of social change, such as the end of a war or the elimination of racism or sexism. An example of an emerging movement in the 1990s is the movement for affordable health care in the United States. Groups in a movement do not have any one kind of organization. Sometimes they carry their existing institutional structures with them, and at other times they create structures to participate in the work for a particular change in society.

Second, what is the relationship of these communities of faith and struggle to the established church? Most of the time this relationship is one of "unity in tension." That is, they still have connections to the traditional confessional groups, either through their members or through an official link or sponsorship. Yet, as will all Spirit-filled communities, they face moments when their prophetic actions and criticisms cause alienation and movements to suppress or co-opt them into the establishment. On the other hand, the communities themselves find that when they are not related to larger institutions they need to create larger networks or new organizations if they wish to provide for continuity and mutual support and correction. At other times communities may decide to join the larger secular movement. This tension between connection to religious tradition and to movements for change is sometimes creative and often debilitating, but it is always present in communities of struggle.

Third, what is the primary task or series of tasks around which the life of the community is organized? Liberation communities arise out of a commitment to act and then provide the basis for celebration and reflection on the ongoing struggle for new life. If they cannot identify their commitment to action they may very well be Christian communities, because of their belief in Jesus Christ, but they are not communities of faith and struggle. Struggle is always very concrete, and often painful and full of conflict and the possibility of suffering. This is because the struggle for justice always runs the risk that those who benefit from injustice or who are unable to see or understand the injustice will oppose such actions. Out of common tasks, or focus on what I would call a "third thing," groups discover the gift of a community that was simply not there when they only talked of their unity in diversity.

Fourth, what is the commitment of the community to the empowerment of all women as co-strugglers in the gospel? In asking about feminist liberation ecclesiology, it is important to include a question about how various movement-connected communities include feminist advocacy with concern for hospitality to many different groups. How diverse is the community and what is the class, race, gender, sexual orientation, ability or disability, and age of their members? There is no one membership requirement for liberation communities, but it is important to make clear what their relationship is to the oppressed groups with whom they are connected. To be a white middle-class group in solidarity with peasants in

El Salvador is quite different from being a group of poor peasants gathering as a basic Christian community in spite of suspicion and surveillance from government forces and U.S.-sponsored low-intensity conflict.[43] Similarly, the position of a man as a feminist advocate is not the same as a woman who engages in advocacy as the member of an oppressed group. The meaning of the gospel and the ways in which we live out that gospel vary with the situation and begin with our own condition of power, privilege, and access to the benefits of society or lack thereof.

Fifth, what is the vision or hope that sustains them in the struggle? It is the conviction that God's intention is for a mended creation, and our participation in that mending often sustains persons in the long haul. Sometimes a community is sustained by specific middle-range historical projects that it shares with others in the movement for liberation. At other times it is the spirituality of liberation, closely connected to Bible study, prayer, and the practice of solidarity and martyrdom, that becomes the well of strength for new life, even in the midst of death. As Gustavo Gutiérrez puts it in *We Drink from Our Own Wells:*

> It can therefore be said without any fear of exaggeration that we are experiencing today an exceptional time in the history of Latin America and the life of the church. Of this situation we may say with Paul: "Now is the favorable time [*kairos*]; this is the day of salvation" (2 Cor. 6:2, Jerusalem Bible). Such a vision of things does not make the journey of the poor less difficult nor does it gloss over the obstacles they encounter in their efforts to defend their most elementary rights. . . .There is a question here, then, not of a facile optimism but rather of a deep trust in the historical power of the poor and, above all, a firm hope in the Lord.[44]

Liberation Communities

It may seem strange that a book on feminist ecclesiology is looking for clues to that ecclesiology among all sorts and conditions of people rather than among feminist communities only. Yet a feminist ecclesiology imaged as a church in the round, where persons gather together at kitchen tables and many other tables to break bread and share the justice and peace of God, is not able to create an understanding of what it means to be a liberation community that would exclude men as long as the men are willing to associate with the activities of the kitchen table. The search for clues to feminist liberation theology does, however, lead to critical questioning of any group that does not include in its commitment specific ways of including women in the work of empowerment for participation in God's Mission.

Although the angle of vision of this investigation is not focused exclusively on women and women's communities, it does focus on the feminist commitment to struggle for the full humanity of women of all abilities, ages, classes, races, and sexual orientations. This commitment is frequently most clear in communities of women seeking to develop their own self-identity and self-understanding of what it means to be participants in the mending of creation. These communities, who sometimes call themselves Women-Church, gather to express their commitments as feminists through worship, study, reflection, and action, but they share these commitments with many other communities of struggle and are not the only source of emerging clues to the meaning of church in the round.

Renewed Christian communities

Renewed congregations represent the continuing ferment in the lives of established church institutions that breaks out from time to time at all levels of church life and calls people to use their ecclesial and social power in advocacy for those who have been marginalized in society and in the church. The result is local churches or regional church bodies that are renewed as communities of faith and struggle. One such example is that of the Downtown United Presbyterian Church in Rochester, New York.[45] This church was formed in 1974 when three of the oldest Presbyterian churches came together as one congregation committed to a continuing ministry in the central city. A long and intensive period of goal setting had a profound effect on the life of the newly merged congregation. An oral history of the goal-setting process records that they came to a style of partnership in ministry and round table churching that led them to shape the ministry of the church according to the needs and challenges of the downtown area as well as the struggles for justice in the wider society.[46]

The church symbolized its commitment to partnership with a nonhierarchical leadership group of four co-pastors who rotate responsibilities. The group includes both men and women and, in 1991, sought also to include Jane Spahr, the first openly lesbian Presbyterian minister ever called to serve as a church pastor.[47] There are a variety of forms of expression of worship; education is intergenerational and includes members from a nearby group home for developmentally disabled persons. Bible study and social change issues are correlated in study and worship. Two church buildings were given away, and the space in the third has become permanently available for non-profit community action projects as well as for community cultural events. Proposals for ministry and mission in the church are only developed in cooperation with the people for whom the programs are intended and are spun off for others to continue whenever possible.

The various projects that connect to movements are organized by councils of the church and by task forces that include the persons who are most affected by the issues. The church is a sanctuary church and ecumenically active as a host in that movement, working to defend its refugee family when they were twice arrested in Rochester. It is also a "more light church," facing dismissal from the Presbyterian Church (U.S.A.) for its advocacy of the ordination of gay and lesbian persons as elders and ministers. The church also includes within it a Women-Church that meets monthly to share in feminist liturgies. From this brief description it is clear that this church, like many others, has moved to a pluralistic ministry in what I would describe as a permanent-availability structure. The church itself is a partnership of persons offering hospitality and support to community action groups who seek to use their facilities, such as Parents Anonymous, Jail Ministries, a housing council, a day-care center, and an employment support center, but it also acts in advocacy for the urban poor, for persons with disabilities, and for welfare rights, as well as for Latin American and gay and lesbian liberation.

As a community of faith and struggle the Downtown Church is a diverse congregation, but it is still identified as a white mainline congregation in which power and possibility for actualizing its Spirit-filled commitment to solidarity in struggle comes through church endowments as well as ongoing gifts. Like other churches of this kind, it provides a leaven and a hope to those who search out a new paradigm of partnership, and its feminist vision of round table churching is carried out in the style of its leadership and decision making as well as its advocacy for justice.

The model of a permanent-availability structure that nurtures both hospitality to the community and social justice ministries exists in other parts of the country and has been used successfully by large urban African American congregations. Preston Washington gives us an example of this in his book *God's Transforming Spirit: Black Church Renewal*. In it he describes the Memorial Baptist Church of Harlem in its journey toward renewal, a Spirit-filled journey that leads a congregation to become "relevant in relation to its community and world."[48] Renewal of the congregation has also led to ecumenical renewal programs in the community, especially in the areas of housing renewal and development and in support for single-parent families and a home for mothers and babies. This large institutional model is difficult to sustain without church resources or grants from foundations or governmental agencies. Although less accessible to direction from poor people's movements, it has the advantage of combining many different groups and classes and churches in one umbrella organization that can deal with larger political and social structures and problems.[49]

Another model of renewed congregations is the Metropolitan Community Church of San Francisco. The Universal Fellowship of Metropolitan Community Churches (UFMCC) was founded in 1968 in Los Angeles by the Rev. Troy Perry, "a former Pentecostal minister who aimed to spread the new gospel that God loves gays and lesbians."[50] The denomination numbers thirty thousand members and two hundred churches worldwide.

MCC San Francisco is part of a denomination which itself is a community of faith and struggle. Its direct connection to the movement for lesbian and gay liberation has placed it in the forefront of the struggle for their rights and for the development of gay, lesbian, and bisexual power in the San Francisco area and in the struggle with the AIDS epidemic. At first the church and the denomination saw their contribution to the wider church as clearly in the area of issues of human sexuality and homophobia, but the AIDS crisis catapulted them into what MCC San Francisco's late founder, Howard Wells, called "eschatological living." The focus is on spiritual growth and on understanding what it means to live the resurrection hope here and now, to live with AIDS.

Kittredge Cherry and James Mitulski, ministers of MCC San Francisco, write about this challenge in the life of the church community of faith and struggle.

> In a sense, all of our worship services are AIDS healing services. Every Sunday we provide a gay-positive, gay-affirming environment, where scripture is related to lesbian and gay experience and same-sex partners can receive communion and laying-on-of-hands prayer as a couple.[51]

Although the church was started as a community for gay white men, it is evolving into a vibrant community of hope that is connected not only to the gay and lesbian movement but also to the feminist movement, through its lesbian members and staff. Its primary tasks have to do with building an open and affirming community of hospitality; caring for the spiritual needs of a community faced with rejection, discrimination, and great suffering; and doing extensive community outreach and education with other churches. Its largest membership is white male, but it includes many white females and a modest number of African Americans and Hispanic Americans. Without a doubt the resurrection vision of this congregation is one of the full humanity and dignity of all gay and lesbian persons, of an ecumenical community of acceptance, and of a world free of weeping and pain as young persons of all races and classes find themselves struggling to live with AIDS.

MCC churches work ecumenically with smaller denominational organizations in major church bodies that advocate and minister with and to lesbian and gay Christians. The structures of the churches are not different from those of other denominations, and the majority of the membership is conservative theologically. Another quite different renewed structure for ecumenical life among church denominations is the recent reformation of an ecumenical body of Protestant and Roman Catholic churches in New Zealand. In speaking about the organization of the Conference of Churches in Aotearoa–New Zealand (CCA-NZ), Janet Crawford describes it as a journey toward "non-patriarchal community."[52] It is organized in such a way as to be a partner organization to the ecumenical council of the Tangata Whenua, the Maori people of the land of New Zealand, and uses a Maori name, Aotearoa, for that land. It is also organized to include as many voices and groups as possible in its deliberations and voting process, not just denominational representatives.

Its particular goals are those of bicultural partnership, with leadership in this respect coming from the ecumenical council of the Tangata Whenua. Inclusiveness and diversity is stressed in its ongoing life, and it affirms the dignity and equality of women through ensuring full participation of women in consultation, decision making, and action. At least 10 percent of the annual forum will be from the Tangata Whenua and includes participation of groups not specifically represented by member church structures. The decision making of the council forum is by consensus, in order to move toward unity within the community of different traditions, and it is led by three co-presidents. The movement for liberation with which this council is allied is clearly that of the indigenous people's movement of Aotearoa, but the partnering structures for encouraging empowerment are also connected to the feminist, peace, and ecological movements in that country. The council carries out the usual tasks of councils and includes many white middle-class men and women, but its commitment is to stop "business as usual" and to work as a Christian community that lifts a sign of Jubilee for all to see.

Not far from Aotearoa is another conciliar community of faith and struggle that at the moment has the shape of renewed traditional churches but is multiplying rapidly from the bottom as a base community movement. The Church of Christ in China, an ecumenical Protestant denomination, has been growing rapidly since it was allowed to open in the early 1980s and is constantly seeking to develop and train leadership for the many new churches that begin in people's homes. The Roman Catholic Church in China is run by the Patriotic Association, is not allowed to establish ties with the Vatican, and is even more strictly regulated by the government than the China Christian Council. Yet the governmental fears about the expansion of the Christian churches may be very real. In the years from 1986 to 1991, Protestant churches grew from 4,000 to 7,000 and the distribution of Bibles tripled. Catholic churches are growing as well, and it is estimated that there could be as many as 20 to 60 million Christians in China today.[53]

The Protestant church in China calls itself the "Three Self Movement: self-governing, self-supporting, and self-propagating." It exists under close governmental supervision from within its organization, yet its proclamation of the gospel is very closely related to the eagerness of people for a supportive voluntary community and freedom of expression. A new church is being born in China, and it is emerging in a people's movement of house churches. Those struggling to organize this movement of the Spirit can only dimly discern its new shape, but at the moment its structures are very much associated with older Protestant or Roman Catholic traditional structures recognized by the government, and its struggle is to provide the basic resources for Christian community, service, education, and worship.[54] Although the China Christian Council includes women in its seminaries, and most certainly women are an important part in the spread of the churches, the leadership and direction of the churches is still in the hands of older men, most of whom were trained abroad before the Revolution.[55]

These examples of renewed congregations and denominational structures could be multiplied in various parts of the United States and the world. Their significance in this discussion is twofold. One is to show that it is possible to respond to the movements for change and to be part of these movements even when the congregation or organization decides to reform an existing traditional structure. The other is to demonstrate that it is possible to talk of communities of faith and struggle at the larger denominational and ecumenical level as well as at the level of smaller basic Christian communities (BCCs). Such larger church bodies can also work with, and share in, the lifting up of new ways of being church in the round.

Basic Christian communities

As we have seen, small communities of faith and struggle first emerged in large numbers in Latin America, although they are found on every continent. Just to give a small flavor of this diversity and variety, James O'Halloran, in his book *Signs of Hope: Developing Small Christian Communities*, describes BCCs in Dublin, Ireland, and St. Paul, Minnesota, as well as Quito, Ecuador, and Freetown, Sierra Leone.[56] Here I will try to show their variety by describing communities in Korea, the Philippines, and the United States as well as some in Latin America. If these communities are found in many different contexts, how are they to be distinguished from the countless small prayer groups, Bible study groups, and charismatic meetings that have been a part of Christian community life over the centuries? Without claiming a unique new structure for the BCCs, it is possible to say that they are communities that unite "theological and biblical reflection with social analysis leading to action for justice."[57] They make use of tools for social and political analysis in order to understand their own predicament and work for change.

This linkage of the communities with liberation theologies is very important for the formation and development of these theologies out of the experience of struggle. In turn it provides a theological framework for the action/reflection of the communities on the meaning of their faith. Even if there is a wide variety in the quality of life, commitment, reflection, and Christian praxis in such communities, there is at least a discernible pattern of development. Many of the communities are formed by a pastoral worker within the life of a parish and focus on prayer and gospel-sharing with emphasis on development of ecclesial and sacramental life. They begin to be concerned about one another in the context of struggle and move to mutual aid and neighborhood improvement. Gradually some come to see the possibility of change in society and respond to situations of poverty and oppression by demanding change.[58]

In Latin America the communities were usually formed by priests and bishops in response to the shortage of priests and the need for lay leadership in the parishes. But as they became a vehicle for the response of the poor against a situation of social and political oppression, these communities became a new form of church life that sought to provide courage, strength, and hope to the people. In situations of extreme poverty and oppression such as Brazil or the Philippines, where the population is around 90 percent Roman Catholic, the BCCs become more than parish communities. They become the people at the grass roots organizing their lives in such a way that they can live them out in faith and struggle. And the potential of these communities for new life and organization is not ignored either by those whose power is threatened by their activities or by those who see them as part of the rebirth of the church. In Brazil alone there are more than fifty thousand BCCs; on the island of Negros in the Philippines, for example, there are over two thousand in the one diocese of Bacolod where Bishop Antonio Fortich worked to develop this system among the farming population as they struggled for land reform and for survival.[59]

Gustavo Gutiérrez helps us to understand the significance of the word "base" or "basic" in the description of these Christian communities by pointing out that it does not refer to those who are at the bottom of the hierarchy of the Roman Catholic church but, rather, to "the poor, oppressed, believing people: marginalized races, exploited classes, despised cultures, and so forth. It is from them that these Christian communities are arising."[60] The basic community is made up of those who make the option to join in solidarity with their oppressed brothers and sisters, and those outside this class or group who make their struggle a basic commitment of their own lives and thus stand in solidarity with them.

This basic commitment is to stand in solidarity with the poor. In Latin American liberation theologies this is understood as joining God in *making an option for the poor.* God is concerned for the poor because they are the marginal ones who have no other protection. In Jesus, God's Jubilee began breaking into our lives as all persons were made welcome into God's household. Jesus lived among the poor, fed them, ministered to them, taught them, and suffered the consequences of making this option for inclusive justice. In the BCCs, God's option is made clear as those who are unwelcome and marginalized begin to speak out about what justice and liberation would mean for their lives and to move together to work for that God-given possibility of mending creation. As we shall see in chapter 4, this does not mean that God does not love everyone, including the rich, but it does mean that the rich and those of privilege are called to make their option for the poor as well. Thus Gutiérrez writes that this work to make the poor welcome is the basis of evangelization.

> By evangelization we certainly mean the proclamation of the word. But we also mean the gesture of solidarity that gives authenticity to that proclamation, the commitment to the poor and oppressed of this world in their lives and their struggles.[61]

In visiting one group of BCCs in Lima I was able to see the way the parish organized itself into four or five communities, each with its own group of leaders who met with a Sister as a coordinating team for the communities. Much of their work was in the squatter areas around the town where people needing housing built homes of cardboard and metal on dusty desert hills. These people in turn had to organize to obtain water-truck delivery, electricity, and transportation. The BCCs were linked not only to their parish, and nurtured by its vibrant and liberating liturgical life, but also to other BCCs in a city, national, and international network. Along with other groups they were working to support another community in its bid for electricity and were joined in turn by others in creating a community soup kitchen for families of workers who were on strike.[62]

The Philippine communities in Negros are also organized with a strong network of support. In the rural area the communities are opposed by the government and find themselves caught in the low-intensity warfare conducted by the government against the New People's Army. Many of the communities are intentionally disbanded by the government, both by torturing and killing the leaders and by a practice of rounding up the families and forcing them to relocate in towns or in "protected hamlets" where they are watched by the military. Yet even in the face of torture and death these communities continue their ministries of faith and struggle. According to Father Rolex and students in a travel seminar from Yale Divinity School in 1990, the communities all have a lay pastoral team whose members are trained by visiting regional teams each month. These teams are composed of a Bible leader, a health worker, a catechetical worker, and a liturgist. When visiting a remote BCC, Father Rolex would travel with a team by truck, muleback, and on foot. The team provided some safety on the journey and then could work with the local leaders when they arrived after many hours.[63]

The structures of basic Christian communities are not the same everywhere. They are very much related to context. For instance, in Hartford, Connecticut, a local parish is organized in a BCC structure as a part of its ministry to the Hispanic community in that area. In Minneapolis–St. Paul the Community of St. Martin is organized around intentional justice and peace-making ministries by persons who are middle-class.[64] Minjung churches in Korea are organized around the struggles of exploited workers as a concrete expression of the advocacy of Minjung theology for the suffering people of Korea. The Minjung are the politically oppressed, economically exploited, socially marginalized, and culturally despised and ignored of Korea.[65] Often the Minjung churches are made up of middle-class persons in solidarity with the workers and with those struggling for democracy, peace, and unification. They started as mission churches of the established churches but are largely independent in their theology and their vision of a more just society.[66]

In response to our questions about communities of faith and struggle, we can say that all these communities are connected to poor people's movements for justice. They are most frequently part of the infrastructure of church life, although they then exist in tension with traditional church institutions and are free to multiply only where bishops favor their ministry.[67] Their tasks include nurture and development of faith and Christian identity, but these tasks are integrated with the development of social commitments to justice and support of the community in struggle.

Although as many as 80 percent of the members of such communities in Latin America are women, and many of the local leaders are women, there is an assumption that the problems of the poor and those of women are identical so that there is little focus on the struggles of women for full humanity.[68] This has an advantage in recognizing that struggles for human rights are struggles for women's rights, but the disadvantage that there is less specific focus on leadership development for women and the overall structures are run by men. Speaking about BCCs, a Latin American report by women suggests that they are limited because they have "not specifically posed the issue of women as a specific challenge with regard to the buildup of the church, its ministries, its organic setup, and so forth."[69]

The vision of these communities is one of jubilee. They share in the recognition of this time as one of *kairos,* and they long for Jesus' words in Luke 4:18–19 to be fulfilled. Meanwhile, they themselves have taken up the ministry of Jesus to bring good news to the poor and release to the captives.

Feminist Christian communities

This vision of Jubilee is also shared by feminist Christian communities, but the vision specifically includes women together with men in the vision of a mended creation. In North America the FCCs are the most widespread form of alternative Christian community. These largely ecumenical Christian groups have emerged out of attempts to bring feminist perspectives to mainline Christian churches. Although we do not yet have a sociological study of what the Hartford Seminary WomanCircle research program calls Women's Base Communities and Support Groups, the program is conducting a two-year study of these communities and their effect on "participants and congregations in Catholic and Protestant traditions."[70]

It is already clear that these groups are growing in number and often have a revitalizing impact on congregations as well as on the lives of their participants. The groups are base or basic not in the sense of advocacy for the poor but in the sense of advocacy for women. They are also base communities in the sense of being predominantly small grass-roots gatherings of women, in the United States and around the world. They are part of a much larger movement of feminist spirituality that, according to Mary Hunt of WATER (Women's Alliance for Theology, Ethics, and Ritual), "encompasses a vast array of faith groups, from astrology to wicca, tarot to tai chi, made up of many women who have roots in mainstream traditions but who find spiritual nourishment beyond those."[71]

Feminist Christian communities are similar to the Korean Minjung churches in that they are predominantly middle-class and are willing to express their spirituality in a variety of forms in order to draw on the tradition and culture of other religions. They also share with Minjung churches the tension between the groups and the churches out of which the participants come, but they are much less likely to be involved in critical class analysis and advocacy of workers' movements. The women's liberation movement to which the feminist Christian communities are connected often reflects the white middle-class bias of the majority of its members in stressing the individual needs of women for meaning and support in their lives, rather than making direct connection to justice struggles against racism and classism, along with sexism and heterosexism.

Among Roman Catholic and some Protestant women these feminist base communities are sometimes called Women-Church. As I indicated in chapter 2, this name emerged from the term "Woman Church," which, according to Rosemary Ruether, was first used at a conference of Roman Catholic women in November 1983 and was later changed to Women-Church, to signify that there are many types of such churches. The term "women-church" is also used to speak of the idea and reality of the *ekklesia* of women through history. According to Ruether: "Women-Church represents the first time that women collectively have claimed to be church and have claimed the tradition of the exodus community as a community of liberation from patriarchy."[72]

Describing women-church in *Bread Not Stone*, Elisabeth Fiorenza says that it is not exclusionary of men but a "political-oppositional term to patriarchy." She describes it as a "movement of self-identified women and women-identified men in biblical religion."[73] The name "Women-Church" is somewhat misleading, as the groups do not intend to be a new denomination but simply to be alternative and nonpatriarchal forms of Christian community. Some women do not like to use the term "church" because it is identified with existing patriarchal institutions, and others consider the term "women" confusing because the groups are not necessarily exclusive of men. But, like any metaphor, it holds a promise that "women" can be an inclusive term for both men and women, helping to correct the fact that women have been ignored, and "church" can be a newly inclusive community that presents a glimpse of what the church might become.[74]

Whatever self-designation is used by these feminist Christian communities, they form a movement for church transformation and renewal made up of women and men who find themselves alienated by the patriarchal structures, liturgies, and theologies of the churches. The groups seem to form around one or more of the following tasks or needs: advocacy, self-identity, transformation of the church, new practice of spirituality. Some groups come together in relation to a social justice issue such as battered women and families, ecology, or women's health. Many are formed around the needs of women for mutual support and a new naming of their reality and their own identity. Others band together to transform a local or national church around issues such as women's ordination, reproductive rights, human sexuality, or inclusive language. Some groups come together primarily for study or for celebration of inclusive liturgies, making use of female imagery for the deity as well as for human persons. Frequently the groups serve a variety of needs and move to new areas as the needs of the group change.

Like many other Christian feminists I am connected to a variety of such groups and have experienced the way they grow, change, and disband as needs or tasks are accomplished or transformed into other areas of need. For twenty years I have been a member of the ad hoc group on Racism, Sexism, and Classism, meeting monthly in New York City in the winter and at my home for an "advance" weekend each June. This group is always changing and is maintained by a mailing list that keeps members informed of the program events that are planned in advance each June. By now many of the original members have moved away or retired, and the group itself has lost four of its members to cancer and one to appendicitis.

The purpose of the group was to support women who worked in national church and ecumenical offices in New York City by doing critical analysis of the ways racism, sexism, and classism were interwoven into our work and suggesting strategies for dealing with these in personal, political, and ecclesial settings. A lot of the work of the group included networking around church issues particularly important to women and providing international ecumenical linkages with the Women's Desk of the World Council of Churches, the National Council of Churches, and the National Board of the YWCA. In our first two phases, we stressed transformation of Christian institutions.

The group was founded in 1971 as the New York Task Force on Women in Changing Institutions in order to present data for a WCC study on Christians in changing institutions that had not included any women's groups. Out of our discussions and work we became one of the groups in the study, and I was able to publish a working paper for the WCC on human liberation in a feminine perspective.[75]

In 1974 the group was re-formed and named POW for Participation of Women (in the World Council of Churches). At the request of women in the WCC, we agreed to work to make sure that women delegates would have their travel funded so they could take their place as 20 percent of the delegation to the Nairobi Assembly of the World Council. Our work included fund-raising as well as preparation and advocacy for women in the U.S. meetings. The Nairobi Assembly was the first in which more than 4 percent of the delegation had been women, and the active participation of women was encouraged by an international network, of which our group was a small part.

After 1975 the group was again re-formed for a task of advocacy around the issues of racism, sexism, and classism (RASC), with particular emphasis on the way these social sins form a web of oppression in society that makes it necessary for women to work as advocates of the full humanity of all women together with men. At this time we adopted our advocacy name and worked as an interracial group on justice for women in the churches, in ecumenical bodies, and in the activities of the United Nations Decade for Women. At the same time we continued our support of such causes as the ordination and placement of women in the churches and the WCC study on Community of Women and Men in the Church. The group was racially mixed, although the majority were white, and included both lay and ordained, employed and unemployed women.

In the 1980s RASC shifted its attention to members in need of support as they lived and struggled with cancer, sickness, and continuing oppression and marginalization in the churches. It also shared advocacy for those who were lesbian and were being forced out of their positions in church hierarchies. A number of the members were connected to work in the Third World, and through that group I traveled to Korea and Japan and began my advocacy of Asian women's feminist theology. As new members joined, looking for support in their own search for self-identity as pastors and church and social agency employees, there was more emphasis on personal development and on the practice of spirituality for justice. More time was spent on study and discussion, as well as on seasonal liturgical celebrations and memorials. The group membership continues to evolve, with only a core attending most of the sessions, and there are also related groups of persons in Philadelphia and New Haven. The loss of the central emphasis on advocacy and of many core members may mean that the group will need to disband or be formed again with a new task for the nineties!

RASC is unusual in that it started as a local group but had many national and international connections. It is usual, however, in the way it

evolved to meet the needs of the participants and their concerns for justice for women. Its network aspect is very characteristic of such groups;
they have very little official structure but function through networks of
friends. One group that sponsors and facilitates such networking and
mutual resourcing is WATER, the Women's Alliance for Theology, Ethics
and Ritual. Coordinated by Mary E. Hunt and Diann Neu, WATER describes itself as

> an educational center, a network of justice-seeking people that began in
> 1983 as a response to the need for serious theological, ethical and liturgi-
> cal development for and by women. We work locally, nationally and in-
> ternationally on programs, projects, publications, workshops, retreats
> and liturgical planning which have helped thousands of people be part
> of an inclusive church.[76]

WATER functions as a facilitator of feminist communities that are
searching for ways to connect their spirituality with political advocacy.
The two co-directors work to develop ongoing programs as well as coordinating cooperative projects with women in Latin America and developing
liturgical resources for the Women-Church movement. The quarterly
newsletter, *WATERwheel,* distributes liturgical and theological resources to
a wide readership in the United States and abroad. This process of networking is frequently the way that groups maintain contact with one another, and almost every coordinating group maintains itself through
regular publication of newsletters, regular requests for money from their
constituencies, and occasional national or regional conferences.

Although the predominant constituency of such groups is white,
there are communities that have emerged out of the needs of women of
color. Two such groups will be discussed in greater detail in chapter 6.
One is the Rainbow Church, "a faith community of Korean-American
women in international marriages" that is affiliated with the Seaford
United Methodist Church on Long Island. As I already mentioned in
chapter 2, the church was begun by the Rev. Henna Han in response to
the suffering and isolation of Korean women who were brought to the
United States by G.I.s.

Another is the Loves Herself . . . Regardless program for African
American women in the Boston area developed by Donna Bivens and
Renae Scott as part of the work of the Women's Theological Center.
Working for ten years on the development of alternative theological education for seminary students and laypersons, the WTC has gathered
women from diverse racial and ethnic backgrounds in programs that confront injustices of race, class, gender, and sexual orientation.[77] One of its
projects is an ongoing community of African American women who share
in programs addressed to their own needs and those of the African American community. New people continue to search out this Loves Herself

community, where women of color gather together as a supportive community for one another.[78]

Feminist Christian communities, like basic Christian communities, are found in North America and all around the world, particularly in Europe, Australia, and Aotearoa–New Zealand. In Korea, for instance, Christian feminist groups have formed a Women-Church that has operated since 1989 and has a pastor who coordinates its twice-weekly services. The church works to seek out the oppressed women of Korea. Its Methodist pastor, Young Kim, quotes the parable of the lost coin in Luke 15:8–10 as a fundamental text for the church. The coin represents not only the lost women of Korea but also what Korean women have lost: God's image in themselves, the mother image in God, their confidence to speak for themselves.[79] As the women gather they celebrate an agape meal of rice and chilled ginger tea in remembrance of Jesus' table hospitality with the outcasts of his society.

In the Netherlands the women have organized themselves in various types of groups on the edge of the churches. According to Lieve Troch, writing in a 1989 issue of the *Journal of Feminist Studies in Religion*, there are "approximately a thousand groups, each including ten to thirty women and more, in different settings," some of which have existed a long period of time and others of which have been recently formed.[80] In this woman-and-faith movement, women go beyond the limits of denomination and social, class, and cultural differences, and sometimes differences in race, to find one another. They are looking for new forms of community "within and through their differences," and they strive to confront the differences and work with them to build sisterhood. Their first concern is not with the church as male institution but with feminist transformation, and they work toward understanding the Bible in new ways and developing new liturgies that emerge out of the struggles of women for liberation. These groups also are developing strong networks outside the churches, but as elsewhere they maintain unity in tension within as well as outside the traditional structures.

As we look at the wide variety of such groups it is difficult to draw generalizations. Yet it is possible to discern that the basic functions of the feminist Christian communities are not all that different from other church structures. Rosemary Ruether suggests that Women-Churches continue a variety of functions that make up church life, such as collective study, liturgy, social praxis on behalf of others, and collective community.[81] These suggestions are not difficult to recognize as those functions in the life of Christian churches often spoken of as *kerygma, leitourgia, diakonia,* and *koinonia.* It would seem that wherever Christians gather, the presence of the Spirit of Christ is made known by these simple acts of shared word, liturgy, service, and community.

These very different communities find their commonality not only in marginality to the churches but in their connection to the feminist movement. Their tasks are varied but usually include both a spiritual search for meaning and self-identity among women and advocacy for justice for women. The constituency remains predominantly white and middle-class, but other forms of feminist Christian communities are emerging among women of many different cultures and races. The vision or goal of these communities is that of Galatians 3:28: a church and a society in which there is no longer division between persons because of race, class, or gender. Young Kim articulated that goal for Women-Church in Korea by saying that the lost coin for which women search is the possibility of true joy that will come when there is no more oppression and sorrow in their midst. When the lost coin is found, "our joy will be God's joy."[82]

Having had an opportunity to look at some examples of communities of faith and struggle and at the many and various ways they are connected to movements and to the Christian tradition, we perhaps can discern a few clues for feminist liberation ecclesiologies from the witness of these groups to the possibility of new life, of resurrection in the church.

First, from them, and from countless others like them, we have learned that the missionary nature of the church as it participates in God's sending and liberating work in the world requires a justice connection. There is no way to be an advocate for partnership beyond patriarchy without working for justice. Kitchen table solidarity requires that persons and their communities share in the struggle for full humanity and human dignity for all people, and especially those too poor and powerless even to think beyond the need to find some food for the family gathering.

Second, we have seen over and over again that the witness of the church is rooted in a life of hospitality when bounded communities who have sought to gain identity behind their particular walls of tradition find themselves broken open by the gospel invitation of hospitality to the stranger in their midst. Communities of hospitality become a living invitation to God's welcome table and, in turn, are developed by those who have found a new openness and welcome in the gospel message.

Last, we can see from our discussion of feminist and liberation communities that the life of the church involves the nurture of spirituality of connection. It practices the presence and connection to God and to the people on the margins of society through the study of the Bible and its interpretation and celebration in the round table community of Christ. In such settings there is an opportunity for life to come together in a way that both transcends and includes the bits and pieces that make up the struggle for wholeness, freedom, and full humanity.

It may be that the gift of faith and struggle in the life of the church today is a way in which God's Spirit is at work to renew the church as well as the whole earth. This has happened before in the history of the church, and perhaps God will again do a new thing in our midst. Only

God knows if the dry bones of the church can live (Ezek. 37:1–6). But of one thing we can be sure, and that is that God has "threatened us with resurrection."[83] It is possible that the response of communities of faith and struggle to the *kairos* of our time will make it possible for churches to choose life, even at the price of many kinds of death, in order to share the new life of God's Jubilee. Jesus calls us to that new life in his warning about the "whitewashed tombs" in Matthew 23:25–28. In his book *Grave of God*, Robert Adolfs has said:

> The gospels speak of two kinds of grave.
> One was whitewashed, the other was empty.
> The whitewashed grave is the symbol of the false façade,
> of the outwardly beautiful appearance that does not last.
> The empty grave was the grave of the God-[hu]man, Jesus
> Christ, the one who was himself emptied. . . .
> Around the emptiness of the grave were born both
> the hope of the future and the Church, which was, is and
> must always be the *Message of what is to come.*[84]

Today we search for that empty grave, knowing that its resurrection power is offered to the church through the sacrifice and struggle of those who share this faith.

$$4 \mid \textit{Justice and} \\ \textit{the Church}$$

The story of justice and the church begins at a very long table piled high with all manner of party food, soft drinks, and coffee. It was stretched out across the chancel of a church, but it did not exactly qualify either as a communion table or as a kitchen table. Due to the constraints of the space, it most certainly was not round, but there was both solidarity and welcome in the many preparations going on around it. I had been welcomed and ushered into the sanctuary of the Metropolitan Community Church of San Francisco along with other members of the Commission on Faith and Order of the National Council of Churches. Around me a vibrant hymn sing progressed. In front of me an ever-increasing mound of food was being heaped up as people moved around the table preparing for a "love feast."[1]

The visit of our ecumenical group had been arranged by Ron Russell-Coons and by our subgroup on Unity and Renewal of the Church as part of our study of how ecclesiology is changing in response to the situations of groaning, struggle, and death. Ron was a member of the clergy staff at MCC San Francisco, a member of our group, and a person living with AIDS. Together with Ron we had arranged for our colleagues to experience with us "the imagination of AIDS."[2] We wanted them to share in the discovery of what it means to be a community of faith and struggle that is not only living with AIDS but also using its imagination to fashion new understandings of the meaning of wholeness, hospitality, and hope in the face of massive rejection and denial of authentic existence by the dominant society and the mainline churches.[3] Unable to face their own fear of sexuality, homosexuality, and death itself, churches have refused to struggle with the need to transform their own theological and ecclesial inheritance and have denied salvation to those who are engaged in the struggle for life. This struggle was all around us as people living with AIDS were escorted from hospital beds to share in a service of healing, walls were hung with quilts from the Names Project in memory of those who have died with AIDS, and the NCC guests were ushered to their seats amid inner turmoil and fear. But the welcome was everywhere as well, and so was the message of hope and resurrection. "When the Roll Is Called Up Yonder, I'll Be

There" was sung with gusto and great joy. Later, Beryl Ingram-Ward commented on the hymn.

> I was hearing it sung by women and men who have been told by their original denominational homes that because of their sexual orientation they most assuredly would not have a place "up yonder" when the roll was called! . . . Here they were, in church, singing wholeheartedly of their faith in the faithfulness of Jesus, who was present in their midst outside the camp. It was, for me, a thundering affirmation of God.[4]

In such a setting, questions about the nature and mission of the church multiply, and we begin to ask ourselves and those engaged in such a ministry what it means to be a community of faith and struggle. It would seem from participating in such an event and from studying MCC San Francisco in chapter 3 that we can at least catch some glimpses here of church in the round: a community of Christ, bought with a price, where everyone is welcome.[5] As we saw in chapter 1, the critical principle of feminist ecclesiology is a table principle. It looks for ways that God reaches out to include all those whom society and religion have declared outside and invites them to gather together. It measures the adequacy of the life of a church by how well it responds to the needs of marginalized persons for justice, hospitality, and hope. Picking up on the clue from chapter 3 that the church requires a "justice connection," I want to examine how our understanding of church is transformed when we look at it from the perspective of those who are suffering from injustice and oppression.

This chapter, "Justice and the Church," reexamines theological discussions of the role of the church in God's saving and liberating action and asks about the nature of the church and its identifying characteristics. The three parts of the chapter will deal with traditional understandings about the church: as a place of salvation, as a sign of Christ's presence, and as a community of word and sacrament. Each time, new understandings of the church are sought by raising the question of justice. Where is justice to be found in the Christian tradition? Where is it to be found in communities that practice kitchen table solidarity with women and men who suffer from unjust structures related to their sexual orientation, race, gender, class, and so much more?

It may be that feminist interpretation of the church will aid us in the traditioning process described in chapter 1 as we reinterpret biblical and ecclesial traditions in order to discover a still living and evolving past with which to shape the future. Authority for this feminist traditioning comes not only from the discovery of cognitive dissonance among those who are rejected by the churches but also from the Tradition of God, acting in Jesus Christ and calling the churches to become communities of faith, compassion, and justice.[6]

Place of Salvation

In his "Letters to Connie," Ron Russell-Coons wrote to his sister that AIDS had been the "catalyst for healing" and inner peace from God.

> So your prayers and concerns can change. Instead of asking God to change my sexual orientation and then, incidentally, to heal my illness, you can thank God for the healings I am experiencing deep within. My faith is full and strong. The negatives of the virus at work in my body can never overshadow the loving touch of God that heals my spirit.[7]

Ron's spiritual journey is grounded in the day-to-day reality of AIDS. These letters are full of suffering, depression, ostracism, and fear. But they are also full of faith and of the conviction that "though outwardly we are wasting away, yet inwardly we are being renewed day by day" (2 Cor. 4:16, NIV). He journeys home to Alabama to see his parents, sister, children, and friends for what is likely to be the last time. He will be able to see his parents and share their southern hospitality. "But, unfortunately, elsewhere in my family the us-and-them attitude will prevent my sharing in their love."[8]

When confronted with such faith and such longing for reunion, we cannot do otherwise than ask ourselves about the traditional Christian interpretations of the meaning of salvation. A feminist interpretation of the church will need to seek out a constructive formulation of some of the changes needed in the theological interpretation of the church as a place of salvation. Such an investigation is not limited only to issues of sexism; a feminist interpretation of the church questions all the structures of patriarchy that deny the fullness of life for those who question compulsory heterosexuality, gender inequality, and every other form of inequality.[9]

Justice and salvation

The church today is often unable to deal with the crisis of AIDS simply because its understanding of who is saved is so narrow that there is no room in the church, or even in God's love, for a man like Ron. Salvation has been sexualized, privatized, futurized, and restricted to a chosen few. Only those who conform to one pattern of sexuality can be saved. Personal morality, particularly in regard to sexual sins, is emphasized, but the injustices of our economic system, racism, and heterosexism are not even named for what they are: human sin. Salvation is given a dualistic interpretation, focusing on the future destiny of the soul and ignoring the fullness of life in the present. Only those who follow the practices of a particular faith community are considered worthy of the gift of salvation.

Such narrow understandings of salvation not only cause great pain to the many persons who are burdened with guilt but also lead the church to false pride and arrogance in its claim to be the "place" of God's salvation.

Perhaps a fresh look at the meanings of salvation, liberation, and justice can help the church confess its own sin and become an instrument of God's love for all humankind.

Like other central biblical and church traditions, the interpretation of salvation is situation-variable. It not only has evolved over time but also continues to take on different meanings in the face of concrete struggles and hopes for wholeness and life. Its gospel meaning is often illuminated most clearly by those whose struggles with death and hopes for life help us understand what good news is all about. This is because salvation is a story and not an idea, a word that describes God's mending and reconciling action in our lives and in the whole of creation. As we respond in faith to God's saving action, we are drawn into the story and God's gift of justice and love is revealed in our lives.

In searching out the story of salvation in the biblical texts, we do not find one simple formula or proof text either for those who would reduce salvation to concern for the individual soul or for those who reduce it to concern for social issues. In the Hebrew Testament a variety of words such as "to deliver" (*hoshi'a*) and "to redeem" (*ga'al*) are used to describe what God has done and will do for the Hebrew people. One of the most important words for the goal of salvation is *shalom*.[10] This word has a wide spectrum of meanings, which include not only its usual English translation, "peace," but also personal, familial, and communal wholeness, well-being, and prosperity. The word represents a summary of all the gifts God promises to humanity in the mending of creation, including those of justice and righteousness (*sedaqah*). Thus Psalm 85:10–12 includes them all together as the gifts of God's steadfast love or covenant faithfulness (*hesed*). The second half of each verse repeats the first in a piling up of parallel images.

> Steadfast love and faithfulness will meet;
>> righteousness and peace will kiss each other.
> Faithfulness will spring up from the ground,
>> and righteousness will look down from the sky.
> The LORD will give what is good,
>> and our land will yield its increase.

In the Hebrew Testament two of the key motifs of salvation overlap and converge in the meaning of shalom. These two motifs have been identified by Claus Westermann as liberation and blessing.[11] The first motif, liberation, refers to deliverance from suffering, distress, death, sin anxiety, pursuit, and imprisonment. From the time of the exodus onward, Yahweh is portrayed as a liberating God whose actions are the basis of continuing hope for deliverance. The second motif, blessing, portrays God as Creator and Sustainer of all creation (Gen. 1:28, 31). The result of God's blessing, given to Abraham on behalf of all the people of the earth, was spiritual and physical well-being and included the happiness of fertility in family and field, as well as victory over enemies (Gen. 12:1–3). Shalom was understood to include this totality of blessing as a description of the goal of God's liberating action as past event and promised hope.[12]

In the Greek Testament, Jesus, Prince of Shalom, is understood as the fulfillment of God's promise to establish shalom with justice and righteousness (Isa. 9:6–7). The Gospels present Jesus as the one who came to fulfill this double promise of salvation (Luke 2:14; John 14:27). Jesus embodies the meaning of shalom through his actions of healing (blessing), as well as his actions of conquest over death (liberation). In Paul's writings and the later epistles, however, the word most often used to connote salvation, *soteria*, is reduced from the wider spectrum of shalom and deals mainly with the divine-human relationship and not the physical and social aspects of well-being. Paul speaks of salvation as a once-and-for-all occurrence in Jesus Christ, as an ongoing process in our lives, and as a future realization.[13]

As we move into the early period of church history, we discover a tendency to reduce and narrow the broader understanding of shalom even further in the light of the Hellenistic view of the separation of the body and soul. The Latin word *salus*, used to translate *soteria*, became focused even more clearly on one aspect of liberation: that of the eternal destiny of the soul in the afterlife. This *salus* was to be mediated by the church through its sacramental life, and it was understood that there was "no salvation outside the church."[14]

In contemporary theology there is wide recognition of the deformation of the doctrines of salvation and the need to confront the way in which they have tended toward exclusion of non-Christians, heretics, and all who are "other." In liberation theologies, especially, there has been a recognition of the need to regain the wholeness of salvation as shalom, and a shift to the use of the word "liberation" to emphasize the importance of social as well as personal salvation. Without denying that salvation includes a message of personal deliverance from sin and death, liberation theologians also place emphasis on the communal aspect of salvation as social and physical wholeness and harmony among human beings and all creation. For instance, Gustavo Gutiérrez says, "Salvation is not something otherworldly, in regard to which the present life is merely a test. Salvation—the communion of [people] with God and the communion of [people] among themselves—is something which embraces all human reality, transforms it, and leads it to its fullness in Christ."[15]

In liberation and feminist theologies the two overlapping motifs of shalom appear again as a description of a still living and evolving past that can shape the future. The first motif, liberation, is seen as a gift of God's action in history as well as the agenda of those who join God as partners in the work of New Creation. The second motif, blessing, is seen as God's intention for full humanity of women together with men and for the mending of all creation. The blessing of Abraham and Sarah is understood as a gift of full personal, social, and ecological well-being, not only for the people of faith but for all of the groaning creation (Rom. 8:22–23). The work of Christ in bringing about this gift of New Creation is understood both as liberation from sin and as liberation from all the consequences of sin: what Gutiérrez names as "despoliation, injustice, hatred."[16]

Just as the larger meaning of salvation as shalom includes both liberation and blessing, it also includes justice and righteousness.[17] As we saw in Psalm 85:10–12, God's covenant faithfulness or loyalty is expressed through righteousness and peace and includes material as well as social blessing. The word translated as "righteousness" is the same word used to speak of God's justice (*sedaqah*). According to Gerhard von Rad, justice has central significance in the Hebrew Testament for all the relationships of human life. It is the standard not only for human relationship to God but also for relationship to other persons, to animals, and to the natural environment, and it "can be described without more ado as the highest value in life, that upon which all life rests when properly ordered."[18]

Justice is understood in the Hebrew Testament not as an abstract principle, or rule for conduct, but as a relational concept that describes the way we relate to God and one another. The Hebrew people are a covenant people, and faithfulness to that covenant requires living justly with one another and joining God in the vindication of the poor, the widow, the stranger, and all who are oppressed. According to Micah 6:8, God requires justice, covenant faithfulness, and "considered attention to another."[19] This understanding of justice appears even in the earliest biblical material. In her song of victory, Deborah rehearses the righteousness (the saving actions) of God in delivering the people from Sisera and his army. The word for righteousness or justice here is *sedaqah*, although it is translated in the NRSV as "triumphs" (Judg. 5:11). According to Krister Stendahl, God's righteous acts mean that "God is putting things right— and that is *tsedaqah*, the righteousness of God."[20]

In his study of biblical justice for the study on Unity of the Church and Renewal of Human Community of the World Council of Churches, Nestor Miguez has pointed out:

> In that sense justice is achieved by reciprocity. It is not an abstract idea of equality, in the sense in which we could equate justice with egalitarianism, but it is rather the activity by which one can expect that his or her conduct will correspond to that of the other party, even taking into account the differences.[21]

Justice is not only about giving each person their due, it is about the restoration of right relationships and about God's judgment (*mishpat*) on those who are unjust. From the time of the prophets onward there was recognition that God's righteousness and justice might not lead to vindication of an unfaithful people but rather to condemnation and judgment on those who violated their covenant responsibilities before God and their neighbor. Prophets like Amos declared that the day of God's vindication will be a day of judgment because the people have broken God's covenant (Amos 5:18–24).

Much of this sense of justice as God's saving action and our response to that action has been lost in the translation of justice as righteousness because the connotation in contemporary English usage is of personal morality rather than of right relationship and responsibility for the well-being of community. Some of the original meaning of justice and righteousness has been preserved through the Pauline use of the term "righteousness/justification" (*dikaiosyne*). His understanding of justification by faith was an affirmation that through God's vindicating actions in Jesus Christ the power and possibility of just living has been restored. Through God's grace, things have been put right or made just, and we are given the opportunity to live in right relationship with God, one another, and the whole of creation.

In Romans, Paul's development of justification by faith rather than works seems to come out of his concern for the inclusion of both the Jews and the Greeks in God's saving actions in Jesus Christ. Thus in Romans 1:16–17 he cites Habakkuk 2:4 in declaring:

> For I am not ashamed of the gospel; it is the power of God for salvation to everyone who has faith, to the Jew first and also to the Greek. For in it the righteousness of God is revealed through faith for faith; as it is written, "The one who is righteous will live by faith."

Paul sets out to show that God's righteousness and justice have been vindicated through the life, death, and resurrection of Jesus Christ. Therefore, the vindication does not come through the works of the Torah, or law, but through acceptance of God's gift. But, as he indicates in Romans 3:9–20, the Jews are still to be included in God's vindication because all have sinned, both Jew and Greek, and all are offered salvation through God's saving action.

Paul does not separate faith from faithful or just living. In fact, he links justification and sanctification by his assertion that the free gifts of God's Spirit make it possible to practice faithfulness in community.[22] As Elsa Tamez has pointed out in *The Scandalous Message of James*, Paul and James are not as different in their perspective on justification and works of justice as we may have been led to believe. Honoring the kitchen table principle of contextual and situation-variable understanding of a particular theological or biblical message, Tamez points out that Paul is speaking in the context of struggle over the issue of Jewish traditions and whether their practice avails to salvation. "At no time does he place the works of justice in opposition to justification. Rather he says they are the fruits of the spirit that are born of faith."[23]

James, on the other hand, is speaking in the context of struggle for survival among those who are suffering social marginality and economic injustice. He refers to the good works as the "liberating deeds of Jesus" and lifts up Jesus' teachings from the Sermon on the Mount as a guide for righteousness and blessing for the poor and outcasts.[24] Like the prophets, James sees that cooperation in justice is part of faith and together are a response to God's action of justification (James 2:14–26). From the perspective of those who are marginal or oppressed, it is clear that one's actions in response to the gift of God's grace are a part of that gracious empowerment. In another time, the reformer John Calvin tried to make this clear by declaring, "Thus we see how true it is that we are justified, not without works, yet not by works; since union with Christ, by which we are justified, contains sanctification as well as righteousness."[25]

No salvation outside the poor

If it is God's actions that justify and put things right, how is it that the church has come to lay claim to itself as the place of salvation, declaring that there is "no salvation outside the church"? In the early church, as in many other times, the struggles to hold on to faith in the midst of persecutions and disputes over authority and doctrine led to the formulation of a doctrine that would both provide assurance of salvation and also reinforce the authority of the dominant church groups over against doctrines they considered heretical. Cyprian is famous for the formulation of this axiom in the third century on the basis of the image of the church as Noah's ark in 1 Peter 3:20. He declared that only the sacraments of the "true church" could lead to salvation and the schismatics were shut off from "the promises of the Church." The axiom was already in use before Cyprian, as the still-undivided church struggled for dominance over schismatic groups. According to Hans Küng, an earlier complete formulation is found in Origen's writings: "Let no one persuade or deceive (themselves) outside this house, that is outside the Church, no one will be saved; for if anyone leaves, (they are themselves) guilty of death."[26]

This idea of God's preferential option for the church and the claim to exclusive control of the powers of salvation through the sacraments of baptism and eucharist went largely unchallenged in the church for centuries because it consolidated the power of the church, both East and West, in its struggles for dominance in the state and also consolidated the privilege of the clergy in their exclusive position of administering the bread of life. In medieval society it was assumed that all the known world was already Christian and that those who did not believe, like Jews and Mohammedans, were heretics. In the patriarchal dualistic paradigm of reality, it was easy to assume that if 1 Peter 3:18–22 said there was salvation inside the "ark" through baptism, then there was no salvation outside. If the dominant church group was right, the others were wrong and needed to be suppressed or exterminated.

That same dualistic either/or world view could hold that, if Christ is identified with the church as Christ's body, then Christ is not identified with the world outside; if the one, holy, catholic, and apostolic church has been given the responsibility to proclaim the gospel and guard the tradition, then no one outside the church has authority to interpret that gospel tradition. At the time of the Protestant Reformation this world view was not challenged directly by the reformers. What was challenged was the question of which church was the *true* church and would have exclusive rights to dispense this either/or view of salvation. As we shall see in the last part of this chapter, the Protestant discussion of the marks of the church was framed around the question of which church was the true "ark of salvation."

Although there are plenty of persons and churches still laying claim to God's preference for their form of Christianity, the discovery of the whole inhabited world and the many faiths of that world has made the claim to salvation for only a few seem less and less credible. Feminist theologians, as well as most other contemporary theologians, would say that a God of vengeance who shows extreme partiality is not "seriously imaginable," or at least is not a God with which one would fall in faith.[27] While recognizing the closed patriarchal contexts in which such an exclusive view of God could be held, those who seek to serve a God whose wish is to mend creation and restore human community largely reject this earlier formulation and seek out a God of justice and love, a God of hospitality (Rom. 2:11).

Churches and theologians, both Roman Catholic and Protestant, have gradually reinterpreted the meaning of this tradition, seeking the still living and evolving part of its teaching that could shape the future of a world desperately in need of justice, peace, and the integrity of creation. They recognize that at the root of the tradition is the conviction that the church is the locus or place of salvation because God has chosen to be present in the community that shares the life of the risen Christ through faith and action. It is a place of salvation *because Christ promises to be present there.* The traditioning of this doctrine has also led over the centuries to an emphasis on the church as a mediator of salvation. This idea of mediation was developed further in the Roman Catholic Church by the time of the Second Vatican Council. In Küng's words, the council affirms "salvation inside the Church" but also states that "salvation is open to all, not just to schismatics, heretics and Jews, but to non-Christians too and even to atheists if they are in good faith."[28] The church is understood as a sign of salvation or of the New Creation, rather than as an exclusive vehicle of God's saving work.

From the perspective of feminist and liberation theologies, the dualistic and negative formulation of the idea of God's preferential option for the church has to be challenged from the perspective of the margin. In Latin American liberation theologies, this challenge comes through the axiom of God's preferential option for the poor. Looked at from the perspective of those seeking liberation from the structural sins of social, political, and economic domination, the issue of the place of salvation is re-traditioned by examining the biblical traditions of God's justice and righteousness. From this perspective, as Robert McAfee Brown says, justice "appears to be God's middle name"![29] In the light of these traditions there is no doubt that God chooses to be on the side of the oppressed and that Jesus lives out that decision by welcoming the marginal, the poor, the outcasts into God's household. Gustavo Gutiérrez makes this very clear in his discussion of the Beatitudes in *The Power of the Poor in History.*

> To assert that the proper, original message of the Beatitudes refers first of all to the "material poor" is not a "humanization" or politicization of their meaning. It is a recognition that God is God and that God loves the poor with all freedom and gratuity—and that God does so not because the poor are good, or better than others, but just because they are poor. That is, they are afflicted, they are hungry, and this situation is a slap in the face of God's sovereignty, God's being the Go'el ("Savior, Redeemer"), the Defender of the poor, the "Avenger of the lowly."[30]

The power of this message leaves no doubt, in the minds of those who have experienced the tradition of the privilege of the church, that this preference of God for the poor can mean condemnation for the rich and affluent of every nation. But it is only patriarchal either/or thinking that leads persons to assume that if God is for the poor, God is against everyone else. In fact, to assert God's presence among the poor is to use the same theological traditions as those of God's presence in the church, and to run the risks of patriarchal exclusivism. God has chosen to be among the poor in Jesus Christ, as Matthew 25:31–46 makes abundantly clear. This does not mean that God isn't also among others but that God, whose special concern is for those who are suffering, invites us to find Christ through solidarity with the least of our brothers and sisters.

In the same way, the poor become mediators of salvation, not because of their righteousness but because they help us to understand what salvation and liberation mean from the point of view of those who hunger and thirst for justice. The poor are also a sign of salvation because we find Christ there when we work in solidarity with those who are marginalized and deprived of their humanity by society. They are a place of salvation *because Christ promises to be present there.* And those who seek access to God's justice and righteousness have the opportunity of becoming betrayers of their own class privileges and working in solidarity with the poor.[31]

God's option for the poor is an option for justice. It is a sign of God's desire to mend the whole of creation, and especially those parts of creation that are the most broken. In this perspective, to be saved is to receive the gift of God's welcome into a covenant relationship of justice and shalom with ourselves, with God, and with our neighbor. When this gift of acceptance and empowerment for new life happens, there is a desire to live in a way that is accountable and hospitable to those around us. Thus our human actions of justice and love flow from a restored relationship with God rather than from fear of retribution.

Just as with the understanding of the locus of salvation in the church, the locus of salvation in the poor is not to be an end in itself but an eschatological sign of God's work to mend and liberate the creation. But there is a difference here between the two loci. In the latter case Christ is found everywhere in this groaning and suffering world, and God's love is available to all, whether or not they are permitted to break bread in a particular church.

This recognition of Christ's presence outside the church leads in turn to an even wider perspective that would speak of God's preferential option for all creation. Edward Schillebeeckx, in his book *Church, The Human Story of God*, hints at this when he speaks of "no salvation outside the world."[32]

As we shall see in the discussion of the doctrine of election in chapter 5, the shift in paradigm that leads feminist theologies to reject the either/or patriarchal framework pushes us to frame the question of salvation in a different way. Looked at from the perspective of God's work of New Creation, it would seem that God desires the whole of the groaning creation to be saved, liberated, and mended, and not just one or more particular groups within that creation (1 Tim. 2:4). Like the church and the poor, the whole creation is a place of salvation *because Christ promises to be present there.*

Through the incarnation, God has chosen to be among us in the midst of suffering humanity. There is no way to ignore the fact that God is with us in our midst in and through material and historical reality, not just in some otherworldly reality. God has a "passion for justice," and that passion extends to creation in all its parts.[33] The creation is a mediator of God's love and care, for it provides an ecology of life and support and reminds us of the beauty and goodness of the earth. The groaning and struggling creation described by Paul is a sign of longing for the New Creation. It points toward the need for "nature rights" as well as "human rights" and reminds us of our calling to share in partnership with God for the care of the earth.

To make it clear that the world is not just some discarded fast-food wrapper to be crumpled up and thrown away, Sallie McFague has developed the image of the "world as God's body," to suggest the presence of God both in and beyond the world. She uses three alternative models of God, along with this nonhierarchical description of the realm or household of God: "God as mother, lover and friend of the world as God's body is both transcendent to the world (even as we are transcendent to our bodies) and profoundly immanent in the world (even as we are at one with our bodies)."[34]

Whether or not we choose to think of the world as God's body, or as God's household, it is clear that the gospel traditions point to a world in which God is involved. It is a world where Christ's incarnation, life, death, and resurrection point to the power and possibility of New Creation as both present reality and future hope.

Double sin of the church

If there is such an abundance of suffering, injustice, and need in the world, why is it that the white male-dominated mainline churches in the United States have such a difficult time joining in solidarity with those who are poor or marginalized? If there is such an abundance of biblical evidence that God is a God of justice who is concerned to re-create the world as a home or community of justice and shalom, why is justice not a primary mark of Christian community? In this brief investigation of justice and the church it is not possible to do the careful social, political, and economic analysis of particular churches in their own concrete social location and time in order to identify the structures of sin that hold the churches in a pattern of indifference to the world.[35] Yet having looked at some of the communities of faith and struggle in chapter 3, we can at least recognize that the majority of white mainline churches in the United States do not recognize that the struggle for justice is an expression of faith in a world of injustice.

These churches have also participated in a deformation of the doctrine of sin along with that of salvation, so that even the naming of sin is done in a way that conceals the injustice of our social and ecclesiological systems. The connection between personal and social sin has been "split at the root" so that the church can preach love of neighbor and yet confirm the social status quo that perpetuates oppression.[36] This dualistic view, which conceals reality, is taught both in society and in the churches. In her ground-breaking book on white racism, *Killers of the Dream*, Lillian Smith describes the process of learning to deny the reality of sin and injustice while growing up in a "deep south" town:

> I learned to believe in freedom, to glow when the word *democracy* was used, and to practice slavery from morning to night. I learned it the way all of my southern people learn it: by closing door after door until one's mind and heart and conscience are blocked off from each other and from reality.[37]

In the Hebrew Testament, the connection between social and personal sin is much more clear. In the context of shalom and Israel's covenant of blessing and liberation, sin is understood as a breakdown of the covenant relationship caused by disobedience.[38] Frequent words for sin are *chatta'th* (missing the mark), *pesha'* (rebellion or violating the covenant), and *'awon* (disobedience). As we saw in the discussion of salvation and justice, the breakdown of the covenant relationship is frequently described as a violation of God's justice and righteousness, as the people refuse to live justly with one another. Going back to a root meaning of salvation as *yeshu'ah* (to be broad and spacious), sin is understood as denial of this room or space in which to live.

The Gospels often present Jesus as one who fulfills the prophets' call for justice and inclusion of the poor and the outsiders in God's community, and sin is understood as refusal to do God's will on earth (Matt. 6:10). Sin in the context of *soteria* in the Greek Testament is often focused on lack of obedient faith. One misses the mark (*hamartia*) by refusing to have a relationship of trust and obedience with God in Jesus Christ. Paul speaks of sin as "hatred of God" and rejection of Jesus Christ and the gift of God's grace (Rom. 8:7, 14–23).[39] In later church traditions, sin as *peccatum* takes on a quantitative aspect in relation to overcoming sins through participation in the life of the church.

In this context of the separation of personal and social sin, liberation theologians have sought to emphasize oppression and injustice as dimensions of sin. Just as Isaiah 49:19–20 symbolizes the oppression of Israel as a land "too crowded for your inhabitants," and Psalm 4:1 speaks of salvation as the gift of "room when I was in distress," liberation and feminist theologies point to sin as a refusal to give others room to breathe and to live as human beings. The situation-variability of sin is emphasized by looking at its meaning from the perspective of those who have been oppressed.[40] Like the use of "liberation" together with salvation, the use of "oppression" or denial of room to breathe is intended to make clear that sin includes social as well as personal injustice in which real persons are denied the possibility of their own human dignity and of life itself.

Willingness to split off issues of sin from issues of injustice has led to the double sin of the church.[41] It is this double sin that makes it so difficult for white mainline U.S. churches to repent and begin to work for social as well as personal transformation. They cannot respond to the need for justice and liberation as a fundamental part of their calling as the church of Jesus Christ because they have reversed the teachings of Paul that we need to be "in, but not of, the world." According to Robin Scroggs, Paul reminds the Corinthians that they are to continue to participate in the life of their communities, but they are to live as if the New Creation were already at hand (1 Cor. 7:29–31).[42] Instead, the churches of our day often live of, but not in, the world. Their lives, structures, class divisions, sexual orientation, and prejudices all reflect the culture of which they are a part rather than the New Creation. All the while they refuse to be involved in social, economic, and political advocacy for justice.

This double sin is particularly difficult to address because various attempts at turning away from one side of the sin are blocked by the other sin that remains. Thus, as we noticed in chapter 3, the human sexuality debate in the Presbyterian Church could not be resolved even though many persons recognized the need for social advocacy and ministry with those who are victims of sexual oppression. They recognized a need to be *in* the world, serving those in need, but they did not recognize that they themselves were *of* the world, holding to a view of reality that looked upon persons who were victims of injustice as "others" who "bring these things on themselves" by their own actions. As the report put it, the problem or sin of sexuality was not homosexuality or nonmarital sex, the problem or sin was the churches' "conformity to the unjust norm of compulsory heterosexuality and gender inequality."[43]

A move toward repentance of this double sin on the part of the churches would require a recognition that justice must be a key ingredient in both halves of the axiom. Being *in* the world requires active struggle for the harmony and right relationship of that world. Being *not of* the world requires a recognition that God's justice calls us to live now, as if we are part of the mended creation rather than participants in a broken one (John 17:14). Without this the churches go on functioning as if justice were not even supposed to be part of their lives. They need to be called to repentance of what "The Kairos Document" discussed in chapter 3 calls "the fundamental problem of church theology": a dualism of individualism and otherworldly spirituality separated from the worldly affairs of public life.[44]

Recently, a church in Connecticut called a pastor, but before she could accept the call it was rescinded. They had read about her work with another pastor on peace and justice issues and didn't want a "troublemaker" around. Another church formed a special committee to discuss whether the pastor they were calling would be able to separate concern for peace and justice from concern for religion. Yet another church placed an invitation in the local newspaper of a struggling old industrial town in the northeast to come and worship where the town's "first families have worshiped for centuries."[45]

The same double sin is apparent in large megachurches like the Willow Creek Church mentioned in chapter 3, with their outreach and welcome to the "baby-boomer" generation.[46] Here we see churches that are most certainly responsive to the needs and interests of the large number of people who live in what Robert Bellah calls "life-style enclaves" where people are socially, economically, or culturally similar and concerned primarily about enjoyment of private life with those who share their life style. But they recruit people on the basis of being totally *of* such a privatized enclave, and not *in* the world that is struggling with economic and political realities of survival.

Only true repentance and willingness to be in, but not of, the world will lead members of the churches to search for just and responsible relationships in community. Bellah calls this the difference between community and life style. "Whereas a community attempts to be an inclusive whole, celebrating the interdependence of public and private life and of the different callings of all, life style is fundamentally segmental and celebrates the narcissism of similarity."[47] In an earlier time Paul called this search for just relationships "being political." Thus he urges the Philippians to be part of the *polis* and discharge their obligation as citizens in a manner that is worthy of Christ.[48]

Imaginative and constructive repentance leads us toward a desire for social transformation, beginning with the church. But this is very difficult and requires a willingness to risk the suffering that comes to those who try to change the status quo of any society. Adrienne Rich has pointed out that she was greatly helped in making a decision to risk in her own life by a quotation from James Baldwin: "Any real change implies the breakup of the world as one has always known it, the loss of all that gave one an identity, the end of safety."[49]

The world as we know it *is* unjust, and to share with God in the building of a community of justice is to call for a breakup of the world as we know it and for a New Creation! Three possible clues as to what it would take for such imaginative and constructive repentance of double sin are conversion, transformation, and liberation.

The first clue, that *conversion is necessary,* indicates why it is so difficult to help churches see and reject the patriarchal understanding of reality that allows justice and salvation to be split off at the root. As we saw in chapter 1, patriarchy is the designation for a variety of social systems of domination and subordination in which women's realities are defined by the status (race, class, country, religion) of the men to whom they belong as daughter, wife, mother. But patriarchy is also to be understood as an interpretive framework or paradigm of that social system in which authority as domination is understood as a description of social reality that justifies the domination of subordinate groups by those who are dominant. In order for the churches to see the need for repentance they must be converted to seeing and understanding that God's justice springs from a vision of mended creation in which reality is based on responsibility for just relationships with our neighbors, whoever and wherever they may be. Until the paradigm of partnership and justice makes more sense than that of domination and injustice, the churches and their members have not begun to repent of the sin of being *of* the world.

The second clue is that *the goal of conversion and new life is social transformation.* As we noted, the churches often move toward social outreach and social action and thus recognize a need to be in the world, but they are not about to take up Baldwin's call by transforming the patriarchal world of oppression. Social outreach and works of compassion are important for those they assist, as well as for the possibility of new insight and conversion on the part of those who reach out beyond their own enclave. However, it is not truly a move to be *in* the world, unless the churches and their members begin to recognize and move to oppose the root causes of the social, economic, and political problems that deny persons the power and material resources to solve their own problems.

In 1992, at a Hartford Theological Seminary consultation on Women-Church, Marie Augusta Neal noted that the power and possibility of social transformation is both spiritual and political. Prayer, liturgy, study, and care for neighbor, as well as demonstrations, political campaigns, and similar actions, can all be part of the work for justice *or* part of the support for the status quo. The issue is not in what way one works for justice, but whether one's work is on behalf of transformation of the society so that God's justice is done on earth.[50]

The third clue is that *justice involves a liberation journey.* The church shares in the journey of salvation as it takes part in the story of God's love affair with the world. This is a liberation journey that is shared with all of God's creation as it struggles for the power and possibility of being put right. It is a journey with God, ourselves, and others and for God, ourselves, and others. The church seeks to live out the great commandment: "You shall love the Lord your God with all your heart, and with all your soul, and with all your strength, and with all your mind; and your neighbor as yourself" (Luke 10:27; Deut. 6:4). But it can only do so as it comes to understand the needs of the neighbor for just relationships, and for wholeness in community, and takes action in solidarity with the neighbor in need. The journey of liberation takes the church in many new paths, but it can only be part of the repentance of double sin if the churches and their many members begin to show by their actions that they live *in* the world, with responsibility for that world.

These clues are themselves not so unexpected, for they are similar to church teachings about the process or order of salvation as justification, regeneration, and sanctification. The ordering of the clues is not important, for they are all part of the response to God's gracious reaching out to us, to the church, and to the world to put things right. They are all part of what Calvin calls "double grace" as he describes the process of justification and sanctification. God has set us free in Jesus Christ and granted the power of the Spirit to restore our humanity and enable us to do God's will as we share in the mending of creation.[51]

Sign of Christ's Presence

When the church does seek to become a sign of Christ's liberating presence in creation we are often surprised to find a great reversal of things as usual. In ways reminiscent of Matthew 25, we often find it is the outcasts and the persons who are marginal to the life of the church who provide insights needed in a specific time and place. This was certainly true of Ron Russell-Coons and the Universal Fellowship of Metropolitan Community Churches. The UFMCC's application for membership in the National Council of the Churches of Christ in the U.S.A. has been rejected because of its ministry to the lesbian, gay, and bisexual community. Yet it has continued to send delegates as observers and participants wherever this is possible. Ron was the delegate to the Faith and Order Commission, sent to our group by his church to help us in our study of how the imagination of AIDS brings new insight into the meaning of church from the perspective of those on the margin.

The very churches that have been rejected by the NCC because of their openly gay, lesbian, and bisexual ministry have not abandoned the churches of the NCC in their homophobia. Instead, they have continued to provide a much-needed ministry to the wider church, urging it to reexamine its own understanding of sexuality and of the meaning of salvation so that it can come to make sense to persons whose faith is challenged at the breaking points of their lives. Even though he was frequently too sick to work on the book our group was writing about AIDS and the church, Ron continued to provide a ministry of contacts, experience, energy, and love to all those who had become partners with him in creating the book.

What happened in Ron's three years of partnership in our group was that many persons had to discover that God also works through the witness of gay and lesbian Christians. In fact, his presence in the group and his continuing courage in the midst of diminishing strength was, for many, more of a sign of Christ's presence than the traditional signs. In carrying out his ministry with our group, Ron helped us to see what it would mean to "hunger and thirst for justice" and to become a partner in the mending of creation.

Household of God

The story of this mending begins at the other end of history with the fulfillment of God's justice in the New Creation (Isa. 65:17–25; Rev. 21:1–4).[52] The Gospel accounts portray Jesus as both the witness to the coming of God's reign and the one in whom that reign is taking place. In coming to know the story of the one who is called Jesus (Yeshua, the one who saves), we look for Christ's presence among us as a sign of this New Creation or household of God.

The life, death, and resurrection of Jesus Christ are a witness to the world, and not just to the church, that God loves the world and intends to reverse the structures of domination and sin that rule that world. His death and resurrection witness both to the power of injustice to cause suffering in the world and to the power of God's just love in overcoming that injustice. This action of God in Christ is the firstfruits of the coming New Creation which is offered on behalf of all creation (Rom. 8:28–39).

In Jesus Christ, God has elected all of creation to be made new. Not all of creation acknowledges that election, yet different persons of different faiths and ideologies witness to a divine desire for love and justice in many and various ways. As we shall see in chapter 5, God's choice of the whole world indicates God's desire that all will be saved and become part of the mended creation, but it does not indicate that everyone must be a Christian in order to be welcome in God's creation or loved by God. According to Karl Barth, God has elected or chosen Jesus Christ on behalf of all people.[53] Jesus is elected both to witness to and embody the New Creation, and it is the risen Christ's presence among us that continues to convey the justice and peace of that new reality.

As a way of expressing that new reality without using the patriarchal language of kingship, domination, and subordination, I have come to speak of the kingdom of God as the household of God. As I noted in my book *Household of Freedom: Authority in Feminist Perspective,* a metaphor often used in the parables to convey the message of God's hospitality is the household, or *oikos.* Domestic images of the kingdom abound in the Gospels, especially the images of table fellowship that were described in chapter 1. And the word "household" is sometimes used interchangeably with "kingdom" to indicate the place where God's will is done. Thus Mark 3:24–25 says: "If a kingdom is divided against itself, that kingdom cannot stand. And if a house is divided against itself, that house will not be able to stand."

In this eschatological sense of God's householding activity in and beyond this world, "household of God" does not refer to the church, as it does in later Greek Testament books such as 1 Peter, but rather to God's New Creation.[54] The church as a household of faith is called to be a sign of God's power at work among all the nations of the *oikoumene,* but there are other signs that point toward God's mended world house. Those who "fall in faith with Christ," and desire to share the faith and struggle of Christ's community, witness to Christ as the way to the New Creation. They affirm with Paul: "So if anyone is in Christ, there is a new creation: everything old has passed away; see, everything has become new!"

But Christ is not the only way to discover God's will for mending creation, nor has the coming of Christ completed the New Creation that has happened, happens even now among us, and will happen in the future. As Rosemary Radford Ruether has said, "We must see christology, not only as proleptic, but also as paradigmatic."[55]

The work of Christ is proleptic or anticipatory of the completion of the mending of creation. For those who accept God's love through Christ, his work is a full revelation of that love and purpose, but for Jews and for persons of other faiths there is still more to come. Christ's work is also paradigmatic in that it shows Christians clearly what God's love and justice are all about, but that work does not negate the possibility of God's love and justice working through other religions and other social structures.

Discerning God's preferential option for the poor and marginalized can become a baseline for dialogue with other groups when we acknowledge the possibility of the signs of God's work in all creation. In feminist theologies, according to Marjorie Suchocki, justice becomes a fundamental criterion of value and focus of dialogue among different religions as we seek out common ways of living together in a very diverse and complex world.[56]

When we universalize the Christian story of God in Jesus Christ as the only message of salvation for all people, we deny the power of God to work through all the poor and through all creation. To universalize our very concrete and particular faith is a form of imperialism over people of other faiths and ideologies.[57] In humility we can witness to the faith that God has indeed begun the New Creation in Christ, and that for us this is the message of salvation, but still look forward to God's fulfillment of the promise of salvation and liberation for all.

Honoring its humble role as part of God's concern for creation, the church becomes a witness to the presence of Christ. It is that presence that creates the church and not the other way around. And it is that presence that is the power and possibility of life now in anticipation of the household of God. If the church can only find itself where Christ is present, it needs to be very careful to look for the places where Christ has promised to come.

Jürgen Moltmann points out that there are three different groups of assurances of Christ's presence in the Greek Testament.[58]

The first set of promises is related to Jesus' promise to be present in the witness to the gospel, in word and sacrament, and in the gathered community. For instance, Matthew 28:18–20 declares the promise of Christ's presence in witness, baptism, and teaching. In fact the traditional signs of Christ's presence in the church are all anticipated in this text as it speaks of baptism in the *one* name, *holiness* through the continuing presence of the Spirit, *catholicity* as an invitation to all the nations, and *apostolicity* through faithful preaching. First Corinthians 11:23–26 declares the gift of presence in the Lord's Supper, and Matthew 18:20 declares, "Where two or three are gathered in my name, I am there among them."

The second set of promises is related to the presence of Christ among the poor and marginalized. This promise has already been discussed, but it is good to remind ourselves of the importance of Matthew 25:31–46 in making this promise and its word of judgment clear. According to Matthew, Jesus seems to be telling his own story of identification with the poor and outcast so that, together with the Messiah, all who hunger and thirst, all who are naked, sick, or in prison, become the real presence of God's mending work.[59] In solidarity with the least of Jesus' brothers and sisters, we find a social biography of struggle that continues Jesus' own story. Just as the Christians of faith and struggle call out *"¡Presente!"* when the lists of the martyrs in Central America are read at the eucharist, Christians everywhere can call out *"¡Presente!"* and know that Jesus lives through the continuing actions of solidarity with the poor and oppressed.

The third set of promises, related to Christ's future coming and the fulfillment of the household of God, is also linked to the parable of the last judgment in Matthew 25. Jesus promises to be present wherever God's will is done until the time comes when that will for justice and peace is done on earth as in heaven (Matt. 6:10). Moltmann underlines this justice connection, saying that

> the one who is to come is then already present in an anticipatory sense in history in the Spirit and the word, and in the miserable and helpless. His future ends the world's history of suffering and completes the fragments and anticipations of his kingdom which are called the church.[60]

Signs of the church

The church has no nature of its own because its existence is derived from Christ's presence. Yet over the centuries it has claimed that the presence of Christ is manifest in particular signs that make it possible to identify where the true church is located. These are also signs that are understood to be derived from Christ's presence in the church, but they need to be tested from the perspective of the three different assurances of Christ that are described in the Greek Testament to see if they actually do make clear the mandate of the church to be present where Christ is present and to share in God's work of New Creation.

As Robert Schreiter has pointed out, the defining characteristics of the church that are clearly evident for all to see are usually drawn from "the addition made to the Nicene Creed by the Council of Constantinople in 381: 'and in one, holy, catholic, and apostolic church'"[61] Discussion begins here with a common creed recognized by Orthodox, Roman Catholic, and Protestant traditions, but it moves to other signs as well, and it becomes controversial as one confessional body considers the marks of another invalid. Thus, at the time of the Protestant Reformation the discussion of whether the Protestant Church or the Roman Catholic Church had the true marks and was truly church was very much part of the persecution and the religious wars of the sixteenth and seventeenth centuries in Europe. Unity among churches, based on mutual recognition of one another as communities of faith in Jesus Christ, still involves us in the question of the identity of the church of Christ.

The question of identity is a continuing issue because churches must always be looking to find where Christ is present in a particular time and place. In times of change a new process of traditioning is particularly important as we seek to understand the identity of the church in a new situation. Our National Council of Churches group studying how the crisis of AIDS confronts the church with the need to understand what it means to be the body of Christ, sharing in suffering and in the ministry of Christ in today's world, is but one small example of the many Christians who are searching out the identity of the church in the midst of social, political, and economic upheaval.

As we begin to explore the self-understanding of the church, we find that historical descriptions are helpful for locating ourselves within the Christian tradition and discerning indicators of faithfulness, even though they are clearly *not* helpful as rules used to exclude others. We also find that these traditional signs are not nearly as self-evident as they were once considered to be, for they themselves require considerable explanation and verification even among churches who continue to accept the four signs spelled out in the Nicene-Constantinopolitan Creed. For instance, the World Council of Churches Faith and Order Commission has been studying the creed for ten years as part of its program on "Towards a Common Expression of the Apostolic Faith Today." It has taken many consultations and volumes to try to establish that the creed is, in fact, a common basis for "confessing one faith."[62]

The understanding of the church shifts when we interpret one, holy, catholic, and apostolic from the point of view of those at the periphery of life, society, and the church. As with the other identifying marks, what is of most importance is not the presence of certain characteristics but their use and practice. According to Hans Küng, "Unity, holiness, catholicity and apostolicity are therefore not only gifts, granted to the Church by God's grace, but at the same time tasks which it is vital for the Church to fulfill in a responsible way."[63] The signs themselves cannot make the presence of Christ clear if they do not show that presence forth among the poor and as signs of a mended creation, as well as in the witness, liturgy, and gathering of the community.

In our study group on Unity and Renewal of the Church we tried to discern the ways in which the marks of the church are traditioned from the perspective of those engaged in ministry with those living with AIDS. Moving to the margins of most official church bodies, we shared stories, sermons, liturgies, and case studies like those of Ron Russell-Coons that enabled us to catch a glimpse of what the signs of the church would look like at "breaking points of life." The clues that we discerned and tested out together are described by Robert Schreiter in his article "Marks of the Church in Times of Transformation."[64]

The *unity* of the church is a gift of the Spirit or presence of Christ. The church is one because all who call on Christ's name discover Christ in their midst. As God in Christ and the Spirit are one, the many parts of the church are gathered together through one divine action as the sign of the coming household of God (Eph. 4:4–6). The unity of God with humankind brought about by God's reconciling action in Jesus Christ is imaged by the unity of the church across barriers of diversity.

In actuality, churches live out their unity in Christ neither with one another nor with the world. In the face of the differences caused by confessional splits and the deep differences caused by racism, heterosexism, and other forms of oppression, it is perhaps best to emphasize the need for diversity, rather than unity, for it is at this point that the churches are unable to live out their calling to unity. As we will see in regard to racism in chapter 5, a clue important to communities of faith and struggle is that the church cannot be a sign of unity if it achieves unity by marginalizing those who do not fit. Unity at the expense of the weak is not a sign of Christ's hospitality welcoming all into God's household. As Mary Tanner has put it, "A united Church in which ecclesial divisions were overcome but in which divisions based upon race, class, sex, or wealth remained would not be a church truly united. The church must be renewed into unity."[65] In the view of the working group on AIDS, the test of how well the church lives out its witness to unity in Christ is *how well it breaks down barriers* at points where people are being excluded.

The *holiness* of the church is also derived from Christ's presence and from the power of the Spirit to transform the church so that it can live in a relationship of righteousness and justice with God. In biblical tradition, holiness is a fulfillment of covenant relationship with God. The community of faith lives out what Paul Hanson calls a "triad of justice and mercy and faith."[66] In the Sermon on the Mount the directive to be perfect as God is perfect is a way of expressing this need to respond to God's putting things right, by living that way ourselves (Matt. 5:48). This intention of holiness extends far beyond the church itself, for, in the words of Marjorie Suchocki, it is part of God's purpose in mending creation by "weaving creation together in a bond of love."[67]

Again, as we look at the actions of local, national, and international church bodies, we are struck by dualism in the interpretation of the signs of holiness. The church is to be holy by being apart from the world, persons are to be holy by being apart from their bodily selves, and holiness is an individual practice of Christian virtue apart from a community that shares in the suffering of those who oppose injustice. As we shall see in chapter 6, a clue to the gift of holiness in the church is that it leads to a spirituality of connection to our whole selves, to a community of faith and justice, and to those on the margin of society. In our working group on the church with AIDS, a test of the presence of Christ's holiness in the church is how well it announces justice and denounces forces that hinder the appearance of God's righteousness in the mending of creation.

Christ's gift of *catholicity* in the church refers both to the universality of Christ's presence in all the world and to the orthodoxy of the church as it witnesses to the story and teachings of Jesus Christ. If God has acted in Jesus Christ to renew the whole earth, then the presence of Christ in the midst of all creation is important for the church's self-understanding. In this sense, to be catholic is to be connected to all of creation in all its groaning parts and to take responsibility for the needs of the many different churches and peoples of the world. In sharing the one story of God's liberating love in Jesus Christ, the church is also catholic as it witnesses to that story, in ways that are faithful to the biblical and church traditions yet works continually to reinterpret and retradition these traditions in new contexts.

This tradition of catholicity has often been honored in ways that have denied the true universality of God's message of love and replaced it with an assertion that one particularity includes all of what God's message might be about. In a traditional patriarchal paradigm of domination, universality is understood as a mandate for the church to dominate all religions and all people and require them to live according to its teachings. In the same way, the patriarchal paradigm of orthodoxy has led to the idea that right doctrine is to be defined by those who rule over a particular community and is more important than orthopraxy, the right practice of communities of faith and struggle as they seek to be connected to the world around them. A clue to catholicity is expressed in the responsibility of churches for one another as well as for their neighbors in all parts of the world, living out a story of faith that witnesses to God's love for that world. A test of how well the church lives out the sign of Christ's universal presence in the world that was formulated by our working group on AIDS was the quality of connectedness in solidarity with those on the periphery of church and society.

The *apostolicity* of the church is a sign of Christ's presence in the life of the church as the true witness to Christ's own story. By the inspiration of the Spirit of God in Christ, the church continues to share in the witness to that story both in word and action. The continuity of the continuing story of salvation is assured in the view of Roman Catholic, Orthodox, and Anglican churches through the passing on of ordination or commissioning of the apostles through each generation of leadership. For others, the apostolic witness is understood in terms of the quality of life of those who continue to live out the biblical story of the Christ and the apostles in their own time.[68]

As we saw in chapter 2, the patriarchal paradigm of domination has played an important part in the idea of apostolicity as authoritative witness and the guarantee of that authority through chosen male leaders. But it is important to remember that an apostle in the earlier Pauline sense of the word is a witness or missionary, someone sent to tell the good news (Rom. 1:1; 1 Cor. 12:28). In this sense it is possible to invite all the community of faith to become part of the apostolic tradition, not just those who are set apart by clerical ordination. A clue here is that the sign of Christ's apostolate is the sign of participation in God's Mission, God's sending and liberating action in the world. Our working group on AIDS helped me to see that a test of Christ's witness in the church would be its constancy in participation in God's Mission, and not just its lack of interruption in the connection to the early apostles and their witness.

Justice connection

The latter two promises of Christ, to be with the poor and to come again to establish the reign of God, are often ignored as the church practices the double sin of living of but not in the world. Therefore, the question must be raised of whether there needs to be a fifth sign of *justice*. Surely the church is not Christ's church if it is not a witness to the presence of the one in whom God made things right. Many creeds have been written since the Nicene-Constantinopolitan Creed, and they have responded to the needs of the churches in their own times. In our time there needs to be an added emphasis on the justice connection that would make all the other talk about signs more authentic.

Many contemporary theologians assert that these dimensions of the church need to include the perspective of people on the periphery or margins, who very much need an emphasis on the dimension of prophecy or justice. For instance, a special consultation on one common expression of the apostolic faith from the perspective of black Christians in the United States, held in 1984, placed heavy emphasis on this dimension. In the report, "Toward a Common Expression of Faith: A Black North American Perspective," they affirm "that the One, Holy church cannot exist apart from ministries of justice and liberation."[69]

Adding the sign of justice is nothing new in the history of the signs of the church. There never has been a set number of signs, and a widespread consensus on the four signs was achieved only in the nineteenth century, according to Schreiter.[70] Roman Catholic theologians have proposed as many as one hundred signs, and some favored a fifth sign of "Romanness" in the late nineteenth century. Leonardo Boff points out this variation in his article "Theological Characteristics of a Grassroots Church," in order to propose fifteen characteristics of a church linked to the subordinated classes.[71] He also makes very clear the way in which interpretation of the signs is related to the place one is related to one's economic, political, and social position in a society. Protestant theologians, already working with the "extra two" of word and sacrament proposed by sixteenth-century Reformers, have strongly suggested adding a third additional mark of participation in God's Mission to stress the life of the church as a participant in Christ's liberating action in the world.[72]

Some theologians, such as Marjorie Suchocki, prefer to make this clear through the reinterpretation of holiness to reconnect it to God's righteousness and justice. Others, like Schreiter and Moltmann, specifically argue that the reinterpretation is better done within the four creedal signs so that the prophetic dimension is seen throughout.[73] I myself have stressed this dimension in interpreting the signs by lifting up diversity with unity, justice with holiness, connectedness and orthopraxy with catholicity, as well as mission with apostolicity. A shift in perspective to those who are oppressed is crucial, however, and it seems to me that this perspective is very difficult to maintain even if we seek the three aspects of Christ's presence in each of them.

There is so much injustice both within and outside of the church that a clear reminder of Christ's presence calling the church to be one, holy, catholic, apostolic, and *just* is crucial for its identity. This reminder needs to push all churches to constant repentance of their double sin and a constant "hunger and thirst for righteousness [justice]" (Matt. 5:6). Even the churches described in chapter 3 stand in need of this reminder of the justice connection. For example, the historic black churches have been steadfast in their advocacy of racial and economic justice but have often ignored the issues of justice for women and for homosexual persons.[74] The latter issue has contributed to the reluctance of many black churches to be involved in programs addressing needs of persons with AIDS. This picture is beginning to change, especially with increasing numbers of IV drug users, women, and children of color who are HIV positive. More and more black churches are making the justice connection in regard to AIDS as well as to the rights of gay men and lesbians.

The same need for continuing self-criticism in the light of the mark of justice is needed in white feminist theology and in Women-Church. We have seen that Women-Church is an exodus movement of women seeking out communities that express their full humanity and liberation from patriarchy. Small feminist base communities gathered for shared worship seek to live out the mark of justice for all women. Often, however, they neglect the issues of justice for persons of all colors and classes because they are largely white and middle-class. In a similar way, the Metropolitan Community Church of San Francisco has had to struggle to include men of color and women of all colors in its programs.

In traditioning the signs of Christ's presence in the church it is important to recognize that the signs themselves are always changing according to the different cultural, historical, political, and economic contexts of the churches. If the signs are to be helpful in locating the church they need to be descriptive rather than prescriptive, avoiding a patriarchal pattern of dogmatism. Yet it is possible to say that the churches' actions in living out those signs need to be connected to the places where Christ promises to be present. The church finds its own identity as a sign of Christ's work in the bringing of God's household by being a community of faith and witness, a community of struggle for the poor and oppressed, and a community of hope in the fulfillment of God's New Creation.

Word Preached and Celebrated

When the NCC Faith and Order working group on Unity and Renewal finished its work on *The Church with AIDS: Renewal in the Midst of Crisis*, the book was dedicated to Ron Russell-Coons with thanks for the gift of life he shared with us. Ron did not see the final fruit of his ministry with us, but he did see the galley proof, specially bound and sent from Westminster/John Knox Press, and that book went with him to his funeral as a sign of the word he preached and celebrated. Although his failing health had forced him to retire as pastor of a Metropolitan Community Church church in Seattle just before his fortieth birthday, Ron relocated with his partner, Chuck, in San Francisco and continued his ministry through MCC–San Francisco and through the NCC working group of the Faith and Order Commission.[75]

Ron was preaching on the day our commission visited the San Francisco church. He preached on the resurrection that has already begun in Christ and welcomed us to the love feast as a sign of God's welcome table. The church did not serve a regular communion at the service, not because the visitors were afraid to commune with the community living with AIDS but because some of these same visitors represented Roman Catholic, Orthodox, and Protestant churches that did not practice intercommunion.[76]

The feast we celebrated was a resurrection feast, and surely the community experienced a word purely preached and celebrated! If that is the case, then what is missing from our understanding of these marks that frames them in such a way that they serve once again to exclude rather than to include all who search for God's love? It would seem that one of the major missing pieces here is again the dimension of justice. For when justice becomes the criterion for sharing in community, then life is shared with those who have been excluded from so many tables and, as we shall see in chapter 5, the question of sharing at Christ's table becomes a question of hospitality rather than of ecclesiastical unity.

Word purely preached

In the Reformation of the sixteenth century and beyond, there was a long period of controversial theology in which Protestant Reformers and their descendants argued against Roman Catholic reformers and their descendants about what made the church *truly church*. The Protestants claimed that the true church was not only recognized by the visible signs (*signa*) of Christ's presence in oneness, holiness, catholicity, and apostolicity but also by what they called the marks (*nota*) or distinguishing characteristics or functions of the church.[77] These marks of the church were claimed to be what obviously constituted it as true church: namely, the word truly preached and the sacraments rightly administered. Thus John Calvin says, "For whenever we find the word of God purely preached and heard, and the sacraments administered according to the institution of Christ, there, it is not to be doubted, is a Church of God."[78]

The Protestant Reformers did not deny the importance of the Nicaean formula, but they wanted to build their reformation on the scriptures. For this reason they tried to discern in the biblical tradition how the church might be faithful in its preaching and sacramental life. Today it is generally recognized by Roman Catholics that the witness of the scriptures to Jesus Christ is the basis of the life of the church.[79] It is also recognized generally by Protestants that, as Jürgen Moltmann says,

> A church in which the gospel is purely preached and the sacraments are rightly used is the one, holy, catholic and apostolic church. The two Reformation signs of the church really only show from within what the traditional attributes of the church describe from without, so to speak.[80]

The word was understood as pure and the sacraments rightly used if they were administered by the duly ordained male clergy, according to the scriptural promises, and conveyed the gospel to the believers through preaching or signs of bread and water. Ecclesiastical discipline or the fencing of the table became for some a third mark, in that it made sure that God's word was truly preached and celebrated.[81]

From a patriarchal point of view the duly authorized preachers, presiders, and disciplinarians ensured that things be done according to established church order, but it did not free the church or its marks from a denial of the full humanity of women. Through the invention of the printing press, the scriptures were available to laypersons in their practice of prayer and study. Great pains were taken to educate the people in reading and studying the Bible in the vernacular so they could know what was "true." For instance, John Calvin wrote his *Institutes of the Christian Religion* in order to guide the interpretation of scriptures so that students of theology could be prepared for "the reading of the divine word."[82] Yet the interpreters and preachers were all men with clerical privilege, except in left-wing Reformation groups like the Anabaptists and some of their descendants, such as Shakers and Quakers.

As we saw in chapter 2, this increased access to the word of God did not do away with male clerical privilege and power. It also did not do away with what feminist theologians would call "the idolatry of the Father." As long as this personal metaphor for God was used as if "Father" were God's name, the "fathers" of church, family, and state remained as direct representatives of a patriarchal and dominating male God. According to Sallie McFague, "It is not just that 'God the Father' is a frequent appellation for the divine, but that the entire structure of divine-human and human-human relationship is understood in a patriarchal framework."[83]

Women and other subordinated groups could not be trusted to interpret the good news and could not discover themselves as fully human persons made in the image of God.[84] But unless God is imaged as both female and male in speaking and enacting God's word and in the metaphors for God's self-revelation, this word of welcome to women is not clear.[85] Unless God is imaged in verbal metaphors such as "creator, liberator, and advocate," as well as in personal metaphors, this word of justice in the household of God is also lost.

Then as now, true interpretation of the Bible was a difficult task, and we cannot be surprised that the leaders of the Magisterial Reformation conformed to the world view of their own social and political context. They did at least make it clear that the interpretation and understanding of the word were the work of the entire congregation. In every time and place we have to seek out again what is the true gospel message for our time. The Gospels witness to the story of a man who proclaimed God's reign and welcomed people, all people, as children of God. Jesus proclaimed the good news that outsiders were welcome and promised to be present when the church shares in proclaiming that story.

Whatever else the true preaching of the word would need to include, it at least would have to be a word that speaks from the perspective of those who have been crushed and marginalized in our society. It would need to be a word of solidarity, healing, and love in situations of brokenness and despair and a disturbing and troubling word of justice to those who wish to protect their privilege by exclusion. It is a word that often is not fully heard by women in search of their full humanity, nor by those with disabilities in search of an accessible community that celebrates their otherness, nor by other marginal groups such as lesbians and gay men. Yet it is marginalized persons like Ron Russell-Coons who are often the first to reach out to others with AIDS and to other churches in ecumenical coalitions of caring. The scriptures have very little to say about homosexuality, but they have a great deal to say on the necessity of hospitality and of justice for the oppressed (Luke 4:18–19).[86] As we listen to the scriptures as good news to the poor and suffering, and listen to the poor explaining the meaning of Jesus' welcome to us, we may more truly understand the gospel message of God's love.

Sacraments rightly administered

The sacraments were understood by the Reformers as instituted and administered according to the teaching of the scriptures. Protesting against the abuses of the sacraments in the sixteenth-century church, they emphasized baptism and the Lord's Supper as the only two sacraments instituted by Christ's words and actions. They made sure that the preparation for the sacraments included instruction in their biblical meaning and practiced "fencing of the table" by allowing only members in good standing to receive the elements of bread and wine. There also continues to be much discussion over the meaning of baptism and eucharist, although there is much that churches can say together about their institution and meaning. For instance, the Baptism, Eucharist, and Ministry document of Faith and Order says that Christian baptism is rooted in the ministry, death, and resurrection of Jesus of Nazareth (Matt. 28:18–20). "It is incorporation into Christ, who is the crucified and risen Lord; it is entry into the New Covenant between God and God's people."[87] Eucharist is interpreted through the words of 1 Cor. 11:23–25 and is "a sacramental meal which by visible signs communicates to us God's love in Jesus Christ."[88]

When we seek to understand what it would mean to administer the sacraments *rightly*, consideration needs to be given once again to what the biblical meaning of "rightly" would be. Certainly that meaning would go beyond proper preparation, administration, and celebration of the words and actions of Jesus. In fact, the word "rightly" probably would include the need for the community of celebration to live out a life of righteousness or justice.

In regard to baptism, this would mean that a great deal more attention needs to be paid to what this sacrament conveys from the perspective of feminist ecclesiology. As Marjorie Procter-Smith says, "What women need to know from the sacraments of baptism and eucharist is that Christ is present in our struggle to live out our baptismal equality and dignity, and that God has not forgotten us."[89]

Much work has already been accomplished by feminist theologians on the question of the meaning and interpretation of the sacraments, both in biblical and church tradition and in liturgical tradition. Some of the work of Elisabeth Fiorenza and Rosemary Ruether on interpretation from the perspective of women-church has already been cited in earlier chapters.[90] And the already abundant feminist literature on ministry, preaching, and liturgy has received the very helpful additions of Ruth Duck's *Gender and the Name for God* and Marjorie Procter-Smith's *In Her Own Rite: Constructing Feminist Liturgical Tradition.*[91]

From this literature I would like to highlight two problems that relate to the continuing traditioning process of baptism as a sacrament of new life in Christ. The first is that baptism is understood as a cleansing of our sins. These sins are inherited by birth from our mother, who conceived us through sexual intercourse with a man and conveys to us both our mundane and bodily existence and our mortal and sinful existence. Baptism is often administered quickly, to give the child a "better start" and a "new family." In church tradition this service happened without the mother, who was required to remain away from the church immediately after baptism because she was "polluted" by blood in giving birth as well as in menstruation. The new life the baby receives as God's child conveys the message that the life of salvation comes through the males who administer and control the rite, not through the mother's gift of life.

There are many other ways to symbolize baptism, by lifting up such actions as the use of water as a reference to the life-giving waters of the mother's womb, and as naming as an incorporation into the life story of Jesus who was baptized by John. The new United Church of Christ baptismal liturgy helps in this with a long memorial of biblical images of water in creation, exodus, and in the gospel accounts.[92] Many feminist and liberation theologians also argue that the important symbolism of conversion and exodus into freedom in Christ is better served through the practice of adult baptism. This also helps to make clear that, although the gift of grace in baptism is based on God's free choice in Christ to welcome all God's children into the household of God and is administered only once, baptism is a response to that gift through a lifelong process of struggle for life in covenant relationship with God and our neighbors.

A second problem in relation to baptism is that of the trinitarian baptismal formula, "In the name of the Father, and of the Son, and of the Holy Spirit." This formula represents years of development in church tradition, especially in the period of the early church creeds when the relationship of Christ to God and of the three persons of the Trinity was being hammered out. As Ruth Duck notes, the triadic formula is found only in Matthew 28:19. The wording is from Matthew, although it is presented as part of Jesus' great commission, and it appears that in early times baptism in the name of Christ or of Jesus was a more frequent formula.[93]

In contemporary settings, when these words are heard as the formula for entrance into life in Christ, the exclusive meaning of the male language makes this formula particularly inappropriate. There is no easy answer to how to find a way of expressing the truths of the Trinity through common metaphors that would be acceptable in all Christian churches. Some have gone the route of Riverside Church in New York City and amended the formula to read, "I baptize you in the name of the Father and of the Son and of the Holy Spirit, One God, Mother of us all."[94]

But this and similar formulations retain an emphasis on parental relationships that are most certainly not the only type of metaphor available. Ruth Duck proposes the use of a declarative statement that is an adaptation of Elisabeth Fiorenza's translation of Galatians 3:26–28:

> You have been baptized into Jesus Christ;
> you are now a child/children of God;
> you have put on Christ.
> There is no longer Jew nor Greek,
> there is no longer slave nor free,
> there is no male and female,
> for we are all one.[95]

I myself have also urged the regular use of 2 Corinthians 13:13, both as an inclusive benediction and as the basis for an inclusive baptismal statement: "The grace of the Lord Jesus Christ, the love of God, and the communion of the Holy Spirit be with all of you."

In any case, we can rejoice that behind the sacrament of baptism is the promise of Christ to make us new so that already we can begin to live beyond the former barriers that denied the full humanity of those who were of the "wrong religion, class, race, or gender." The ancient baptismal formula quoted by Paul in Galatians 3:27–28 reminds us that the divisions of old creation have been overcome, and old forms of domination no longer belong to life in Christ. Just as the original division of male and female in Genesis was overcome, that of Jew and Gentile, slave and free were understood to be overcome in the context of the early house churches. Some would argue that today the list needs to be much longer, to include heterosexual and homosexual, able-bodied and disabled, rich and poor, capitalist and socialist.[96] It is the overcoming of these divisions, and the new life of freedom, that is the sign of Christ's presence. As we shall see in chapter 5, however, the question of sacraments rightly administered remains when we discover that the divisions and the old life are alive and well in the institutions that claim to partake of this gift of God's grace.

The sacrament of holy communion partakes of this same ambiguity. Although it is administered frequently in the community as a continuing gift of God's forgiveness and empowerment for life, it is also frequently administered in a setting that contradicts Jesus' promise to be present as we show forth his death until he comes (1 Cor. 11:26). The church has been careful to say that it is God in Christ who makes the sacraments efficacious, and not the ones administering the sacrament or the community in which they happen. But at the same time it has fenced the table by requiring that only those ordained and authorized in a particular pattern officiate. As we have seen earlier, the requirement for right administration has become not a commitment to justice, and doing what is right, but a commitment to the "right" religious institution in which salvation is located. Women, especially, discover communion as a sacrament of *disunion* as they begin to analyze the way they have often been denied access to the eucharist itself, because of ritual impurity, and denied the privilege of sharing in serving the meal.[97]

There are so many different versions of the words of institution in the Gospels in addition to 1 Corinthians, so the exact words used in the liturgy have not been in as much dispute as their meaning. Building on the seven Greek Testament motifs of eucharist as "joyful thanksgiving, *anamnesis* [remembrance], *koinonia* [community, partnership], sacrifice, the presence of Christ, the action of the Holy Spirit, and the eschatological banquet," the various confessions have traditioned the meanings most appropriate for their own contexts of origin and continuing life.[98]

In an area where there have been so many problems, and in which there is so much written, it is difficult to characterize the problems of unjust administration of the meal. Here I want only to mention two additional problems as examples of the continuing struggle to be present where Christ promises to be present. The first is one that will be developed further in the discussion of spirituality in chapter 6. It concerns the connection of the eucharistic tradition with other exclusive rituals that are used to guarantee male privilege in patriarchal societies. Studies in social science and religion by feminist scholars have shown that the usual pattern of blood sacrifice is that it takes place as an exclusive male ritual in which the pattern is one of taking life and shedding blood, in contrast to the women's role of shedding blood to *give* life.

In her article "Sacrifice as Remedy for Having Been Born of Woman," Nancy Jay details gender-related features of sacrifice in various cultures in order to show that blood sacrifice is practiced in many parts of the world and shares cross-cultural features that are gender-related, "such as an opposition between sacrificial purity and the pollution of childbirth, and a rule that only males may perform sacrificial ritual."[99] This gender relationship appears to have been what has attracted leaders in the men's liberation movement like Robert Bly to adopt secret male initiation ceremonies to provide a second "birth from men." These rituals of bonding between old and younger men who are searching for maturity are modern versions of tribal blood rituals of initiation.[100]

According to Nancy Jay, there is an affinity between blood sacrificial religion and patrilineal social systems that make the relation between father and son the basis of social order and continuity. This lineage is maintained by sacrificial worship, not by giving birth, and often provides an eternal inheritance that overcomes the mortality of being born of a woman.[101] The sacrificial system can be a symbolic means of maintaining the social continuity, such as that of the blood sacrifice in the eucharist, but it is linked to the same patrilineal social structures and privileges. Thus, Jay says,

> The Eucharist as "blood sacrifice," the Christian clergy as a specific sacrificing priesthood, and the unilineal organization of that priesthood as exclusive inheritors of apostolic authority, all came into being together and developed together; and the rejection of one entailed the simultaneous rejection of the others.[102]

An example of this was the Protestant Reformation, in which the mass as sacrifice was rejected along with apostolic succession. However, patriarchal imagery of sacrifice continued in the Christology, and the patriarchal social context ensured that the claim to exclusive male privilege of ordination would continue.

The sacrificial aspect of the eucharist, like the second birth of baptism, needs to be carefully retraditioned from a feminist perspective. It is possible to celebrate at table in memory of the sacrifice made necessary by the injustice of the religious and political authorities of Jesus' day and the victory of God's justice and love over injustice. In this way the table could be administered rightly as a place where such sacrifice is no longer necessary, and each and every person is welcomed to share in Christ's presence through the power of the Spirit. A second problem concerning the right administration of the Lord's Supper is that of unwillingness to tradition the meal in such a way that people in different circumstances and cultures have full access to its administration, its offer of abundance, and its meaning for those who are struggling for life.

In situations where bread and wine are not the staff of life, it might well be that some other food, like rice and tea, cola and chips, or bananas and oranges, might be the most appropriate food at a particular moment, even though the historical elements are important to keep the story alive. In the Aladura churches in Nigeria, for instance, the fellowship of thanksgiving comes through a communal meal in which the Spirit is celebrated in testimony and gifts of produce from the farms are offered up. In most cases this eucharistic or thanksgiving offering is made up of bananas, oranges, mangoes, groundnuts, and pineapples. This is the food available to the churches, and it too can be a sacrament of Christ's presence.[103]

In many situations the presence of Christ is in no way correlated with the restrictions of clerical administration. For instance, on July 3, 1986, a funeral mass was held in New York City for Sister Marjorie Tuite, national coordinator of the Women's Coalition to Stop U.S. Intervention in Central America and the Caribbean and staff member of Church Women United.[104] The mass was a celebration of her life and what she had stood for, in spite of the fact that the priest in charge tried to prevent non–Roman Catholics from approaching the table. Both women and men from the peace and human rights movements began to stand up and give homilies and testimonies. The mass itself was transformed by the spontaneous participation of the whole group in consecration and commemoration, and the linking of her life and struggle and that of the people of Nicaragua continued. And that mass continued beyond the church walls in people's lives and hearts as her ashes were taken to Nicaragua for burial among the heroes and martyrs of the revolution. Christ *¡Presente!* Marjorie, *¡Presente! Presente* whether or not authorized by the church.

And then there are the children of South Africa and so many other places that are being sacrificed needlessly on the altars of racism, nationalism, and international capitalism. Are these children taken up into Christ's sacrifice? How are they to take part in this meal of solidarity in suffering when many churches do not recognize their place at the table? On January 14, 1990, a Third World travel seminar I conducted for students at Yale Divinity School visited Roman Catholic, United Methodist, and Anglican church services in Soweto in South Africa. Even worshiping in different languages did not conceal from us the powerful presence of Christ's Spirit among the people of those churches.

In the Anglican church I attended, the service ended with a

tremendous hymn sing by the congregation during which all the children of the parish filed by the congregation and received a blessing from the priests. The congregation had begun to include this blessing procession around the church when the schoolchildren became involved in the struggles against apartheid and began to be massacred, detained, and tortured by the police. From the children's point of view, every day might be their last. They needed a sign of Christ's solidarity and presence with them every moment, not just when they were old enough to understand! Surely this, as well as the testimonies for Marjorie and the bananas and oranges, is a sacramental sign, to be shared among the household of faith every bit as much as other forms of table fellowship.

Table fenced with justice

The sacraments are about God reaching out on the cross, to make things right, and about God's continuing action on behalf of groaning creation. Here we find the gift of righteousness and justice and are called to right administration of those gifts, together with others in need of God's justice within and beyond the rubrics of our particular traditions. The fencing of the table at the Lord's Supper refers to the need to be properly prepared to receive God's gifts of love and grace, but from a feminist perspective this preparation consists of a discipline of living justly in solidarity with those who are marginal to church or society.

Perhaps the place to begin a discussion of those who are welcome to bring their gifts to the table is with one of Paul's many difficult and ambiguous quotes. In 1 Corinthians 11:17–22, Paul reprimands the church, and particularly the women prophets in the church, for divisions and refusal to share at the Lord's Supper and clarifies the meaning of the meal with what we know today as "the words of institution." Then in verses 27–29 he says:

> Whoever, therefore, eats the bread or drinks the cup of the Lord in an unworthy manner will be answerable for the body and blood of the Lord. Examine yourselves, and only then eat of the bread and drink of the cup. For all who eat and drink without discerning the body, eat and drink judgment against themselves.

According to Antionette Wire, Paul's words are directed at the women prophets, "Chloe's people," who see the meal as an eschatological feast of resurrection in which they are already set free from the domination of their husbands to be partners in Christ and to eat and drink together rather than at home (1 Cor. 1:11; 11:22).[105] In a manner not unexpected, if Nancy Jay is correct, Paul does not think they take the meal seriously as a memorial of Christ's death. In his view they are too busy already living their new life in Christ's Spirit. His words about misuse of the meal are one of the origins of the tradition of fencing the table; making sure that no one who is unworthy or "unorthodox" may partake. Yet they seem to indicate that God, not the church, is responsible for the table and the salvation situation of all who participate. The church is responsible for making clear the meaning of the presence of Christ in the sacrament, and this meaning—which was in dispute between Paul and the women—still is a source of division today among many different churches.

If we look carefully at the text we are reminded of Judas, the first disciple to eat and drink the meal and not discern the love of God present therein. Even Judas was welcomed to the table by the one whom he would betray, but his actions brought God's judgment. It would seem that we are unworthy to partake of the table, and cannot discern Christ's body and blood and what it signifies, when we contradict the meaning of Christ's sacrifice and thus join Judas as betrayers.[106]

When the church tries to limit the size and shape of the table and who will serve the meal, it needs to be careful that it is not betraying the work of the one who is called Just (Luke 23:47; Acts 3:13–15).[107] Whether or not we agree that Paul had a right to claim God's judgment on those who disputed his patriarchal authority, or that he was correct in saying the judgment is visited physically, the intention of this difficult text seems to claim that it is *God* who fences the table. Those who partake are called to come with repentance and sharing of new life in Christ, but the welcome table belongs to God.

In responding to Christ's invitation to come to the table, we bring many gifts, including those of gender, race, class, sexual orientation, and physical ability. As persons seeking to be whole, we bring all our gifts as an offering to God. But in making that offering we are also asked if we have been serving our neighbor with our whole heart, mind, and self. In what way have we made it more difficult for others to know of God's love and acceptance and prevented them from sharing the many gifts that God intends for all persons and creatures?

Matthew 5:23–24 reminds us that one of the ways to discern Christ's presence is by risking the difficult action of reconciliation with those whom we have harmed. Seeking the forgiveness of our neighbor includes a lot more than conformity to the old patriarchal fencing of the table by excluding those who are not members in good standing. It means the action of *removing the fences* so that all may bring their gifts to the table and seek to discern the presence of Christ in their midst. Fencing the table with justice is crucial to the way we approach the Lord's Supper. The fenced table becomes what in the black church tradition is called the welcome table.[108] As we will see in the Introduction to Part Three, this welcome table is the communion table and every other church table gathering that symbolizes that those who have been denied access to the table of the white, rich masters are welcome at God's table and offered a foretaste of that final moment of full partnership with God.

In one of her early stories entitled "The Welcome Table," Alice Walker tells of this powerful message of God's welcome by sharing the story of an old black woman who, upon being thrown out of the white church where she has tried to rest and pray, meets up with Jesus on the hot dusty road and walks and talks with him. How long she talks no one knows, but at least long enough to find her way home to God's table. They find her body alongside the road the next day.[109]

The sacraments are the foretaste of God's future. The table rightly prepared is a table that belongs to God, where all things are clean (Acts 10:15; Rom. 14:20). Coming to the table we discern Christ's body not only in the broken bread but also in the broken people of the world. And if we welcome them with us we may receive the gift of a renewed church, a church that makes outsiders welcome as they sing, "We're gonna sit at the welcome table one of these days!" It is no accident that this is the table spread at Metropolitan Community and other churches carrying out an extensive AIDS ministry. At the love feast the Faith and Order Commission attended in San Francisco everyone was welcome, and even those with AIDS who had to be carried by others were greeted and encircled with love at a table rightly administered in the name of God's justice and love. The sharing of the agape meal without eucharist was in itself a way of making everyone welcome. No one was excluded by being of a communion that fenced another out because of a lack of apostolic orders or apostolic life style.

When we look at the Reformers' marks of the church from the perspective of how well they connect the church to those on the margin of society, we notice that the marks themselves involve us in actions of justice and love that prepare the table. From a feminist and liberation perspective it seems that the word truly preached and sacraments rightly administered may need to be found in communities of faith and struggle. For the church's identity is derived from the story of Jesus' own word and action on the cross in solidarity with the oppressed. This is our word and action as well, as we struggle for justice and life itself together with our sisters and brothers caught in the patriarchal structures of domination, subordination, and exclusion.

The search for identity in the church and the discussion of descriptive marks have caused a great deal of suffering and mutual condemnation over the centuries. Yet that search could also become the basis for making the justice connection. A church in the round follows the one who is working still to call us all to take part in the work of mending the creation and putting it right (John 5:17). What our NCC working group learned through reflection on shared ministry with persons with AIDS is that love with justice is at the heart of what the church is about. For the church continues to be a community baptized in the troubling waters of the Spirit and called out by God to participate in the New Creation.

A lot of questions about feminist interpretation of the church remain, because the life of a community of faith and struggle includes more than its self-description. For instance, in chapter 5 the need to share God's hospitality leads us to question the way the church claims the privilege of God's special election for itself. And in chapter 6 the need for a spirituality of connection that nurtures feminist ecclesiology leads us to ask how God's Spirit connects us more deeply to ourselves, to those on the margin, and to the traditions of our faith communities.

This chapter raises a question about tables, for here we have Christ's table administered with justice as a traditional mark of the church. Does that mean that church in the round really has a *fourth* table, along with the round table, the kitchen table, and the welcome table? Indeed, there is no limit to the number of tables that are part of church in the round, just as there is no limit to the signs of Christ's presence. Christ's table is central to the gathered life of Christians as a symbol connected to the other three tables. But Christ's table and the others are all metaphors for the one table of God, the eschatological table of New Creation, where there is justice and peace, and there are no longer any tears, hunger, or thirst (Isa. 25:6–10).

At home, in church, and wherever people gather, each and every table draws its meaning from its connection to the present and coming reality of New Creation. And each and every discussion of the signs of the church ultimately is tested by how well those signs convey the good news of God's Jubilee of liberation and justice that was at the heart of Jesus' Spirit-filled ministry. In the words of Luke 4:18–19:

> "The Spirit of the Lord is upon me,
>> because [God] has anointed me to bring good news to the poor.
> [God] has sent me to proclaim release to the captives
>> and recovery of sight to the blind . . .
> to proclaim the year of the Lord's favor."

Part Three
Welcome Table Partnership

In his book *Fire in the Belly: On Being a Man,* Sam Keen speaks of a world which is largely run by sedentary males. "The symbol of power is the chair," and those who occupy these chairs "make the most money."[1] Perhaps this is why the furnishings for church in the round tend to run to tables, many of which, including those of Jesus' time, are low to the floor so that persons can recline or sit on cushions (Matt. 26:20). Of course, having no chairs does not eliminate preferred seating. The welcome table, on the other hand, changes the seating pattern no matter what the style of the gathering, for its intention is to make very welcome those who feel least welcome. Insofar as there is preferred seating at all, the honor goes to those who have been the least of our brothers and sisters (Luke 14:7–11). Lathrop's poem reminds us:

> Roundtabling means
> no preferred seating,
> no first and last,
> no better, and no corners
> for "the least of these."[2]

The welcome table is part of the black church tradition. It symbolizes the communion table and every other gathering at table. At God's welcome table those who have been denied access to the table of the rich white masters are welcomed and may welcome others as a foretaste of the final moment of full partnership with God. Voices are lifted in singing:

We're gonna sit at the welcome table!
We're gonna sit at the welcome table one of these days; Alleluia![3]

This table of hospitality is just the opposite of the household codes or lists of cultural norms adopted as the duties of the Christian patriarchal household in the Pastoral Epistles to keep everyone in their place (Eph. 5:21–6:9; Col. 3:18–4:1).[4] At this table there is a great reversal of "things as they are" so that they may become part of God's reality of love and justice.

The theme of hospitality is basic to the life of any church, yet it is often ignored when that hospitality requires including those who are "outsiders." Perhaps this is why there is so much emphasis in the Gospels on the way that Jesus welcomed the outsiders into God's household. For instance, the story of Jesus and the woman at the well in Samaria tells us a lot about animosity between Jews and Samaritans and their unwillingness to worship together in "spirit and truth" (John 4:1–42). But it tells us even more about Jesus' willingness to break these taboos as he talked with a three-time loser who was foreign, fallen, and female.[5]

The animosity between the Jews of Jesus' time and those of "mixed blood" who lived in Samaria and worshiped God on Mount Gerizim rather than in the temple in Jerusalem was such that the woman was surprised that Jesus even spoke to her. Her past history of more than five husbands made her unclean not only as a foreigner but as a sinner according to Jewish religious regulations. Just how no-account she was as a woman is revealed in the disciples' surprise that Jesus was talking with a woman and in the townspeople's hearing her good news about Jesus but not fully believing it until they go to see him themselves. Nevertheless, this uppity woman, who was not afraid to talk with Jesus as she shared her water with him, was made welcome by the one who reversed all religious expectations in order to share the "living water."

In Part Three: Welcome Table Partnership there is a reversal of our expectations about who is invited to God's eschatological banquet, as we consider ways that God in Christ has reached out to make us all partners in the celebration. Our search for the meaning of church in the round will move in chapter 5, "Community of Hospitality," to an examination of the way in which the doctrine of divine election has often fenced the table so that it reads NOT WELCOME. It looks at the doctrine of election from the perspective of those who have been excluded from the church and calls for a shift in our ecclesiology toward an understanding that particularity is not to be equated with partiality (Acts 10:34).[6] Chapter 6, "Spirituality of Connection," will examine the character of life together when persons who, though very diverse, become connected as a circle of friends. It lifts up spirituality as a choice to be connected to our bodies and ourselves, to those on the margin and to justice struggles, and to tradition and our particular communities of faith and struggle. Such a gift of spirituality, when discovered in the midst of church in the round, will truly be one that lives out Christ's offer of partnership to all those who come to the welcome table searching for the "living water" of God's love.

5 | Community of Hospitality

An open door is a rarity in a place like East Harlem in New York City. A typical door in one of the low-income housing projects or six-story walk-ups is a door with several locks, tightly bolted, with a peephole to examine all those who wish to enter. Often the doors are dented and scarred from unwanted attempts to break into the apartment. In such a situation, where danger lurks in the halls, elevators, and streets, hospitality does not flourish. Yet in these communities there are always those who will welcome a friendly visit from someone who is not a robber or an estranged husband, someone who is not a welfare investigator, a loan collector, or a truant or police officer. Perhaps they would welcome a person whom they identified as a clergyperson, but most likely they would be more willing to open the door if the person was known to them.

In the church we tried to encourage welcome table partnership and openness to neighbors wherever possible by continual visitation, by organizing community action projects or events, and by holding small house Bible studies in the homes of those who would open to others in their building. The groups helped to prepare the sermon by studying the lectionary texts, raising questions, and sharing stories that could become part of the people's theology on Sunday. But, more important, they took time for "show-and-tell" so they could share concerns, lift up the need for prayers, and do community organization work. The study was led by laypersons and staff who studied the text together in advance. Other members of the group took care of the worship and spread the welcome table with steaming cups of coffee and a variety of goodies.

Those who were willing to risk opening their triple-locked doors and admitting semi-strangers into their homes were also encouraged to go further and put a sticker on their door, which displayed clasped hands and a cross and greeted all who approached with the words:

WELCOME IN THE NAME OF CHRIST

BIENVENIDO IN EL NOMBRE DE CRISTO

Such a sign was a way of making clear that it was possible to welcome other persons and to reject the alienation so pervasive in a community of persons who faced rejection in the dominant white middle-strata society and isolation and fear in their own neighborhoods. As Henri Nouwen points out, hospitality creates a safe and welcoming space for persons to find their own sense of humanity and worth. Unlike *xenophobia*, hatred of strangers, *philoxenia*, or hospitality, is a welcoming of strangers out of a delight in the possibility that in that opening of community God might be present.[1]

There are many kinds of fears and hatreds that fuel xenophobia, but one of the root causes of the conditions of division in society are structures of oppression such as those of racism. In Euro-American culture, the barriers created by the daily practice of white racism have long been recognized as a church-dividing issue. When the World Council of Churches, through its Program to Combat Racism, made a stand against apartheid and the evils of racist exploitation by providing humanitarian aid to liberation struggles in Africa, member churches began withdrawing funds and threatened withdrawal from the Council.[2] In the late 1960s, when members of the United Presbyterian Church found that some of its mission funds were supporting the legal defense of Angela Davis, a Communist Party member and advocate of Black Liberation who was implicated in a shooting but acquitted in 1972, the discovery caused a controversy second only to the 1991 debate on the sexuality report that affirmed openness to extramarital sex and the ordination of gay and lesbian persons.[3] The controversy at the WCC Assembly in Canberra in 1991 around Professor Chung Hyun Kyung's use of Asian traditions in Christian theology was in part a debate over whether a woman from Asia can set the agenda for traditional white Western male theology.[4] As the ecumenical theme of unity and diversity becomes more of a reality by the inclusion of Third World churches, the ecumenical status quo is responding with talk of the limits of acceptable diversity.

Local churches are just as divided as denominational and ecumenical bodies over issues involving white racism. Some urban churches are inhospitable to the persons of color who often live in apartments crowded around their doors, and some suburban churches are inhospitable to persons of color who are often excluded economically from living anywhere near their doors. In these predominantly affluent white communities, churches look around and declare that they don't have a problem of diversity instead of recognizing their economic and cultural insularity as part of the problem of white racism.

This chapter reexamines the doctrine of election as an indicator of divine preference often used to close out persons of a different race, class, sexuality, or nationality. The first section discusses white racism as a church-dividing issue. We then examine the contradictions that we face in talking of unity and diversity and raise the question of whether it is possible to take diversity seriously when unity is anchored in a tradition of divine election. The final section argues that divine hospitality is a more helpful starting point in developing a theological pattern of diversity and welcome for all people.

White Racism: A Church-Dividing Issue

Working against racism is not easy for anyone! It is dangerous for persons of color, who risk "rigged conflict" in which the person or group with least power pays the greatest cost. It is dangerous for white persons, because they risk loss of power and admission of their own fear of difference and complicity in maintaining structures of white privilege. Racism needs to be specified as *white* racism because the economic and political power to create this system of oppression at home and abroad belongs to white persons of Euro-American descent. Others suffer from white racism and are also every bit as prejudiced, but they nevertheless live in a global culture in which the major sources of power are in white hands. This form of structural sin and dehumanization divides persons, churches, societies, and the world. We can do no other than join in the struggle against such division if we believe that Christ has broken the dividing wall between us so that all may be one (Eph. 2:14).

Divided self and divided ministry

As I indicated in chapter 3, I have been a member of a National Council of Churches subgroup on Unity and Renewal in Faith and Order for eight years. In this group we have also been reflecting theologically on congregational case studies that show how white racism divides churches and hinders the sharing of God's hospitality with all people. This chapter on issues of God's hospitality and racism takes its starting point from the story not of Ron Russell-Coons but of Gladys Moore, another member of our group, about her ministry in Bethany Lutheran Church, Jersey City, New Jersey, from 1984 to 1990.[5] Using a process of action and reflection, the working group, Gladys Moore, and I discussed her case study and sought to identify the generative theological issues that emerged. In reflecting on these issues we were searching for ecclesial clues to the ways churches might become antiracist communities of faith who join with oppressed groups in the struggle for racial justice.

In beginning with Gladys Moore's account of racism in her life and ministry as a pastor in an Evangelical Lutheran church it is important to recognize the risks Gladys takes in telling her story from an African American perspective of pain, anger, and survival. It is also important to acknowledge that my reflections as a white Presbyterian woman currently teaching at Yale Divinity School are a secondhand interpretation of her story. My theological solidarity in the reflection is just one very small part of the continuing actions and reflections needed to work against my own racism and that of church and society. Gladys sets out in the following manner:

> As I understand it, my task here is to do a case study on my experience as the first (and perhaps, only) Black and female pastor of Bethany Lutheran Church, Jersey City. I will pay particular attention to our denominational call process and note the differences between what happened in my case and what "normally" occurs. I will also attempt to describe how serving as the Black pastor of a racially mixed Lutheran congregation was both a self-dividing and church-dividing issue. Finally, I will try to draw some conclusions related to the question, "Is racism ever a church-uniting issue?" (p. 1)[6]

Gladys describes her continuing journey toward wholeness, working against racism that is "self-dividing and church-dividing." The story begins with her decision to move out of traditional black denominations and join the Immanuel Lutheran Church in East Lansdowne, Pennsylvania. She was the first African American member and saw her role as "proving to white people that African Americans really were worthy of their respect and their love" (p. 2). This period of self-denial continued as she became a candidate for a Master of Divinity degree at the Lutheran Theological Seminary in Philadelphia in 1980, and it took its toll on her as she struggled with this burden of proof.

Fortunately, her intern year at St. Matthew's Lutheran Church in Jersey City helped her begin to acknowledge how much she had "internalized the racism, sexism, classism, and homophobia which [her] parents had taught [her] to struggle against" (p. 2). She describes this as a "conversion" to her own people.

> But my "conversion," as it were, was more profound than simply realizing that my choices for calls were circumscribed [because of my race]. During internship, I also came to understand that the city was where I belonged. I "belonged" with my people, and for the first time in my life, I *knew* that these beautiful, over-exploited, struggling folks of African descent—both Black and Puerto-Rican—were *indeed* "my people." (p. 3)

In May of 1984, Gladys graduated from seminary and, after a nine-month search, was called to Bethany Lutheran Church. This struggling church, given no other choice of candidates, indicated to her that they thought her gender was a major problem but not her color. As she began her ministry in this church that had no "race problem," Gladys soon discovered that it was not sexism but "issues related to race" that had the greatest effect on her life and ministry in the almost six years that she served as pastor. Having moved out of her own period of denial, Gladys found herself in a *church* of denial. In this small, racially mixed congregation of 200 baptized members, about 60 percent were white, with a predominantly

Swedish cultural background, and 40 percent were black from many different cultures. The church sought to be a liberal church.

> Difference was down-played as much as possible; [but] while lip-service was given to the "rainbow" of peoples at Bethany, the power structure basically remained in white hands. (p. 4)

Over the years Gladys worked to make the church self-supporting and to find ways to make it a church of hospitality. She wanted Bethany to become a place where folks would not have to become "white Lutherans."

> I wanted the congregational climate to be one in which "strangers," i.e., those whose worship and lifestyles were different from the norm, would be warmly received. (p. 5)

At first, Gladys was not allowed to make changes in the worship life of the church, even to the point where she was reprimanded for "swaying back and forth" when listening to a gospel choir. But with the help of two dynamic black Lutheran couples who joined the church, she was finally able to change the power structure to include "newcomers" in decision making. Yet key white leaders still considered Gladys to be the problem.

> *I* was the problem, they thought; not racism. If I just concentrated on being a pastor instead of a *Black* pastor, everything would be all right and things would be like they used to be. (p. 6)

Slowly, however, membership shifted so that the congregation became about 65 percent black and 35 percent white, was self-supporting, was led by a council representing the makeup of the congregation, and had joined an interfaith community organization and moved out into community projects. She also finally found support from a black male seminarian who came to the church as an intern. He provided another strong black Lutheran presence and also helped Gladys sort out and articulate her ongoing ministry at Bethany, in the struggle to become a place of hospitality for all persons. This reflection, coupled with attendance at a conference on Black Theology and the Black Church at Union Theological Seminary in New York, pushed Gladys Moore to a new stage of consciousness as she began to ask herself what difference Bethany had made to the lives of people in the community and when, if ever, the congregation would deal with racism directly.

Gladys Moore came to realize the magnitude of white racism as a system of oppression that just kept denying the life and the very existence of herself and other persons of color. Her own pain, frustration, and anger with the entire church structure, and her realization of the difficulty of change, seemed overwhelming.

> And for my part, I was tired—tired of trying to share my pain and the collective pain of my people with folks who did not even want to hear it,

let alone enter into it; tired of dealing with the fragility of urban ministry; tired of trying to be "all things to all people"; and simply tired of all the parish pettiness. But I was also angry—I was angry with a denomination that gave much lip-service and tons of paper to the "issue" of inclusiveness but did little to examine the structural, institutional forms of oppression which it perpetuated. (p. 9)

Angry at herself for being willing to participate in her own oppression and self-division, Gladys struggled to sort through the contradictions of her existence by dealing with her own color and culture. But finally Gladys found that, at this stage in her ministry, she needed to resign in order "to rest, to heal, and to reflect" (p. 9). Her conclusion in reflecting on this experience was that racism can become a church-uniting issue

only insofar as we are willing to be anti-racist by living in solidarity with those who daily suffer the psycho-spiritual, physical, and economic effects of this structural form of sin. . . . We are separated from each other in a way that God did not intend for us to be. But through Christ's victory won on the cross of Calvary, we too can claim the victory—the victory that unites us in the struggle against oppression and *for* life—the abundant life that Christ offers to all. (p. 9)

Forms of structural sin

There are many factors to acknowledge in this powerful account of life in a predominantly white, racist church. First, of course, we must acknowledge that much of what happened to Gladys happens to persons of other cultures, races, genders, and sexualities. Much of it has to do with the problems and challenges of clerical church structures, of ways of learning to be a pastor, of being a woman in a traditional male role. But the fact that there are recognizable problems in the life of the church in no way means they should *be* that way. Nor does this in any way take away from the basic problems of institutional racism experienced by Gladys herself.

The white church members here could have been in any white-dominant denomination or any urban community with a mixed population who respond to growing diversity with attempts at retreat, fear, and denial. Many persons of color have similar experiences of racism in multicultural settings and respond with pain and anger at the violation of their own humanity. But none of this takes away from the concrete description of Gladys's particular journey and what she came to see as the cause of her pain: systemic white racism as a form of structural sin or oppression.

White racism is a social system of domination and subordination that assigns persons of color to subordinate roles and ensures that, all other things being equal, those persons of color will always come out in the subordinate position. Along with other structures of oppression that support a hierarchy of domination and subordination on the basis of gender, sexual orientation, class, nationality, age, or physical ability, racism forms a web of oppression that operates to crush those caught in the web. The social structures that support this web include unfair distribution of political power, inadequate access to financial and material resources, inability to set cultural standards of behavior, and lack of power to name reality and define truth.

Dominant groups perpetuate structural sin because they have control of the political, economic, cultural, and educational forces that define the standard of life for the entire society and justify the status quo of that society to their own benefit. There is no way out for dominated groups except to work together to change this unjust distribution of political, economic, and social power in order to eradicate the web. The removal of one strand or another still leaves the system in place and other persons entrapped in a "simultaneity of oppressions."[7]

As we saw in chapter 4, God's justice and the putting of things right through the mending of creation calls for eradication. It calls for a year of Jubilee when God sets at liberty the oppressed (Luke 4:18–19). Those who follow the messianic ministry of Christ are called to antiracist work because a root cause of oppression in American society and around the world is white racism. White persons and churches working on racism cannot understand themselves as recovering racists because there is no way in U.S. society to be free of the racism virus. When one is a recovering alcoholic one works to abstain from alcohol. But it is impossible to abstain from white racism in a society in which all structures conspire for racist oppression. The only way to keep this structural sin from continuing to divide us in society and the church is to work constantly for racial justice, taking steps for personal, social, and ecclesial change together with others.

White racism as a form of structural oppression divides the church and calls into question ecumenical attempts to move toward unity in diversity. As John de Gruchy writes from South Africa, we have inherited confessional divisions from Europe, but

> it is equally true, and more painful, that these confessional divisions have been exacerbated by separation along racial, cultural and ethnic lines. These issues, normally regarded as nontheological, must now be seen as equally confessional, because they have to do with the truth of the Gospel as much as those that, for example, traditionally separate Catholics from Calvinists.[8]

As Gladys Moore indicates, racism can become a church-uniting issue only when churches join in the struggle to become antiracist by living in solidarity with those who endure the direct and dehumanizing effects of this sinful social system. In their daily actions of breaking down dividing walls, they can seek to be one in the truth of the gospel that

Christ has made us one. This leads us to the next question on our search for ecclesial clues: What are some of the steps in becoming an antiracist community of faith?

This is a very large question and one that is answered only through a long road of continuing antiracist actions and reflections. Yet one way to begin becoming an antiracist community of faith is to become aware of contradictions in the way those of us who are white see reality and the way that social, economic, and ecclesial reality is experienced by persons of color. Why is it that many persons find difference fearful and threatening? And how are we caught in contradictions because we cannot even see the racism that is all around us?

Caught in the contradictions

Diversity has to do with difference. Diversity is not just an ecumenical slogan that is often contradicted by our largely homogeneous church communities. It represents a description of the differences of race, culture, gender, sexual orientation, age, abilities, economic and political status, and much more that are part of the world in which we live. Many differences are God-given actions of creation and lend beauty and excitement to this world. Yet the connotation of difference seems to be that persons and groups who are not like ourselves cause threat and discord to our way of life and our particular community.

As Parker Palmer has pointed out in his book *The Company of Strangers,* communities are usually formed "by *an act of exclusion* —'we' are in and 'they' are out."9 Some communities, like many black churches or the Universal Fellowship of Metropolitan Community Churches, are formed because they have already been excluded, and they need to form a sense of identity in a situation of involuntary exclusion. But many other churches are formed to exclude persons of color, persons of a lower class, or persons of a different sexual orientation. As soon as they search out their identity through exclusion and putting others down, they are not only unable to welcome those who are different but also caught in a community that survives by surrounding itself with walls. These walls frequently include myths and false information about those who are excluded and most certainly lead to a false sense of identity for those who say who they are by putting others down or by admitting them only if they conform to the in-group's cultural pattern.

It is possible, however, to have a deep sense of God's love and hospitality toward us as children of God. Usually this happens where persons have experienced that deep love and caring through persons and communities who have cared for them. Such a sense of personal and communal self-worth may help us risk showing hospitality to strangers and those with different cultures, experiences, and ideas. One way of expressing this in Christian communities is to say that the community gains its identity through the gift of faith in Christ. At the center is trust in God's love in Christ, and at the ever-changing edges is the practice of hospitality and service. When Christ breaks down the walls between us, "the world becomes an open house."[10]

In our competitive and capitalist society, and in churches that are very much a part of this society, it is difficult to resist a way of life in which certain persons are excluded as surplus, unneeded, inferior. In her essay "Age, Race, Class, and Sex: Women Redefining Difference," Audre Lorde says:

> Certainly there are very real differences between us of race, age, and sex. But it is not those differences between us that are separating us. It is rather our refusal to recognize those differences, and to examine the distortions which result from our misnaming them and their effects upon human behavior and expectation.[11]

Audre Lorde says that institutionalized rejection of difference justifies the need for "surplus people" in a profit economy and leads us all to handle difference either by ignoring it or, if that is not possible, by copying it if we think it is dominant or by destroying it if we think it is subordinate.[12] At Bethany Lutheran Church, as at most other predominantly white churches, difference was ignored by saying, We are all alike; "we're all color-blind" (p. 4). It was destroyed by prohibiting call-and-response and rhythmic motions in the service: "Don't ever let me see you swaying back and forth again" (p. 5). Perhaps African culture might be incorporated into worship in the form of a "sanitized" spiritual or two.[13]

Learning to recognize the distortions in the misnaming of differences is key to learning to value difference and to welcome those who are different from ourselves. Thus, for example, it is not possible to see the contradiction in the statement of the white Bethany church leaders that everyone is welcome but that we are all alike here, unless we recognize the way that "white privilege" is an assumed norm of U.S. society. Peggy McIntosh points out in her powerful paper "White Privilege and Male Privilege" that the privilege of white persons is assumed in every public and private aspect of their lives. Just to be clear about this, she lists forty-six conditions white persons can count on that African American persons cannot. Among her sample list we find:

1. I can if I wish arrange to be in the company of people of my race most of the time.
2. I can avoid spending time with people whom I was trained to mistrust and who have learned to mistrust my kind or me. . . .
14. I can arrange to protect my children most of the time from people who might not like them.
15. I do not have to educate my children to be aware of systemic racism for their own daily physical protection. . . .

42. I can arrange my activities so that I will never have to experience feelings of rejection owing to my race.
43. If I have low credibility as a leader I can be sure that my race is not the problem.[14]

In her random listing of these and other conditions of white privilege, McIntosh discovered that she was listing conditions from daily experience that she "once took for granted, as neutral, normal, and universally available to everybody, just as [she] once thought of a male-focused curriculum as the neutral or accurate account 'which can speak for all.'"[15] Out of this she came to see that what is happening in racism and other systems of oppression is that certain persons have an unearned advantage and conferred dominance simply by virtue of birth. Such difference is most certainly not neutral, for in this situation difference connotes not only difference in value but also in unearned social power.[16]

Seeing the value of diversity, both as a God-given gift of creation and also as an enrichment of our lives, becomes a possibility as we become aware of the way in which difference carries with it the negative value of dominance, of divide and conquer in our society, and take steps to change this. As white persons begin to see the contradictions in saying we value difference and then ignoring the way it functions to support racism, classism, sexism, and other oppressions, we can begin to practice antiracist behavior and work against our own white privilege.

The traditional mainline predominantly white churches are caught in many contradictions. There are as many contradictions as there are ways that white culture conceals and rejects difference. These contradictions between our assumptions and the reality experienced by others serve to deny the possibility of unity and diversity. The primary contradiction is the one we have already analyzed, that of community and uniformity. Established churches seek to build community by eliminating diversity: by excluding the "others" or by welcoming them to become like "us." We have been taught by patriarchal structures of domination that community means sameness, uniformity, and control.

As we saw in chapter 3, this patriarchal paradigm or way of thinking and acting does not refer only to the subordination of women. Elisabeth Fiorenza says that patriarchy as a male pyramid of "graded subordinations and exploitations . . . represents a social-cultural system in which a few men have power over other men, women, children, slaves, and colonialized people."[17]

In using patriarchy as a critical, interpretive tool in reference to the Christian biblical and church tradition as well as to society, Anglo-American feminist theologians join with womanist, *mujerista*, and Asian feminist and liberation theologians in analysis of the structures of sin that perpetuate division through a web of simultaneous oppressions.[18] This pyramid functions in the same graded subordinations in regard to all aspects of the web of oppression, including racism. In this way of thinking, community is formed in a hierarchy that pushes those of low status to the bottom and those who do not fit to the outside.

According to Fiorenza, the contradiction between democratic aspirations and rhetoric and patriarchal structures of domination is at the heart of Western society.[19] Democracy as it emerged as the political form of the *polis*, the Greek city-state, was itself contradictory. It provided political freedom and participation for all free white propertied males. All women and children, as well as male workers both free and slave, were excluded and lived in the patriarchal economic and social structure of the *oikos*, or household.[20] As we can see from the history of white racism in the United States, we still live with this flawed concept of democracy, which uses economic, cultural, and political power to justify the limitation of participation in the decision making of society.

The churches, along with other institutions, seek to work out democratic structures of equality, but these are constantly undermined by the patriarchal structures of domination that shape the way our democracy is played out. When dominant groups seek community by exclusion and subordination, they end up subverting community because unity and uniformity are a contradiction in terms. Community is built out of diversity. We do not need community if we are all one family or one social or economic group; we already are alike in significant ways that hold us together and allow us to communicate. We need community as a way of participating together in some task or commitment that provides a bond of commitment to one another in the struggle to *become* a community.

From a Christian perspective, community, or *koinonia,* is a new focus of relationship in Jesus Christ that sets us free for others.[21] The community of faith and struggle is formed by its central commitment to Christ, but it is nurtured by its common struggle to live out the ministry of Jesus and his message of good news for the oppressed (Luke 4:18).

The purpose of the community is to extend this welcome of God's household to all people, especially to those who have been excluded by society.[22] Christian community is built up out of the creative potential of difference through the gift of God's Spirit. When the community is also being built up in structures of patriarchy and exclusion, community is deformed for the sake of uniform order. As the Gospel of Matthew reminds us, there is no cheap reconciliation. "So when you are offering your gift at the altar, if you remember that your brother or sister has something against you, leave your gift there before the altar and go; first be reconciled to your brother or sister, and then come and offer your gift" (Matt. 5:23–24).

From the point of view of those of us who have benefited from unearned advantage and conferred dominance, imaginative and constructive repentance includes seeing the contradictions in our ways of life and taking steps for change. From the point of view of those who have suffered un-earned disadvantage and conferred domination, powerlessness is a call to actions of empowerment for justice, and pain and anger are a call for new forms of community, coalition, and solidarity. For Gladys, antiracism is the daily struggle for self-identity and empowerment in our society. The contra-dictions are written into her very existence in this society, contradictions that are perpetuated by white indifference and unwillingness to see.

Contradictions of Divine Election

The contradictions arising from the search for unity and diversity in the life of white mainline U.S. churches raise important questions for Chris-tian tradition. In what way does biblical and church tradition help or hin-der the understanding of unity and diversity on the part of churches seeking to become antiracist? Are there particular doctrines that rein-force the need for uniformity over against diversity? As soon as we begin to take these questions seriously in our theological investigation, we dis-cover that the doctrine of divine election is in many ways ambiguous if not contradictory in its teaching of divine choice for service to the na-tions. Often the chosenness of the community manages to swallow up the mandate for outreach to others. In fact, the doctrine of election itself may be one of the reasons it is so easy to practice unity without diversity.

Caught with his compassion down

Jesus himself is part of this tradition of the chosenness of God's peo-ple, and both the Gospels and Paul struggle with whether the teaching of Jesus about welcome into God's household is only for the Jews or for all people. One story that captures this tension in the ministry of Jesus is that of the Syrophoenician woman in Mark.

> From there he set out and went away to the region of Tyre. He entered a house and did not want anyone to know he was there. Yet he could not escape notice, but a woman whose little daughter had an unclean spirit immediately heard about him, and she came and bowed down at his feet. Now the woman was a Gentile, of Syrophoenician origin. She begged him to cast the demon out of her daughter. He said to her, "Let the chil-dren be fed first, for it is not fair to take the children's food and throw it to the dogs." But she answered him, "Sir, even the dogs under the table eat the children's crumbs." Then he said to her, "For saying that, you may go—the demon has left your daughter." So she went home, found the child lying on the bed, and the demon gone.

This story, recorded in Mark 7:24–30 and again with additions in Matthew 15:21–28, has many layers in its formation, as does the history of its interpretation and the consciousness of its listeners. In different racial and cultural contexts, persons see quite different and unique aspects of the story of the woman who talked Jesus into healing her daughter by claiming the right to at least the crumbs under Israel's table!

The story is similar to other Gospel narratives in its emphasis on the faith of the woman which leads to exorcism as well as to controversy and dialogue. Most important for many of the Asian churchwomen with whom I have discussed this passage is the great faith of the mother that leads her to break out of all cultural expectations and speak to a Jewish rabbi in public. Their own experience of struggle against great prejudice on behalf of their daughters and themselves makes her courage and faith really good news. In cultures where submission and silence are virtues for women, there is a changing understanding of women's "self-image, which has been obscured by the roles that have been assigned to them by patriarchal society."[23]

Another dimension, emphasized by many biblical scholars, is the need of the early Gentile church to emphasize Jesus' mission to the Gentiles, those outside the Jewish community. This would explain the inclusion of the story in the Gospels in spite of its uncomplimentary view of Jesus as one who calls the Gentile woman and her daughter not "saints of God" but "dogs," who should not eat the food offered to the Jews.

An equally important layer, however, is the social location of this poor, single, foreign mother. The woman sets out to convince Jesus of the importance of healing "nobodies" like her daughter. This is what liberation theologies call "the hermeneutical privilege of the poor." Those who have been "left out" become the very ones who understand most clearly why God's welcome is such good news and where that welcome is needed. Many of us have grown up in eucharistic traditions that use Jesus' words in the confession before communion, "We are not worthy to eat the crumbs under your table." Because of the woman's reinterpretation, the confession indicates that no one is worthy, and therefore *all* are accounted worthy to be invited to the Lord's Banquet!

This uppity woman becomes a role model for many women as one layer of the story underscores the element of reversal. Here a woman does her own naming and calls Jesus to use God's power to help her daughter. In this reversal of role models we have the one who is the nobody do the educating and the one who is the teacher do the learning! It might be upsetting to think that a woman helps Jesus to discover (or redefine) his own calling more fully, except that is exactly what happens for us. We don't own the call we receive in baptism or ordination. We all share in the one call of Christ. In baptism our call is confirmed, but it is not complete, and neither, it seems, was Jesus' call. When the Syrophoenician woman caught him with his compassion down, she witnessed to Jesus about the need to broaden his ministry of hospitality to those outside the house of Israel. [24]

Out of its many layers, this text from Mark 7 provides a few clues to the reinterpretation of the doctrine of election. First, it reminds us that the understanding of election, like that of salvation, is situation-variable. This story is part of a long and evolving biblical tradition about the meaning of God's choice of Israel as a light to the nations. Because the meaning of election changes over time and in different contexts, we should not be surprised to find it happening in the Gospels. Second, the ministry of the Syrophoenician woman models for us the importance of understanding what the gospel is about from the perspective of outsiders, those marginal persons who are hungering and thirsting for good news. Last, the way in which Jesus is portrayed as changing his mind and learning new perspectives on his own ministry is a model for us as we seek to gain new perspectives on issues of chosenness and exclusion in the life of the church. Jesus' willingness to change is a model for all of us of what it means to face the contradictions of our lives that serve to exclude the least of our brothers and sisters.

Rereading the story of the chosen people

At a conference entitled Gender, Race, Class: Implications for Interpreting Religions, Renita Weems raised a key question about racism and election that has led me to search for the way these two are interconnected, not only in her writings but also in those of Cain Felder and other biblical scholars particularly interested in issues of election and community.[25] A womanist perspective, Weems argues, must criticize theological and cultural assumptions and biases of the Bible by beginning with an analysis of election, for

> the Bible's renown, I believe, is grounded in large part in the claim of Israel's (and later the Church's) election. Therefore, to identify the biblical world as patriarchal (or parochial, for that matter) is only to talk about symptoms. Those who have been excluded from Judeo-Christian theological discourse and structures must begin their work with an analysis of "election."[26]

The understanding of election in the Bible is frequently ambiguous and contradictory. For instance, to be chosen by God is to be chosen as a *partner* in the care of the earth and of all God's creatures. Yet to be chosen as a king or as a people is to exercise *domination* over those who are not so favored.

From my perspective, the problems of patriarchy and of election go together. For, as we have seen, the web of oppression always includes a paradigm of domination and subordination. In the Bible we discover over and over a cycle of deformation that is in part owing to pervasive patriarchal social structures that turn the idea of election for survival and service into election for security and superiority. This pattern is what Judith Plaskow has called a cycle in which the oppressed become oppressors.[27]

In the Hebrew Testament it is not until the time of Deuteronomy in the seventh century B.C.E. that the tradition of the uniqueness of Israel is developed as a model of relationship to a God who chooses out of love (7:7–9).[28] Nevertheless, the understanding of uniqueness as a people chosen (*bachar*) by God can be seen in the development of Yahwist religion among the tribes of Israel. In *The Tribes of Yahweh*, Norman Gottwald contends that Israel thought of its God as different from other gods because Yahweh was "the god of such a different people."[29] He contends that their difference was that they were a federation of liberated tribes who understood that their God had covenanted together with them to provide support for their egalitarian social structures. Without a sense of uniqueness, the tribes would have been swallowed up by their surrounding neighbors. "The Chosen People is the distinctive self-consciousness of a society of equals created in the intertribal order and demarcated from a primarily centralized and stratified surrounding world."[30]

When the monarchy develops in Israel and Judah, tension appears between the old understanding of Yahweh as one who has chosen to help the weak and the new understanding of Yahweh as a cult figure sanctioning domination, but it is only with the prophet Amos that there emerges a prophetic critique of the understanding of election as privilege. According to Renita Weems, "the book of Amos is a model dissenting voice within the Hebrew Testament."[31] The prophet from Tekoa appears in Jerusalem to criticize the dominant interpretation of Israel's election traditions, saying that election gives no special privilege. "Are you not like the Ethiopians to me, O people of Israel? says the LORD. Did I not bring Israel up from the land of Egypt, and the Philistines from Caphtor and the Arameans from Kir?" (Amos 9:7).

To be elected by God is not to practice elaborate festivals but to practice justice and care for the needy, and not to do so will bring God's judgment (Amos 4:1–3; 5:18–24). Amos opens the way for the prophetic task of recalling the people to remember their roots as an egalitarian covenant community. By the time of the exilic period, Deutero-Isaiah confirmed that God could indeed destroy the chosen people, because of their covenant unfaithfulness, but offers hope for Israel's continuing task.[32] "It is too light a thing that you should be my servant to raise up the tribes of Jacob and to restore the survivors of Israel: I will give you as a light to the nations, that my salvation may reach to the end of the earth" (Isa. 49:6).

Yet in the continuing cycle of election, the tradition was again narrowed to a very particular focus against other people in the time of Ezra and Nehemiah and the rebuilding of Israel. This in turn was criticized in such books as Ruth and Jonah. Ruth the Moabite becomes the ancestor of King David, and Boaz becomes a model of hospitality to the widow and foreigner in a direct challenge to the Chronicler's view that foreign wives should be excluded from Israel. Jonah represents Israel in his attempt to refuse God's command to assist in saving the city of Nineveh.

In Jonah 4:11, God reprimands Jonah for his selfishness. "And should I not be concerned about Nineveh, that great city, in which there are more than a hundred and twenty thousand persons who do not know their right hand from their left, and also many animals?" Phyllis Trible portrays the book of Jonah as an example of "scriptural subversion."[33] We are drawn into the story in which Jonah is convicted, only to find that not only Israel but we ourselves are Jonah, refusing to share the message of love and rejoicing when others repent and are saved.

The strength of the biblical message is reflected in this cycle, in which bounded community is repeatedly broken open. When election as assurance of justice and survival is deformed into election as privilege for the dominant political and religious authorities, it is broken open by election as prophetic critique and calling to service and witness. As Paul Hanson says in *The People Called,* election was criticized over and over in the Hebrew Testament to make it clear that "election based not on merit and dedicated not to self-glorification, but based on a call to self-transcending task and dedicated solely to God's purpose and God's glory, maintained a touchstone for persistent criticism of all human efforts to exploit election for personal or national gain."[34]

Bounded community

It is not surprising that this same pattern continues in the Greek Testament. As we have seen in Mark 7, Jesus himself is portrayed as participating in this continuing cycle in which the understanding of election is broken open in new ways. Like the prophets of old, his message is that the constrictions of the Pharisees on God's choice and welcome are a form of idolatry. The household of God is open to all persons, especially those who have been excluded and marginalized. In her response to Renita Weems's lecture, Pheme Perkins speaks of this as the formation of a "bounded community" for the sake of unity in relation to God, which then has to be broken open again by a new expression of universalism.[35] The problem is that social, political, cultural, and economic structures that make "bounded community" a viable expression of religious self-identity change over time, leaving the tradition of "bounded community" where social realities now call for "open community."

Jesus breaks open the boundedness of the Jewish religious community by reaffirming the vision of justice, mercy, and faith in the classical Hebrew pattern of community. According to Hanson, Jesus practiced all of life as an act of undivided *worship,* proclaimed God's *righteousness* as an order of communal justice and responsibility, and broadened and deepened the meaning of *compassion* in the context of his eschatological vision and his own passion.[36] The interpretation of this message in the Gospels varies, but, as we saw in chapter 4, the parables of the reign of God make very clear both God's choice to call those at the periphery of Jesus' time to the center of the community—the poor, landless, religiously unclean, women, foreigners—and the urgency of responding to that call.

Matthew 22:1–14, the parable of the Wedding Banquet, presents Jesus' critique of self-assured religious leaders who refuse to answer God's invitation to share in the household of God. The parable ends with the saying, "Many are called but few are chosen." The ones chosen are those who repent and accept God's grace. As the Beatitudes remind us, all who hunger and thirst will be satisfied (Matt. 5:6).

Luke and Mark also emphasize Jesus' offer of the good news and his welcome of all persons. In Hanson's words, the invitation to the eschatological banquet in Luke 14, verses 12–14 and 21–24, reads like a "guest list derived from the announcements of the Jubilee Year in ancient Israel."[37] In the transfiguration and the passion story, Luke understands Jesus himself as the chosen one in whom God identifies with those who are in bondage and oppression and moves them into the center of the community (Luke 9:35; 23:35).[38] In Luke the ministry of Jesus as suffering servant breaks open the understanding of election as the calling to the oppressed (Luke 4:18–19).

In Mark the focus of the passion is that the new covenant in the blood of Christ is "poured out for many" (Mark 14:24). With John, however, we see the cycle of election begin to turn again as the emphasis on bounded community and love of God and one another within the community leads John to neglect the margin where the community touches those in need of hospitality and service. This in turn permits castigation of the Jews and the accusation that those who differ are children of the devil (John 8:44; 9–10).[39]

The idea that the Christian community has replaced the community of Israel as the chosen ones of God is very much present in the Greek Testament. The dispute about inclusion began with Paul's commission to spread the gospel to the Gentiles (Gal. 2:1–10). Here the early church was called to extend its ministry to all persons regardless of race, social status, or gender. "There is no longer Jew or Greek, there is no longer slave or free, there is no longer male and female: for all of you are one in Christ Jesus" (Gal. 3:28).

Later the churches were presented with the reverse question of election. Are the Jews still the elect or have they been rejected? Paul, as a Jew and a rabbi, is eager to make clear that God's mercy includes both Gentiles and Jews. In Romans 8 he declares that the assurance of God's love is based on God's election and cannot be taken away by suffering or even death itself (8:28–39). In Romans 11:25–35, he extends the argument for salvation of the Jews and argues that as regards "election they are beloved, for the sake of their ancestors" and they will be included when all the Gentiles have heard the gospel message. "Just as you were once disobedient to God but have now received mercy because of their disobedience, so they have now been disobedient in order that, by the mercy shown to you, they too may now receive mercy. For God has imprisoned all in disobedience so that he may be merciful to all" (Rom. 11:30–32).

As the churches developed, many of those who were poor and outcast, struggling for survival, heard God's welcome and accepted the invitation. For instance, both 1 Peter and James are written to communities that are in need of support in their struggles as displaced foreigners, or diaspora. In *The Scandalous Message of James*, Elsa Tamez says that "we find in the Letter of James a community or communities of Christians . . . marginated or deprived of the civil, social, and political rights of the cities or regions in which they lived."[40] No wonder it is 1 Peter who speaks of the community as those "chosen by God," for again they are in circumstances that call for a strong sense of identity for survival.

On the other hand, Ephesians picks up a lofty and universal understanding of election as the writer makes clear that being chosen in Christ before the foundation of the earth is for the purpose of letting the whole world know that God cares. The church is not to be a new Israel, a holy assembly set apart to the Lord (Deut. 23:3), but the beginning of a new humankind sent into the world to show forth the new inheritance offered to all (Eph. 1:1–14).

Throughout the Greek Testament the cycle of election in which bounded community is repeatedly broken open continues as resurrection communities of faith struggle to interpret the Christ event as a gift of God's grace for salvation. As in the Hebrew Testament, it is necessary to study all the allusions to God's choice in connection with the actual social reality in which they were formulated and to emphasize that they are situation-variable like the gospel itself. Thus the cycle of scriptural subversion also continues with the Bible subverting itself, even while we subvert it by our interpretations and traditioning, only to find, as Trible says, that it has subverted *us* by "turning our theologies upside down."[41]

Hospitality and the Church

The various contradictions emerged in biblical interpretations of election as the social, political, economic, and religious structures of the people of faith became dissociated from an election tradition appropriate to their situation, and the traditions themselves became ideologies used to protect the religious and political privilege of those who were dominant in the society. This cycle of election for survival, subverted by election for superiority, only to be subverted again by election for service, happened repeatedly in the history of the Bible. Indeed, even the breakthrough of the Greek Testament did not fully solve the relationships of Jews and Gentiles, and it barely touched issues of inclusion of slaves and women as full members of the community (1 Cor. 11:2–16; Gal. 3:28; Philemon 2). The women whom white feminist scholars have emphasized as leaders of house churches were probably women of sufficient privilege to own the house, and we have little knowledge of how egalitarian relationships between free and slave women or rich and poor women were worked out.[42]

Need for identity

The teachings of Jesus and the insights of Paul about an egalitarian community of hospitality have continued to be subverted in the history of the Christian church. In the formation of church doctrine, as the early church tried to make sense of its faith and present it in the context of the Greco-Roman world, the doctrine of election served not only as a source of identity, mission, and calling of the church but as a means of exclusion, domination, and privilege. In this very brief discussion of its development I will select three key points about election that are shared in the biblical and church tradition. In each case I will argue that the clues for reinterpretation of the doctrine of election mentioned in connection with the story of Jesus and the Syrophoenician woman in Mark 7 are key safeguards if the church tradition of election is not to reinforce a narrow view of unity that excludes the "others."

In the history of the church, the doctrine of election points to the need for identity as human beings in the world. Those who are nobody affirm their own self-worth as children of God by claiming that God has chosen them and enabled them to live faithfully. In this sense, to be chosen of God is to be granted full human identity and worth as a gift of God's love. No wonder not only the tribes of Israel, and the nobodies of the early church, but also those in every culture who have been considered less than human, or outcasts, have found reassurance that God has chosen them as covenant partners. In this aspect the idea of election enables communities to resist racism and other forms of oppression.

The social factors that emphasize God's choice as a source of faith and identity were present when Augustine fashioned election into the doctrine of predestination. Predestination refers to God's choice that some will be saved. According to Augustine, all persons since Adam are lost in sin and are in need of God's grace in order to have faith. God's grace is irresistible but is given only to a limited number of persons, who are thereby saved through faith.[43] The Council of Orange in 529 C.E. rejected Augustine's view of predestination, in which some are saved and some rejected, but it adopted his view that God's grace was necessary for faith. Augustine's view reflected his debate with Pelagius over whether human beings were able to exercise free will to do good and evil, as well as his own experience of Christian conversion as a gift of grace, not an act of free will. Augustine also was bishop of a church under siege and was constantly seeking resources that would strengthen the identity of those who had been called to faithfulness in Christ.

The next major development of election as a doctrine of predestination came with the Protestant Reformation in the sixteenth century. In debates with Roman Catholic theologians the Reformers argued that salvation was by God's grace alone, received through faith, and did not entail human merit.[44] John Calvin, one of the chief exponents of predestination, spelled it out as part of his doctrine of salvation and the practice of the Christian life.[45] The persecutions and difficulties Protestant Christians were facing in France and other parts of Europe made it even more important for Calvin to fashion predestination as an assurance of God's grace sufficient to sustain faith even to martyrdom.

In Calvin's understanding, eternal life is foreordained for some and eternal damnation for others, quite apart from any reference to human righteousness.[46] With members of the church assured by the knowledge of their faith that God had chosen them in Jesus Christ, it was possible by either/or logic to come to the conclusion that those without the same faith had been consigned to damnation by God's will. Election for anyone is an expression of God's grace in Jesus Christ, and rejection is always deserved, for all have sinned and fallen short of the glory of God. Those who have the certainty of salvation are much more confident in living out their daily Christian lives, but this confidence seems to be gained at the expense of others.

The social factors in Calvin's struggles as a reformer in Switzerland, and the martyrdom of many of his followers, most certainly helped to make his teaching fit the reality of his situation, but it soon became clear that this same teaching could be used as a powerful political weapon to expel those of a different faith. A source of identity in the formation of a struggling community of faithful people quickly became deformed by a hierarchy of orthodoxy and exclusion by those who became the dominant political and religious leaders in Protestant areas of Europe and North America. In much the same way today, the history of South Africa demonstrates the power of the idea of election and exodus for white Afrikaner settlers, but this same myth of election has become a prime ingredient in the racist doctrines of state theology in its "justification of the status quo with its racism, capitalism, and totalitarianism."[47]

This deformation of election combines the idea that election is a free gift of God's grace with the idea that election is a form of privilege that justifies the exclusion and domination of others. One clue to resisting this deformation of election is the recognition that election changes meaning and emphasis in the light of a particular context. It's interpretation must be situation-variable, so that what is a word of hope in the situation of the oppressed does not become a word of exclusion and privilege in the situation of a dominant group. Election provides a source of identity in a particular social-historical reality, but it becomes contradictory when abstracted as a doctrine that is applicable in all realities. Without grounding in a reality of oppression, election quickly moves from a gift of grace to a justification of privilege.

In the history of the church, election has also pointed to the church's calling to witness and service. Here the emphasis in biblical and church tradition has been on the task for which the community has been chosen. This aspect of election has received emphasis by twentieth-century theologians such as Karl Barth. Barth has rightly criticized Calvin's doctrine as unbiblical in its idea of a hidden decree of condemnation.[48] Barth agrees with Calvin and most other Christian theologians that the grace of God is the only source of salvation. He emphasizes, however, that God's election is focused not on a particular people but on the one who represents the chosen people, Jesus Christ. Jesus himself is both the elected one and the one who in his suffering, death, and resurrection elects us all to faith and service.[49]

In the helpful way that he makes use of the tradition of Jesus Christ as the chosen one, Barth has moved away from the contradictions of election. If the one elected is Christ, then all have been elected in Christ and are called to respond in faith. The task of witness and service has been carried out by Christ, and those who follow do so as members of a community of witness and service. In Christ, God has created and chosen all humankind and taken the part of both those who are elected and those who are rejected.[50] Barth still accepts the doctrine of predestination, in that whether we reject or accept our election is a matter of the grace of God. He stops short of universal atonement, because he wants to guard the sovereignty of God and the freedom of God's action.

Our discussion of the changing interpretation of salvation in chapter 4, as well as this discussion of election, indicates that from a feminist perspective there is a need to go further in our traditioning process by coming to understand the atonement as an act of God's universal solidarity.

In my opinion, God's freedom is seen in the choice of Jesus as the suffering servant, who takes on the task of becoming a light to the nations and of serving those in need. Those who see themselves elected with Christ through faith are called to take up his life style of compassion and hospitality to our neighbors in need. When the doctrine of election reminds us of this task or calling, a different perspective is needed from that of Barth's emphasis on God's transcendence and on predestination of some to salvation. What is needed is an emphasis on God's choice of incarnation and identification with those in need. Just because Jesus is the chosen one, we find ourselves with God in the midst of the world willing that all might be saved (1 Tim. 3:16). God who is free from us has chosen to be free *for* us and therefore chosen solidarity with all humanity.

The clue to resisting the deformation of election so that service is replaced by a justification of superiority is the importance of solidarity with the outsiders. Such a perspective means that we, like Jesus in Mark 7, have to learn what it means to carry out the task of service by responding to those who define the need for us. If God has stood in solidarity with *all* "outsiders," including ourselves, then we are called to the task of being for others and standing with them in their struggle.

In the history of the church, election has also been a way of pointing to God's promise. This important element of God's choice to covenant with a people is an alternative way of maintaining some of Barth's emphasis on the sovereignty of God. God is "free for us" yet always "free from us" and all our idolatries and manipulations. Thus, although election seems like a doctrine that leaves no questions in the minds of the elect, the Reformers who taught election were also clear that they did not know the mind of God. They spoke of the gospel message in terms of promise and not guarantee, of certainty in God's promise and not security. They maintained that God's promise of forgiveness and salvation was never guaranteed. This is because the broken relationship with God, restored through the actions of God's love, is accepted in trust and faithfulness but still awaits fulfillment in God's household. The offer of new life in God's household was made possible in Christ's death and resurrection, but we continue to live out our salvation in fear and trembling, and in the expectation that one day we will be fully set free to be with God (Phil. 2:12).

This Pauline understanding of the journey of salvation or liberation is at once a gift and a continuing task to be fulfilled in the future. The Reformers spelled out the unfolding of the order of salvation as justification, regeneration, sanctification (Rom. 8:28–30). They debated whether Christian perfection was possible in this life through God's grace, but even John Wesley, who believed that sanctification could lead to perfection of our lives as Christians, affirmed that the good news was one of promised gift, task, and expectation, and not guarantee.

This idea of the nature of God's promise is in tension with the conviction of predestination, but it serves as a safeguard against misuse of religious practices to "guarantee" that we are chosen. God is beyond our manipulation because God is the one doing the choosing, and those who respond in faith must trust in a promise and not a guarantee. This leads us to a clue to resisting the deformation of election as promise into a guarantee of salvation. In a real sense, election is always temporary election. It is not temporary in terms of God's act of electing humankind in Jesus Christ, but it is temporary in terms of the need to be willing to change our understanding of election as new aspects of God's promise become clear to us. The future of that promise stands open and we can trust that there is "more to come."

Diversity and hospitality

Even in this brief sketch of the cycle of election in biblical and church tradition we can see the way our theologies need to be subverted over and over, in order to prevent the contradictions between free gift from God and privilege of the elect from becoming an excuse for racism and exclusion. In regard to our original inquiry about the contradictions of unity and diversity in the church, it seems at least probable that the idea of a chosen people, united in Christ, is in part based on this difficult doctrine of election and shares its ambiguities and contradictions.

The difficulty with unity, uniformity, and exclusion pushes us to look at alternative descriptions of the unity of the church for mission in a pluralistic world. One possibility would be to speak of hospitality and diversity rather than unity and diversity. In this way we move away from chosenness as a basis for unity in Christ toward the metaphor of compassion and hospitality as a basis for unity. The self-understanding of the church as one body, united in one faith in Jesus Christ, would be interpreted in terms of the purpose of that unity in mission. The church is a community called to share in the passion and compassion for humankind shown by God in Jesus Christ. It is called as Christ's partner to live as a community of faith, compassion, and justice.[51]

Hospitality is an expression of unity without uniformity, because unity in Christ has as its purpose the sharing of God's hospitality with the stranger, the one who is "other."[52] As Jesus points out in the parable of the Good Samaritan, the neighbor whom we are to love is the person in need, not just someone like ourselves (Luke 10:25–37). The Greek Testament abounds in exhortations to hospitality. John Koenig says in *New Testament Hospitality* that

> *philoxenia,* the term for hospitality used in the New Testament, refers literally not to a love of strangers per se but to a delight in the whole guest-host relationship, in the mysterious reversals and gains for all parties which may take place. For believers, this delight is fueled by the expectation that God or Christ or the Holy Spirit will play a role in every hospitable transaction [Heb. 13:2; Rom. 1:11–12].[53]

Koenig describes hospitality in the Greek Testament as "partnership with strangers" and understands hospitality as "the catalyst for creating and sustaining partnerships in the gospel."[54] *Philoxenia,* as hospitality, is the opposite of *xenophobia,* as hatred of the stranger and the one who is different. Hospitality can become a "third thing" around which partnerships are formed as each of us welcomes another as Christ has welcomed us (Rom. 15:7).[55]

In his book *Reaching Out,* Henri Nouwen says, "Hospitality is not a subtle invitation to adopt the lifestyle of the host, but the gift of a chance to the [guests] to find [their] own."[56] Hospitality creates a safe and welcoming space for persons to find their own sense of humanity and worth. Hospitality protects pluralism, according to Parker Palmer, because the church becomes a "community of compassion" where God's love for the world is practiced without motives of proselytism and God's covenant "to do justice, to love kindness, and to walk humbly" is lived out (Micah 6:8; Matt. 25:31–46).[57]

When God's call is to hospitality, the unity of the community still is distinct, because its task is distinct, but it sees itself not as the chosen number one but as one in the many.[58] As Judith Plaskow has put it in *Standing Again at Sinai:*

> What must replace chosenness, then, as the model for Jewish self-under-standing is the far less dramatic "distinctness.". . . The term distinctness suggests, however, that the relation between these various communi-ties—Jewish to non-Jewish, Jewish to Jewish—should be understood not in terms of hierarchical differentiation but in terms of part and whole.[59]

As one in the many, the religious community can see itself as only one of many valuable pieces of the whole. Hospitality becomes a style of interaction with the other pieces that make up the whole of God's cre-ation. In Plaskow's view, "It is not in the chosenness that cuts off but in the distinctiveness that opens itself to difference that we find the God of Israel and of each and every people."[60] It is this unity without uniformity that makes hospitality and diversity possible.

In going back to Gladys Moore's story about her ministry at Bethany Lutheran Church, a persistent theme in her struggles with racism was that of hospitality. For instance, the white leaders' rejection of black customs of worship led her to say,

> I wanted the congregational climate to be one in which "strangers," i.e., those whose worship and lifestyles were different from the norm, would be warmly received. That was my vision for Bethany's worship life, and sadly, it fell far short of the ideal. (p. 5)

At the point of crisis in her ministry, Gladys began to question whether the six years had made any difference to the struggles of persons in the community surrounding Bethany.

> What difference *has* Bethany made in the lives of the people in our com-munity? Have we been actively engaged in the liberation and empower-ment of the oppressed people in our neighborhood? Have we preached good news to the poor, or have we been a part of the problem? (p. 8)

Hospitality was on Gladys's heart, and a unity based on this was a key step in moving into antiracist work in that community.

This connection between hospitality and justice has also recently been brought to focus in the life of the YWCA of the USA. Since the 1960s this national movement has worked on the unfinished dimensions of its 1967 Purpose Statement and its one imperative, to "thrust our col-lective power toward the elimination of racism wherever it exists and by any means necessary." It was seeking to be a "women's movement, rooted in the Christian faith and open to all."[61] I worked with the national board members from 1970 to 1973 as religious consultant and struggled with them to make the connection between "Christian" and "open." But the dominant position of Christianity in this organization continued to plague a movement of women from diverse cultural and religious backgrounds. To be rooted in the Christian faith did not provide "soul power" for Jewish or secular members.

In 1991 the U.S. National Convention of the YWCA passed a new Purpose Statement after a long process of soul-searching at every level of the organization. They did not deny their roots, but they made it clear that an organization such as the YWCA could only thrust all of its collective power behind an antiracist vision of "peace, justice, freedom and dignity for all people" if the collective diversities were celebrated. The 1991 statement reads:

> The Young Women's Christian Association of the United States of America is a women's membership movement nourished by its roots in the Christian faith and sustained by the richness of many beliefs and values. Strengthened by diversity, the Association draws together members who strive to create opportunities for women's growth, leadership and power in order to attain a common vision: Peace, justice, freedom and dignity for all people.[62]

This decision for distinctiveness and against chosenness is a choice for hospitality and diversity, a choice that was made in part just because that organization has struggled so long and hard as a women's movement committed to join women of all colors in antiracist work. Christian churches are challenged by this decision, not because they should give up their distinctness in their commitment to Christ but because they are also called to live out that distinctness in hospitality and diversity.

Hospitality on the margin

Hospitality is open to diversity because it aids formation of community by moving the focus from center to margin. In her book *Feminist Theory: From Margin to Center*, bell hooks argues that women of color are creating feminist theory that places their concerns about the web of oppression at the center of discussions of feminist theory. Refusing to be pushed to the margins, they are claiming the center for their own contributions to feminist theory and action. "It is essential for continued feminist struggle that black women recognize the special vantage point our marginality gives us and make use of this perspective to criticize the dominant racist, classist, sexist hegemony as well as to envision and create a counter-hegemony."[63]

This most certainly is a way of expressing the gospel welcome of the "outsiders." Yet in the situation of the search for hospitality and diversity of predominantly white mainline churches, the need is to move from the center to the margins in order to share in the very issues of struggle that bell hooks is describing. This is not contradictory, but it highlights the need for situation-variability in dealing both with groups that have been powerless and those that have been powerful.

Christian communities fear difference sufficiently that they usually spend a considerable amount of time tending the margins or boundaries of their communities, not in order to *connect* with those outside but, rather, to *protect* themselves from strangers.[64] Sometimes discussions of church membership are more concerned with who is in or out than about how to be an open and welcoming community. This fear of difference is reinforced by a dualistic view of church and world that assigns good spiritual aspects to the church and evil material aspects to the surrounding world. The result of this dualistic way of thinking is that Christian communities can excuse their refusal to move out to the margins as a calling to practice piety.

Such unity, formed at the expense of true hospitality and compassion for others, is based on dissociation from the world. Yet the calling of the church is to God's mission of justice and shalom. As long as the church considers itself apart from the world rather than a genuine and authentic part of the world, its unity will be based on refusal to share its Lord's passion and compassion "outside the camp" (Heb. 13:11–12). As Jamie Phelps says in "Choose Life: Reflections of a Black African-American Roman Catholic Woman Religious Theologian," in spite of antiracist rhetoric the church refuses its calling to concrete involvement in changing social structures.

> What I have not heard is the rustle of a movement of masses of white and black Christians in the predominantly white Christian churches to address *concretely* the oppressed conditions of black African-Americans. We have been anesthetized by a privatistic and spiritualized interpretation of the Bible and by ecclesial traditions indifferent to the social and spiritual condition of people of different cultures and races.[65]

In resisting religious dualism of church and world, Dietrich Bonhoeffer stressed that the church needs to move from margin to center. Again, this would appear to be contradictory to our clue to hospitality as we move from center to margin. But Bonhoeffer was speaking in a context where the issue was one of unbelief as God is squeezed to the margin of life by modern scientific thinking. His call to meet God in the center of our lives was a refusal to allow a dualism of religious life, in which we have recourse to God only in moments of extremity.[66]

As we meet God in the center of our life, it is not in the increasingly marginal church activities but in the center of the social, political, and economic structures that call out for justice and peace. Bonhoeffer's idea of moving to the center of society is indeed a move to oppose the "privatistic and spiritualized" theology of which Jamie Phelps speaks. In taking up this task of social compassion, the church continues to shift its attention outside its own margins and where it meets Christ into the middle of the struggle for life. "The church stands, not at the boundaries where human powers give out, but in the middle of the village."[67]

The outreach ministry that Gladys Moore was encouraging in Bethany Church demonstrates this move by the church to the margin and out into the center of the community. Her antiracist work involved the community not just as a source of membership recruitment but as the focus of the ministry of the church. Reflecting the shifts that were taking place in the church, Gladys writes:

> Exciting things were happening at Bethany. We had joined the Interfaith Community Organization and were actively seeking to develop indigenous leadership and to be a vital part of our community. (pp. 7–8)

Even when she felt the need to resign as Bethany's pastor, Gladys continued to search out work at the margin; she took up a ministry with the Youth Consultation Service in Newark, New Jersey. This reflected her continuing question about how to make a difference in "the middle of the village" and not just within the congregation.

One of the organizations working on the margins that was mentioned in chapter 3 is the Women's Theological Center in Boston. For ten years I have served on the board of this center, which was formed to provide alternative programs of feminist theological education on the margins of the established seminary programs. The reason for this was twofold. First, there were very few places where women could come to develop a basic feminist understanding of theology through action, analysis, and sharing of life. Second, there was little opportunity in centers of theological education to make the crucial connections between gender issues and those of racism, heterosexism, and classism. The majority of the founders were white women who struggled with their own diversity as white women and often neglected the fact that feminist theology is not truly feminist unless it includes *all* women in its concerns and not just white middle-class students. But gradually the board and center have continued their antiracist work by making sure that the board and the teaching staff include an equal number of white women and women of color.[68]

Not only has the Women's Theological Center placed itself on the margins of white mainline theological institutions, it has also developed a double program emphasis, designing Resource Center programs that respond to the justice needs of women of color in the Boston area as well as a program of study/action for theological students. The result of this "mixing of agendas" is that the funding for the organization is always marginal as well. Foundations and church bodies want to invest in established mainline organizations, not in an organization struggling with a marginalized constituency in the community. By combining theology and social justice analysis, the WTC confuses those who want to keep theology academic and abstracted from the challenges of life. Thus the funding comes neither from sources for theological education nor for social justice and must be raised largely from women and women's organizations who understand that action and reflection cannot be separated.

In 1991 the WTC took a difficult financial step which is, nevertheless, an important part of its choice to identify with the margins. It moved its office and meeting space out of Episcopal Divinity School in Cambridge and Emmanuel College in Boston to an office in downtown Boston at the YWCA. In order to work with women in communities of poverty it is necessary to be in their midst. By moving out of the educational institutions and into a community that is more accessible to women of color, the center has claimed its own marginality as a plus and continued its push for hospitality and diversity. It has encouraged those who have been marginalized by race, class, gender, or sexual orientation to move from the margins to the center of its organizational life and commitment.

In all this talk of hospitality and diversity it needs to be said that there are also limits, for the stranger needs to be welcomed by a community that is able to practice hospitality. If a Christian community has no sense of its identity in Christ as the center of its life, it will not have a great deal of generosity and compassion to share with others. Partnership takes place around a task of service, yet *koinonia*, or partnership among Christians, is a gift of the Spirit in which there is a new focus of relationship in Jesus Christ that sets us free for others. Just as persons cannot give themselves away to others if they have no sense of self-worth to share, churches with no sense of identity and worth have little to share also. The task and the center go together, each strengthening the other, but both are needed as the church seeks to manifest diversity in its life.

A second limit of hospitality is that its practice is just as subject to deformation and misuse as any other aspect of the life of the church. Like election, hospitality can be turned into a means of domination and prestige. This happens as those offering hospitality do so on their own terms instead of on the terms set out by those who are dominated and oppressed. Just as parents, ministers, and social workers can use service and caring as a way of keeping persons dependent, church communities can offer hospitality only to those who conform to their cultural standards. Yet hospitality linked with the struggle for diversity can at least point us beyond the contradiction of unity and uniformity.

There has been a lot of talk in the modern ecumenical movement about the limit of diversity. The movement is afraid that the world diversity of cultures, politics, and economics will engulf organizations like the World Council of Churches and lead to a loss of center or focus. In seeking to define the limits of diversity, Michael Kinnamon has written a very helpful book, *Truth and Community: Diversity and Its Limits in the Ecumenical Movement.* In his reflections on the ecumenical movement he concludes that there are two limits: (1) the absence of love and (2) idolatry.[69] We are "speaking the truth in love" because the gift of God's love in Jesus Christ is the gift we share (Eph. 4:15). This is not a sentimental love but one that carries out God's own concerns for the world as love with justice.[70] The love limits diversity because it opposes all that is a denial of just love in the name of the primacy of love in our partnership with God. Those actions that "have not love" are to be rejected because love is the basis of the community and of its hospitality in the world (1 Cor. 13).

Kinnamon describes the "second unacceptable diversity [as] idolatrous allegiance to things that are less than ultimate."[71] For Christians, as the WCC statement said, our ultimate commitment is to God in Jesus Christ. Therefore, the hospitality of the Christian community is always derivative and penultimate. It is offered as part of our participation in God's justice and love in the world. There has been and is no normative form of Christianity, but there is unity in the conviction that service of neighbor is service of God.[72] These two limits of diversity have been present in other forms in the discussion of this chapter, for they refer to the need for identity as a people who trust in God's promise of love and practice that love in the struggle of justice. Hospitality, God's and ours, is a limit of diversity because it is only as this is practiced that love takes shape and God's will is done on earth as in heaven (Matt. 6:10).

According to Kinnamon the basic impulse of the ecumenical movement at its best "is a call to compassionate living."[73] This call, in my opinion, is the limit of unity and the understanding of the election that undergirds it. The ecumenical watchword of "unity" needs every bit as much critique and discussion of limits as does diversity. Indeed, this is one of the major preoccupations of the Faith and Order Commission as it works to define the various meanings of unity, including that of *koinonia.* Until the churches discover a way of love that allows them to share one common eucharistic celebration, they will continue to retreat from diversity in the name of an elect tradition or community.

At the 1991 WCC Assembly in Canberra, Australia, this issue of the limits of theological and cultural diversity was high on the agenda. At stake was the question of whether the central core of the Christian faith is to be defined by white Western male Christendom or by the many new voices from the Two-Thirds World.[74] The same questions in regard to racism and exclusion that beset Bethany Lutheran Church are also present at the national and international levels of church life.

A statement by the Faith and Order Commission, "The Unity of the Church as Koinonia: Gift and Calling," said the following:

> Diversities which are rooted in theological traditions, various cultural, ethnic and historical contexts are integral to the nature of communion: yet there are limits to diversity. Diversity is illegitimate when . . . it makes impossible the common confession of Jesus Christ as God and Savior . . . [or] salvation and the final destiny of humanity as proclaimed in Holy Scripture and preached by the apostolic community.[75]

It is important to note here that, as always, the question for the church is not whether its center is in the life, death, and resurrection of Jesus Christ but who will decide how the common confession is to be given and how the final destiny of humanity is to be preached. Frequently doctrinal differences are considered legitimate diversity, whereas differences of sexuality, gender, race, or class are to be ignored if they hinder unity discussions on ordination or eucharistic sharing. In recognition of this continuing problem, the Faith and Order statement includes an appeal for "linking more closely the search for the sacramental communion of the church with the struggles of justice and peace." The voices of those who have suffered injustice and exclusion are needed if such a link is to be made, for they are the ones who must decide what hospitality and diversity are all about.

In this chapter I have argued that overcoming the contradictions of unity and diversity can be at least one small step in the antiracist action/reflection work of the white mainline churches in the United States. In looking at the theological reinforcement of the contradictions, I have shown that the concept of unity is intertwined with the doctrine of election. We cannot give up the idea of election entirely in Christian theology because it is a way of speaking of the unexpected grace of God's gift of faith and new life in covenant community. In my opinion we need to understand this gift as mediated through the one elect person, Jesus Christ, who indicates God's free choice to love the whole world.

We also need to be careful with the cycle of election in which an experience of free gift and identity is crucial for an oppressed community, and yet it becomes an excuse for domination and privilege if the tradition remains intact when that community is no longer oppressed. Antiracist work requires a critical understanding of election and unity that is contextual or situation-variable: open to God's promise yet prepared to take up the task of racial justice work, joining Christ on the margins of the church, in the middle of struggle and suffering.

In order to overcome the contradictions that come with a restricted view of unity, churches and the ecumenical movement might well consider that hospitality and diversity provide a clearer way of speaking of the need for community in Christ that engages in reciprocal celebration of the gifts that different persons can offer as they gather together. Unity interpreted by hospitality allows the radical openness to the stranger that is necessary for diversity and for racial justice work. Hospitality calls us to be a community of faith and struggle that connects with those at the margin and celebrates the way God has called a diverse people, so that we may all share together at God's welcome table![76]

6 | *Spirituality of Connection*

Two years ago I was given a quilt as a sort of feminist festschrift for my sixtieth birthday as part of a celebration at a women's reunion at Yale Divinity School. That quilt, designed and crafted by Michele Basche, Sarah Taylor, and Alison Heston, has become the focal point of my office.[1] I hung it on the wall, and then I even redecorated by buying a new purple rug to go with the colors of the quilt pattern! The name of that pattern is Sister's Choice, and this particular quilt is full of sisters' choices, both front and back. The sisters who sat together and quilted the front have all graduated, but they and the others are not forgotten. The back is covered with the many names of women alumnae who are on that journey of choosing to be a woman, assisted by the opportunities to learn about those choices through their years in seminary. For me, to look at the names is a form of what Toni Morrison calls "rememory."[2] It evokes pictures of life and patterns of relationships in a way similar to the powerful panels in the AIDS quilt.

Quilting is a woman's art form, that women can carry out together, no matter how marginal or poor they are. Traditionally, a patchwork quilt is made up of women's lives and of the history of our families, as each piece is worked in from clothing, bedding, and linens used by ourselves, our parents, our grandparents. Once only associated with women's heritage, the patchwork quilt, most powerfully represented by the enormous AIDS quilt, has begun to replace the melting pot as "the central metaphor of American cultural identity."[3] It represents the lives, the loves, and the losses of those who weave the stories of their lives.

Sister's Choice is the same pattern that Alice Walker has Celie and Sofia quilting in *The Color Purple;* to Celie's delight, they were working in some pieces of an old yellow dress of her beloved Shug Avery.[4] The title of the quilt and the gift of the quilt remind us of the way women choose their traditions and weave their lives together in creative ways that move far beyond the pages of any book. In seeking to understand our experiences and how they interface with Christian tradition and our naming of God, we add to the quilt of our lives the many beautiful pieces of the theological action and reflection that come from the lives of the saints of all times. In this process we seek to understand God's call for the mending of creation, beginning with ourselves.

In this chapter I want to develop the third clue from the examples of communities of faith and struggle described in chapter 3: that feminist spirituality is just such a connected spirituality.[5] Spirituality of connection represents the choice to be connected to ourselves and our bodies, to the margin, and to justice struggles, as well as to tradition and to our particular communities of faith and struggle. I want to talk about the spirituality embodied in those choices, not because they are a prescription for the journey of feminist spirituality but because I hope that sister choice, sister outsider, and sister circle will become clues for those of us who, like Nelle Morton, find that the "journey is home."[6]

Sister Choice

We hear a lot about choice these days, in school and in society. There is talk of "pro-choice," "vocational choice," "life style choice," and "over choice"! Here I want to talk about another form of choice, that of "sister choice"—of choosing to be for ourselves and for other women. Margaret Farley, one of my colleagues at Yale Divinity School, once said that there are certain things in our lives we cannot change, but we have the option to choose or reject them. One of those things we choose is our mother. That is, in our lives we can ignore our mother or flee from her, or we can decide that in spite of everything we really wouldn't want another mother and *choose* her.

The same is true for choosing to be a woman. In one sense we have no choice about this and many other "accidents of birth," like race and nationality. Like our birth mother and father, it is almost always a given that we are biologically female or male. Yet just as we have to come to the point of choosing our mothers and making something of that relationship, we also have to come to that same point about other so-called "unconditionals" in our lives. Those of us who were born women often spend a lot of time wishing we were men or being totally ambivalent about ourselves, our size, our looks, our prospects, and so on. Or we can decide that we really wouldn't want to be a man, nor would we want to be some mythical ideal woman, so we choose to be ourselves. This is not an easy decision. It is much harder than choosing marriage or a profession. Yet once we take this option, we have the opportunity to explore all the ways we might want to be a woman, affirming the value of who we are and learning from other women the many and various ways we might live out our lives.

Choosing to be a woman

The journey toward choosing to be our own woman is what I would describe as a journey of self-liberation together with others. It is a spiritual journey in discovery of what God intends us to become. I know myself that it takes a long time and that it happens over and over throughout our lifetimes. As a child I spent time wishing I were not so tall and "tomboyish" as I tried to choose being like other girls (the popular and socially acceptable ones). As I moved into my work in the East Harlem Protestant Parish, I chose to be a misfit in an interracial community of poverty and then to become ordained in 1958 in spite of becoming a female misfit in a sea of male clergy. But it was only in the 1970s that I was helped by other women to see that women who did not fit the cultural stereotypes were always misfits, and then I chose to be a woman and to work for the full humanity of *all* women, together with men. This is what I would call my sister choice: I chose myself as a woman and sister, and I chose to advocate for other women as my sisters.

My contention is that we are all on a journey toward freedom, and we have a chance to choose how that will or will not happen in our lives. In the midst of all the other choices—of courses, careers, partners, and so much else—we are also choosing how the journey will go in regard to our identity as women. One day you will, perhaps, discover that you basically like being who you are as a woman of whatever color, class, or sexual orientation, and that will be a small but important step in the lifelong process of your own human liberation!

Choosing to be a woman or a man means not just settling for what we are but accepting ourselves, in our own body, with our own abilities, race, sexuality, family, class, and culture, as a gift of God. Women of all colors have ultimately to make this choice as they recognize that who they are as a woman is not given but constructed out of their own situations and responses. Men of all colors must make this choice also, but first they have to learn that what it means to be a man is not a given for them but is constructed in the face of all the variables of their life situation, especially in the U.S. context of racism. White men have to choose as well, but as participants in the patriarchal definition of what it means to be human, the acceptance of their self-worth may not appear to them to be problematic unless, as is often the case, their choice has been complicated by painful experiences such as rejection, lack of love, or child abuse. For both men and women the choice is one of moving beyond particular assigned roles of patriarchal culture, religion, family, or society and choosing to be ourselves in our own particular bodies, with our various limitations as well as our gifts.

Men and women of all colors and classes make their choices differently because their social locations in a sexist and heterosexist society are different. Most men of all classes and races grow up assuming that heterosexual masculinity is the norm for their life, and they spend a great deal of energy trying to conform to what their families, peers, and society seem to think it means to be a man. This is particularly painful for gay men, who struggle against their own sexuality because they have been taught that it is at best a disability and at worst a sin against God.[7]

Leaders in the predominantly white middle-class heterosexist men's liberation movement have pointed out that boys are taught to fear and mistrust their own emotions and feelings and often lack emotional support and rituals of passage into "manhood" that once were provided by fathers or older men.[8] They invite men to join other men in seeking out new sources of wholeness and connection to themselves and others. Yet often men of this group as well as other social groups tend to refuse the difficult spiritual journey that might teach them to get in touch with their own bodies and selves. Instead, they substitute patriarchal games of domination and exploitation of "emotional" females and "subordinate" males or blame their mothers and other women for their problems.[9]

Women are not exempt from such patriarchal games and often spend their energies running from themselves and struggling with their oppression by conforming to their culturally assigned role of subordination and by competing with other women for male approval. Again, it is white, affluent, heterosexist women who find the need for choices less obvious because of the benefits they receive from the patriarchal system by their connection to the elite males. But once they discover that there may be ways of affirming themselves and their difference as well as that of others, they have many more resources than women of color, lesbian women, and poor women.

Women of color frequently see the contradictions in their assigned roles but have few resources and little power, and they take greater risks when they make a stand against their situation of multiple oppression by choosing to be the woman they are and to make use of who they are in ways that serve the liberation of themselves, their families, and their people. In her classic novel, *Their Eyes Were Watching God*, Zora Neale Hurston helps us see this struggle to be a woman through the life story of Jane. She begins that story with words that characterize the different paths African American men and women take in searching out the meaning of their life.

> Ships at a distance have every man's wish on board. For some they come in with the tide. For others they sail forever on the horizon, never out of sight, never landing until the Watcher turns his eyes away in resignation, his dreams mocked to death by Time. That is the life of men.
>
> Now, women forget all those things they don't want to remember, and remember everything they don't want to forget. The dream is the truth. Then they act and do things accordingly.[10]

Paula Giddings calls this ability to "invent themselves" the spiritual dimension that informs the history of black women as they transform the image society gave them into an image "that fits their own inner reality."[11]

In the search for self-identity beyond assigned gender roles, white men may move toward the choice to be a man by seeking to be in touch with their emotions and what is stereotypically considered their "feminine side," but this is always suspect for them because their culture has taught them that men who express their feelings may be considered homosexual. White women trying to become more assertive and search out a way of expressing their own agency run into the same patriarchal control mechanism of homophobia when they "act like a man." But those who, with the support of others, manage to persist may come to a point where they choose themselves, as whole persons who claim their own unique embodiment as both sexual and spiritual beings.[12]

When this happens there is also the possibility of a man choosing to be a *feminist* man. Unlike a woman, who is often drawn into liking other women and advocating for them when she learns to choose herself as a woman, men may not necessarily be drawn into advocacy for women because they choose to be men. But as they struggle to free themselves from patriarchal definitions of what it means to be a man and to make their own "brother choice," they too have the possibility of "sister choice," of joining women in forging alternative ways of being embodied selves who are able to partner themselves and one another on the liberation journey.

Choosing to be a woman includes becoming a feminist or womanist, but for Christians it can also be part of a deeper spiritual commitment. In feminism we learn to be pro-woman, and pro-ourselves if we are women, but choosing to be a woman is a gift of connection to ourselves in which, deep down in the center of our being, we know ourselves as loved and accepted by God and loved and accepted by ourselves as well. It refers to those graced moments when we can say, "I would not choose it any other way." This awareness of the gift of connection does not always stay with us. As our bodies change and our lives and relationships change, we have over and over to choose our bodies and ourselves, embrace our gifts, and do something with them in our life journeys.

An experience of such a choice was shared with me by a former student and a friend of mine, the Rev. Henna Han, whose leadership gifts were described in chapter 2. Henna Han is the pastor of the Rainbow Church, a woman-church that includes many Korean G.I. brides and their bicultural families. Some of these women were entertainers at bars around U.S. bases in Korea, and they are rejected by Korean churches. At the same time, racist rejection in U.S. society is multiplied by the rejection, isolation, and misunderstanding that comes from speaking Korean in an English-speaking family and society.

Henna said to me that as a child she had learned that a woman's body is a great masterpiece of God and that she carried that conviction with her when she became involved in the struggle against patriarchal destruction of women's bodies through prostitution and suffering. She founded the Rainbow Church as a United Methodist church because she felt called to protect women's bodies from the evil that so often destroys them.

Until recently she had thought she was called to ministry simply because, over ten years ago, she had come to my class on Women in Ministry and had begun a very long journey toward Methodist ordination. Now she realizes that all of her life God has been leading her to choose herself and other women as she works to protect their bodies, and the bodies of their families, and the bodies of the nation of Korea against the ravages of the neocolonial prostitution industry. She experiences God's call to service as a call to continue the struggle to "reclaim bodies and to show them as true masterpieces of God's creation."[13]

Choosing to be whole

This sister choice is part of a Christian feminist spirituality of connection to ourselves, others, and God. It is part of choosing to be whole, of choosing to become the full human beings that God created us to be. Spirituality is not just part of the Christian tradition, for it is an important aspect of many religious traditions in reference to the dimension of transcendence or meaning in our lives. In fact, the word is very popular in our contemporary society because it is so flexible and open to faith perspectives and journeys of all kinds. But it is also dangerous because it is most often assumed to be a word that describes something other than our bodies and our material everyday life. It is important then to clarify what I mean when I use the words "Christian feminist spirituality."

Francine Cardman describes *spirituality* as having to do with the direction, meaning, and value we give to the totality of our experience.[14] According to Mary Hunt, spirituality is made up of the choices we make about life that give it meaning: choices about our body, our relationships, our work, and our patterns of reflection, worship, and play.[15]

A *feminist* understanding of spirituality is a nondualistic or holistic understanding that affirms the full humanity of women together with men. I would describe this spirituality as the practice of bodily, social, political, and personal connectedness so that life comes together in a way that both transcends and includes the bits and pieces that make up our search for wholeness, freedom, relationality, and full human dignity.

A *Christian* feminist spirituality is one that finds the guidance and source of transcendence in the God of Jesus Christ and finds guidance in our life choices through the life, death, and resurrection of Jesus' story. It makes connections not only to ourselves, to God, and to the needs of the world but also to that community of faith and struggle which is empowered by the Holy Spirit to live out the liberating story of Jesus of Nazareth day by day.

By now I hope it is clear that this form of spirituality rejects the dualisms and hierarchies of domination and subordination perpetuated by patriarchal thought and social systems. Suspicious of all either/or's, it specifically rejects the separation of body or matter and mind or spirit, of male and female, of freedom and structure. These three are spelled out in the Presbyterian report "Keeping Body and Soul Together: Sexuality, Spirituality, and Social Justice."[16]

When *body and spirit* are separated, spirituality can be nurtured through religious ritual and observance, while at the same time no notice is taken of forms of injustice that do terrible things to persons' bodies as they are subjected to rape, starvation, disease, degradation, and suffering of all kinds. Not only are those who suffer told to wait for their reward in heaven, but those who do nothing to stop that suffering, and may even perpetuate it, manage to live out all the contradictions of a split consciousness. This is aptly described in a saying attributed to Dietrich Bonhoeffer during his imprisonment in Nazi Germany. "One cannot sing Gregorian chants if one does not also cry out for the Jews."[17] We celebrate Bonhoeffer's life and theology not just because he wrote letters from prison and died a martyr but because that martyrdom included a spirituality of connection between action and reflection.

Second, when *male and female* are separated and thought of as radically different, this gender dualism allows women to become objectified and commodified as objects to be used by the dominant males to whom they belong. Men are identified with the spiritual and mind aspect of the body/spirit split, and women are assigned to the inferior natural realm of body, which needs to be tamed and controlled.

Last, the dualism of *freedom and structure* posits the importance of human freedom and responsibility in caring for others and for the earth but then develops a structure of accountability that allows great freedom to privileged white males and provides restrictive regulations for the subordinate groups. Thus morality is based on an unjust double standard, and the focus on sexuality and women's bodies and their control obscures the contradictions of such unjust moralism. Such dualistic thinking and acting help to perpetuate the domination of any oppressed and less powerful group through overregulation by those with the power that comes with gender, race, class, and heterosexist privilege.

Refusing this dualistic spirituality and choosing to make something of the gift of our bodies and our whole selves mean, in the words of bell hooks in *Yearning,* "struggling to assert agency," making something of the gift of ourselves through moral agency in the service and love of others.[18] It is an experience similar to that of Nelle Morton, who, long after retirement from Drew Theological School and a life of social advocacy and teaching, experienced the affirming presence of Goddess in her life in a way that allowed her to accept a blood disorder as her *own* wild blood. In an essay, "The Goddess as Metaphoric Image," she writes:

My greatest surprise and shock came perhaps in the last experience—the surprise of relating my internalized male attitudes toward women's blood to my present very serious blood difficulty—"too deep to exorcise." I am able now to receive the "bizarre and wild cells" as a special gift. In that sense the Goddess gave me back my life and called me to live fully with what I have, adjusting my activities to what energy I can summon and use creatively.[19]

With joy she went on to share her journey with all of us in her book *The Journey Is Home,* carrying on a legacy of holistic and self-affirming spirituality that has inspired a generation of younger women.

Kitchen table spirituality

Sister choice is part of kitchen table solidarity in church in the round. The struggle to choose ourselves as sisters and to accept ourselves as a gift of God connects the church community to the everyday realities that happen around countless kitchen tables. An ecclesiology or theology of the church that includes sister choice will not be afraid of connecting issues of spirituality with those of sexuality or embodiment, nor will it refuse the challenge to "put our bodies on the line," knowing the pain and suffering of those who cry out for solidarity in the struggle for justice.

In opposition to the dualistic separation of body and spirit, this kitchen table spiritual discipline would look for wholeness and fulfillment in the moments in which persons are able to express themselves in a way that connects our deepest sense of embodied self, or sexuality, with our strongest feelings of connection to others and to God.[20] Human sexuality itself is not reducible to genital eroticism. Rather, it is an ever-evolving sense of self-identity rooted in, but not determined by, one's biological sex. Our sexuality as male and female is the embodiment of our spirituality. From a feminist perspective, spirituality includes embodiment, and embodiment includes spirituality. As Margaret Farley has pointed out, there is always an overplus of ourselves in relation to our bodies, and an overplus of our spirits in relation to ourselves.[21]

It is this overplus, this connection, that Audre Lorde describes as the power of the erotic to connect our self with our deepest feelings of joy. "For the erotic," she says, "is not a question only of what we do: it is a question of how acutely and fully we can feel in the doing."[22] In her essay "Uses of the Erotic," Lorde is reclaiming the Greek word *eros* as a personification of love and joy, "creative power and harmony," and as the opposite of pornography, which offers physical sensation without any feeling. She writes, "When I speak of the erotic, then, I speak of it as an assertion of the lifeforce of women: of that creative empowerment, the knowledge and use of which we are now reclaiming in our language, our history, our dancing, our loving, our work, our lives."[23]

For Audre Lorde it is the erotic that grounds spirituality in our bodies and empowers us for both personal and political action. It provides the creative power for writing poetry and for the many ways of expressing our feelings, through art as well as through our personal and social relationships. This gift of feeling that has so long been relegated to the body and to sexual intercourse needs to be seen as a gift of embodied spirituality that connects us to others and to the world and to God as it opens us up to the desire for joy, creativity, and self-transcendence toward others.[24]

It is this desire for God and for community that is the basis for worshiping in the Spirit in churches that encourage their members to express themselves through their bodies in song and dance, in the sharing of word and sacrament, in intercessions for the world, and for those who cry out for love and justice. In her book *Touching Our Strength*, Carter Heyward asserts: "The erotic is the divine Spirit's yearning, through our body-selves, toward mutually empowering relation, which is our most fully embodied experience of God as love" (1 John 4:7ff.).[25]

The perspective of embodied spirituality is not absent from Paul's discussion of worship in Romans 12. His admonition to "present your bodies as a living sacrifice" is an invitation to worship God with our whole selves: with our sexuality as women and men, with our minds, and with our actions of righteousness and justice. It is an exhortation to kitchen table spirituality in which the totality of our lived reality is offered to God and to our neighbor and not just one or another part. Paul's spirituality is connected to our bodies, and not just in the sense of a dualistic negation of the possibility of their misuse. "I appeal to you therefore, brothers and sisters, by the mercies of God, to present your bodies as a living sacrifice, holy and acceptable to God, which is your spiritual worship" (Rom. 12:1).

Interpreted in terms of sacrificial theology this passage, with its reference to the sacrifice of our lives rather than that of a slain animal, has been used to reinforce the idea that the suffering and sacrifice of women and other oppressed groups is an appropriate part of Christian discipline. We are to share in the sacrifice of Christ because we have been "bought with a price" (1 Cor. 6:20). Many feminists have rejected this understanding of suffering, instead pointing out that even the suffering of Christ on the cross was not a choice of suffering and was not the choice of the God of life.

When the Gospel of Mark talks about his prediction of suffering, the author is not speaking of sacrifice but, in the words of Joanna Dewey,

> about what the *world* does to those who follow God's way. The Roman Empire executed Jesus for disturbing the peace; Martin Luther King was assassinated for challenging structures of segregation; the four women in El Salvador were murdered for living out the gospel. The world does not love you if you question its ways. It may even kill you, but that is not God's pleasure.[26]

In Gethsemene, Jesus prayed for God to remove the cup from him

(Mark 14:36). His choice of obedience to God's will led to his crucifixion, not because he wanted to die or because God wanted him to die, but because the political and economic power and the religious power structures of his time rejected his call for a new household of God where all are "invited to wholeness and to food."[27]

These same power structures, which continue to crucify countless people through starvation, war, abuse, poverty, and scorn, must be confronted by a church willing to pay the cost of its opposition to the status quo, not a church that reinforces and justifies needless suffering. Nowhere is this stated more clearly than in the work of Asian feminist theologians. For instance, Virginia Fabella writes that in the Philippines they have "developed (or inherited) a dead-end theology of the cross with no resurrection or salvation in sight."

> While we seek in Jesus' passion, death, and resurrection a meaning for our own suffering, we cannot passively submit ourselves as women to practices that are ultimately anti-life. Only that suffering endured for the sake of one's neighbor, for the sake of the kingdom, for the sake of greater life, can be redeeming and rooted in the Paschal mystery.[28]

In this passage from Romans 12 we find more than sacrificial language. We also find Paul's characteristic integration of the personal and the communal, the spiritual and the physical. Through the power of Christ's Spirit the whole community, both female and male, is made holy and is called to live out its connection to the risen body of Christ by the way it offers its life on behalf of the mending of creation. Ernst Käsemann describes *pneuma* or Spirit in Paul as the power of the risen Christ at work in the community, not as some abstract or disembodied spirituality. "Therefore," he says,

> the truly spiritual service of God consists self-evidently, according to Rom. 12.1ff., in the offering of our bodies; and the baptismal instruction in Rom. 6:12ff. teaches that this bodily obedience is the sign that our existence as Christians springs from the resurrection of Christ and moves towards our own resurrection.[29]

In kitchen table spirituality we worship God with our whole selves as women and men, and with all our concerns and commitments. We "put our bodies on the line" as acceptable worship as we make the "sister choice" work for justice and transformation of the world. Empowered by the Holy Spirit, we bring the deep pain of our suffering and alienation and that of our world, that we may offer it up to God for healing. We express the erotic connection between body and spirit as we reach out to God and those around us in the celebration of the deep feeling of joy that comes with being loved in our whole being.

Sister Outsider

Feminist spirituality includes the choice to be connected to ourselves and our sisters in an embodied and holistic way. At the same time it also includes the choice to be connected to the sister outsider and to all who live on the margins of church, society, and the world. Both Audre Lorde in *Sister Outsider* and bell hooks in *Feminist Theory: From Margin to Center* have shown us just how important it is to choose the margin if we are to practice a way of hospitality that includes the needs of those most needy, and if we are to learn about the ways we ourselves perpetuate oppression.[30] Choosing to be connected to the margin is a spiritual discipline that calls us to work for justice, beginning with the agenda of those who are most marginalized or objectified as objects that can be used, abused, or thrown away. It means treating other people as subjects whose particularity and difference are respected and celebrated, rather than as objects of competition and domination.[31]

Finding the margin

The discipline of such connected spirituality involves knowing where the margin and center are located in order to respond appropriately. We make choices about moving from margin toward center or from center toward margin, according to where we find ourselves in relation to the center of power and resources and of cultural and linguistic dominance in any particular social structure. Our connection to the margin is always related to where we are standing in regard to social privilege, and from that particular position we have at least three choices: not to choose, to choose the center, or to choose the margin.

Our first choice is *not to choose.* If we find ourselves marginalized by gender, race, sexual orientation, class, or disability, we have the possibility of doing nothing. In so doing we internalize the oppression, so that we have a low opinion of ourselves and our group and assume that our position of subordination and obedience is natural and our place at the bottom of the table is fixed. Usually not to choose is also not to be in touch with how we feel and with the causes of our particular alienation and suffering. For those who are associated with the privilege of the center or dominant group, not to choose is to continue to be part of the problem, because the system of racism, compulsory heterosexism, and sexism continues to oppress and is supported by our compliance.

A second choice is *for the center.* Those on the margin choosing the center do so by emulating the oppressors and doing everything to pass or to be like those who are dominant and be accepted by them. Of course, survival requires that all of us know how the dominant group functions and learn the "master's tools," but, as Audre Lorde points out, dismantling the master's house requires us to connect to the margin and continue as advocates of those on the margin.[32] Once acquired, master's tools are used to saw off the corners of the table so that it can become round.[33] Those who share the privilege of the center and choose it by actively working to enhance their own privilege do so at the expense of others on the margin.

Our third choice is *for the margin.* Here those on the margin claim the margin by working in solidarity with others from the margin as they move toward the center. They seek a transformed society of justice where they will be empowered to share the center, and no one will need to be marginalized. Those who find themselves related to the dominant center of society can choose the margin by working as advocates of those who are oppressed and sawing off their own table corners as they work against the privilege of their own group. In either case, the choice for the margin is for the purpose of transforming the center. As bell hooks says in *Yearning,*

> I make a definite distinction between that marginality which is imposed by oppressive structures and that marginality one chooses as site of resistance—as location of radical openness and possibility. This site of resistance is continually formed in that segregated culture of opposition that is our critical response to domination. . . . We are transformed, individually, collectively, as we make radical creative space which affirms and sustains our subjectivity, which gives us a new location from which to articulate our sense of the world.[34]

Perhaps the story I have already told of the Rev. Henna Han can help us understand the way that choosing the margin works for one woman who is oppressed by both race and gender yet is privileged by her success, along with her husband, in winning an education and the possibility of service in the ordained ministry of the church.

For Henna, not to choose has often been a temptation for she has had to struggle with her own internalized oppression and low sense of self-worth over and over again. Although she chose the center in emulating the rest of us in wanting a good education, she most certainly found that the education did nothing to break down the barriers of race and gender that have prevented her from ever receiving a regular pastoral appointment.

Following her role model, the Rev. Cho Wha Soon, a pioneering woman pastor in Korean urban industrial mission, Henna Han made use of her education to choose the margin. In founding the Rainbow Church for Korean women who are married to G.I.s in this country, she chose to sit with them as outcasts in both Korean and U.S. society and to seek the empowerment of the one who humbled himself to be among them that they might have life. In their Rainbow Church the communion table/cross is very low and the women sit up higher around it. In this way she can say to the women that the one they worship as high and lifted up is present in their midst, standing with them on the margin and working with them to transform the center so that all will be welcome (Phil. 2:1–11).

Rejecting the contradictions

Because we are at one and the same time marginal and center, oppressed and oppressing, subordinate and dominant, it is often difficult to sort out our connection to the margin. One place we can begin, however, is to be clear about the contradictions of the patriarchal culture in which we live. The more we connect ourselves to the margin and work for transformation of ourselves and society, the more we become aware of the contradictions between the way we experience social reality and the way it has been interpreted for us in home, church, school, and society. Learning to perceive these contradictions and taking steps together with others to change them is part of our liberating spiritual journey. Here I would like to continue with the contradictions in the life of the church as it seeks both unity and diversity (described in chapter 5) by discussing the way that four of these contradictions often show up in our lives, especially in the lives of white middle-class women. I call these the four "misunderstood C's" that make it difficult to be in solidarity with persons struggling for justice: coalition, conflict, community, and celebration.

A major contradiction that white women face along with all women in developing spirituality of connection is having coalitions without risk. We want to work for justice, and we are afraid or unwilling to risk joining in coalition with others who are already at work. Yet coalitions and safety are a contradiction in terms.

There are no coalitions without risk. In a world full of tactics that divide and conquer we need to risk working in coalitions even when it means giving up the security of white dominance and learning a new practice of working for a "third thing": a goal chosen by those most in need of liberation. Bernice Johnson Reagon of Sweet Honey in the Rock helps us know just how it feels to be in a coalition when she says that if you are really doing coalition work, most of the time you feel "threatened to the core."

"You don't go into coalition because you just *like* it," she says. "The only reason you would consider trying to team up with somebody who could possibly kill you, is because that's the only way you can figure you can stay alive."[35]

The good news is that once we are threatened to the core, once we act, we are less likely to waste time being guilty because we are so busy working to survive along with our sisters of color and others on the margin.

A second contradiction that we face is that of trying to solve conflict without sharing power. Those of us who are white middle-class heterosexual women are both oppressed and oppressors. We recognize sexist oppression at home, on the job, in church, and in society. We then generalize our oppression, assuming that our experience is the same as that of a lesbian, a poor woman, a woman of color, or any combination of the above. Thus we are able to feel self-righteous while continuing to act out of our assumptions of privilege and power as we continue to use the master's tools and tactics and ignore the specific and very particular needs of women in each situation.

Persons of privilege cannot solve conflict without giving up or sharing power. In order to do this, those of us who are white women or men need to give up our own privilege and yet at the same time work for empowerment together with others in relation to our own marginality. As Susan Thistlethwaite has put it in *Sex, Race, and God*, we "must come to a forthright knowledge of good and evil and live through the pain with both a hermeneutic of suspicion of racial privilege and a hermeneutic of truth of white women's suffering as [our] tools."[36]

A third contradiction is that we think we can create community without diversity. As women and men of all colors seek to build new ways of being in community as part of their spirituality of connection, we still cling to the patriarchal view that community means a warm, cozy feeling produced by sameness and uniformity. We base our togetherness on what we have in common and ignore our differences, or seek out only those who seem most like ourselves.

The contradiction here is that community is not built on sameness. Community is built out of difference. In fact, you cannot even create community and experience the possibility of new gifts of partnership without diversity. Audre Lorde makes this very clear in her article entitled, "Age, Race, Class, and Sex: Women Redefining Difference." It is not the differences of race, age, and sex that separates us, she says. "It is rather our refusal to recognize those differences, and to examine the distortions which result from our misnaming them and their effects upon human behavior and expectation."[37]

Folks are not all alike, and just because of this there is some hope for new community in which the center is transformed because of sharing and the empowering of differences. One way of talking about spirituality of connection to the margin is to call it the "rainbow connection," not in the sense of dreamers and "over the rainbow" but in the sense of celebrating rainbow coalitions and the diversity that becomes connected and refracted into great beauty out of the storm and struggles needed for the mending of creation.[38]

Finally, we need to develop a spirituality in which we recognize the contradiction of celebrating liberation without struggling for justice. White women working on barriers that separate us from our sisters of color often want to have the celebration before the wilderness experience! We forget that neither men nor women can celebrate liberation without fighting injustice in solidarity with those on the margin of society. Other forms of celebration that are separated from struggle tend to be a premature naming of reconciliation before we have worked on the coalition, conflict, and community. Coming together to celebrate the many small steps on the road to freedom is essential, but each time there needs to be a step, some concrete action for justice that makes the celebration worthwhile for the different sisters and brothers.

The contradiction of celebrating liberation without working for justice can only be overcome as we look for trouble and beauty together. Thus bell hooks says, of choosing space on the margin as a critical response to oppressive structures, "We come to this space through suffering and pain, through struggle. We know struggle to be that which pleasures, delights, and fulfills desire." Carolyn McDade has a song that helps us feel the way trouble and beauty are all around us in the world and need to be celebrated by those "who dare to love, troubling the powerful and all that maintains domination." One verse of her song of trouble and beauty goes this way:

> By these laboring wings we have come thus far
> to this place in the wind where we see
> trouble and beauty, we see trouble, we see beauty,
> and that far wandering star still calls us on.[39]

Perhaps if we can straighten out a few of these contradictions in our own lives there will be a little less trouble and a little more beauty as we practice a spirituality of connection to the margin and celebrate that choice together!

Welcome table spirituality

When we come together to celebrate at God's welcome table with our sister and brother outsiders, part of our kitchen table spirituality will be that of worrying with God.[40] Many years ago I heard Krister Stendahl quote a rabbinic saying that theology is worrying about what God is worrying about when God gets up in the morning. It would seem according to Stendahl that God is worrying about the mending of creation, trying to straighten up the mess so that all of groaning creation will be set free.[41] In order to do this, God has to be worrying about those who have dropped through the "safety net" of society, about those who are victims of injustice and war, and about the destruction of their bodies, their lives, and the environment in which they live. This worrying with God about the poor, the outcasts, the outsiders of society is a spiritual discipline that is rooted in the Gospel accounts of Jesus' own actions and parables about the hospitality of God's household.

One place to look at this Gospel message is in Luke's version of the Beatitudes in the Sermon on the Mount. It seems to be less edited than Matthew 5:3–12, but nonetheless it still contains characteristic Lukan warnings to his readers against love of riches and possessions. "Woe to you who are rich. . . . Woe to you who are full now" (Luke 6:24–25). In reading Luke 6:20–26 it again seems strange that in our capitalist society affluence is not considered a sin against those who are starving, while other topics not even mentioned by Jesus, such as homosexuality and other "sexual sins," have become the focus of condemnation in many of the churches. Yet Jesus' words welcoming the poor, outcasts, and sinners into God's reign are one of the constant themes of the Gospels. "Blessed are you who are poor, for yours is the kingdom of God. Blessed are you who are hungry now, for you will be filled" (Luke 6:20–21).

The poor, the hungry, the sorrowful, and the reviled will be blessed by God because they are welcomed into God's reign and invited to the es- chatological welcome table where all will have plenty. James Forbes has called this new group of followers of Jesus the "kingdom class," those who are blessed and welcomed as God intended from the beginning.[42] Accord- ing to Jesus, the breaking in of God's mending work has redefined com- munity as all those who have repented and accepted God's invitation. The invitation to share in the eschatological community reads like the Beati- tudes, but it could just as easily read like the Magnificat or the sermon in Nazareth that announces the Jubilee.[43]

As we have already noted in chapter 4, there is a strong indication from such texts of God's bias toward the poor. It would appear from the list of beatitudes, as well as from the corresponding list of woes, that there is no salvation outside the poor. All are welcome, but Jesus has chosen to bring God's welcome to those who are strangers to the blessings of "the good life." All of us can find Christ and join him in his ministry, but we can only find him by participating in his story of partnership with strangers (Matt. 25:31–46). In spite of this message, it seems that in Luke's churches as well as in Corinth there had developed class distinctions and divisions at the table, so that not everyone was welcome to eat (1 Cor. 11:17–22). Pre- occupied by deciding who has access to Christ and to God's table, the church has often fenced out many of those whom Jesus welcomed.

Jesus' message is that he is found with the outsiders, not because they are any more righteous than the others but because, as a group, they are the ones who help us know when justice is done and all are included. As the African American spiritual that was mentioned in the introduction to Part Three proclaims:

> All kinds of people around that table
> one of these days! Hallelujah!
> All kinds of people round that table!
> Gonna sit at the welcome table one of these days.[44]

This message of Jesus is not always welcome to those who already have many blessings, and we find that churches often prefer Matthew's ver- sion, which stresses that it is those who are "poor in spirit" who are to be blessed (Matt 5:3). In either case, however, the Gospels make clear that a life of discipleship is not easy because they continue the Sermon on the Mount with a lot more description of what discipleship for the poor and for the non-poor will be like if they are to join the outsider in his invitation.

Luke searches out the meaning of discipleship as a response to Jesus' message of repentance and welcome. It would seem he hopes that the small churches will become what John Koenig calls "banquet communities" where the table of the Lord is spread for all (Luke 22:30).[45] He is intent on teaching the churches of his own time about the importance of welcome table spirituality as they witness to the world around them. We too need to search out what this means for our own discipleship, as we join God in worrying about poverty and injustice and the mending of all creation.

Sister Circle

There is another quilt in my life that resides at the Women's Theological Center in Boston. It has a beautiful modern design created by Meck Groot and is being stitched together by women whose quilting is coordinated by Beverly Smith and Wendy Ritch. The glorious colors are a bright crazy quilt, symbolic of the ten years the center has struggled to create an alternative theology and spirituality for sister outsiders. The feminist symbol worked into the pattern makes one immediately aware that to be part of that crazy pattern is to be part of a sister circle. The pieces have been purchased by donations that honor women and women's groups by dedicating squares of the quilt to them. When I look at that quilt, and at my own Sister's Choice quilt, I think of all the women's lives that have been wasted, but also of the countless women who have chosen themselves and moved on to transform their communities. I also celebrate the way many women have refused to be alienated from the church and have worked to make the connections needed to transform their churches and traditions into sources of life for themselves and other women.

An example of this difficult work of transformation is Beverly Harrison's collection of essays edited by Carol Robb, titled *Making the Connections.* This book does not claim to be about spirituality. Its subtitle is *Essays in Feminist Social Ethics.* Yet it is a deeply spiritual book, as Beverly Harrison herself makes careful connections between the lives of women and their sister circle and the Christian tradition. For her, "keeping faith in a sexist church" involves moving deeply into the feminist critique of Christianity, as we respond to God's call "to be uncompromising agents of transformation of the church" from within the Christian community.[46] Without a doubt Beverly Harrison has chosen to be connected, not only to herself and to people on the margin of society and the church but also to the community of faith and the tradition she seeks to transform. Following her lead, I want to examine ways that our feminist spirituality pushes us to choose a community and the tradition of that community.

Christians are those who have "fallen in faith with Christ." But this gift of faith usually comes to us in a community of faith that teaches us how to name our faith and share the disciplines of the Christian life. This is why we have to create alternative, nonpatriarchal communities where partnership is lived out in order to be able to live in a different way and to understand the tradition in a different way. We need to subvert the church into becoming a church in the round, a church where spirituality of connection becomes a living reality because people are engaged with a faith that connects them to the struggles for justice in a discipleship of freely chosen service in the name of Jesus Christ. Robert McAfee Brown describes this process of talking back to the church yet claiming "church" as part our spiritual journey together with others: "I believe I am part of a further circle beyond [family and friends], who occasionally manage to put others ahead of themselves and God ahead of all, a circle to which I give the name of 'church.'"[47]

We need to subvert theological education as well. Whenever I teach my classes at Yale I always organize coffee and refreshments, and various other social events, including a closing class session that is like an agape meal with breaking of bread, potluck food, and sharing. I don't do this because I am an advocate of women "making coffee and not policy," nor because I am in need of extra nourishment! I do it because human beings are not islands. We need a space of hospitality to make connections to one another in community. A classroom, no matter how hierarchical and rigid in architecture, needs to become the home of a circle of learners who connect with each other, the tradition, and the world around them as partners in learning, in order to be able to risk the kinds of questions needed for growth.

Choosing a tradition

Many of us are afraid of feminism because it may drive us out of the institutional church and beyond the traditions of the Christian church. Most certainly, the risk of growth and new knowledge is that we ourselves may change and experience the kind of cognitive dissonance that drives us to shift our beliefs so that they correspond more clearly with our experiences and actions. The only reason this does not happen more frequently is that the dualism of church patriarchal teachings allows us to believe one thing in the so-called spiritual world of the church and to act quite inconsistently with that in the so-called real world. As we saw in chapter 3 those who wish to worship in a more holistic way often gather in alternative feminist communities, where they share a safe space to integrate their lives as well as work out how to advocate for "sister outsider" in their institutional church settings.

There are also at least two other reasons that patriarchy has difficulty driving Christian feminists out of the church. The first is that the church as the people of God belongs to all of us, and there is no reason why uppity women and men should allow themselves to be squeezed out of the community. Not only are there many men and women who both need and welcome our various ministries and who themselves might be ready for a liberation journey, but there are countless people in our society who look to us to oppose the reinforcement of patriarchal privilege through religious blessings of the status quo.

The second reason is that the call to transform the Christian tradition and to renew it according to the Gospel message of Jesus Christ is an "old, old story." Whether or not our tradition is congregational, reformed, or catholic, if it is a Christian tradition, it is founded on a Gospel story about someone who confronted the unjust religious practices of his or her own time and paid the cost of living as if the reign of God had already arrived. This story has constantly to be retold and our church structures and teachings rethought in order to make clear its message of good news for all those marginal to religion and society who are central to God's love and care. Those who have experienced this story as life-giving know they must work to transform the ways the tradition allows it to become death-dealing in the lives of women and of the many persons who have suffered persecution because the church places them "outside the camp" of God's favor (Heb. 13:13).

Instead of worrying that we will lose our faith as feminists, we should be celebrating the fact that we have been given gifts that will allow us to talk back to tradition. We should be claiming a voice at the center of the church as interpreters of what it means to followers of Christ in contemporary society. As hooks says in *Talking Back,* "It should be understood that the liberatory voice will necessarily confront, disturb, demand that listeners even alter ways of hearing and being."[48]

We need to talk back as feminist interpreters who are no longer willing to allow talk about God, about ourselves, or about the church to continue in its patriarchal framework of understanding and interpretation. Iconoclasm of patriarchy and its interpretation of God is not a loss of faith, as we can see in Alice Walker's description of Celie trying to get the whiteness and maleness of God off her eyeballs. Rather, it is a liberation to experience God in all that is around us and within us in the world.[49]

As you know, feminist theology and ethics are full of this talking back by means of hermeneutics of suspicion and reconstruction of biblical and church tradition. For instance, the topic headings from the recent feminist collection *Weaving the Visions: New Patterns of Feminist Spirituality* represent writings from different faith traditions in order to present theology in a different voice and to reinterpret what the editors, Carol Christ and Judith Plaskow, call "traditional theological categories of history, God, man, and the world" in the light of very diverse experiences of women.[50]

Perhaps if we recall that "tradition" has many meanings it will be easier to see how it is possible to come to a feminist perspective on tradition, work to transform it rather than abandon it, and join the many other women who nurture their spirituality through new forms of religious life. As we saw in chapter 2, we often talk back to biblical and church tradition by appealing to the action of God in traditioning Jesus Christ into our lives. This Tradition of God handing over Jesus Christ into the hands of all generations and nations is a tradition that speaks of the divine intention to mend creation and make it whole. In our work for justice, peace, and the integrity of creation we appeal to the God who reaches out to welcome the outsider. In appealing to this action as known in Christ, feminist Christians honor their Christian commitment as partners in Christ's work and claim the right to give an account of their hope in ways that bring the interpretations of tradition alive in communities of faith and struggle.

Opening the circle

Christian feminist spirituality is being constantly challenged, not only to talk back to tradition but also to be a part of the transformation of that tradition so that it speaks of the love of God as an open circle of welcome to all persons. Often the spirituality practiced by feminists puts together our sense of embodiment and of transcendence with many other rich faith traditions from past and present. As Rosemary Ruether has indicated in *Women-Church,* feminist liturgical communities draw on many traditions in order to counteract patriarchal damage, and we now seek to "go back behind the biblical religion and to transcend it."[51]

One of the many places that the sister circle has tried to open up the tradition in new ways so that women of all colors and faiths can share in an exploration of their faith journeys is the Women's Theological Center that was described in chapter 5. The study/action program provides an alternative year of community living, action, and theological reflection for seminary students.[52] It also sponsors a program for exploring black women's spiritual resources for love and political struggle. The program title is a quote from Alice Walker's description of a Womanist, or feminist of color, as someone who "loves herself—*regardless.*"[53]

In reporting about the Loves Herself program, Donna Bivens and Renae Scott have indicated that this is a program of spirituality that does not talk about spirituality, because spirituality has so often been misused in otherworldly or "pie in the sky" religious teachings. In addition, African American women's spirituality is connected and integrated into their entire life, and when everything is religious it is not always necessary to name it. Instead they seek to widen the sister circle and nurture its growth and support by using the word "community," rather than "spirituality," and nurturing a community that allows women to love themselves and to love their people. Regardless![54] This is "spirituality without a name," a spirituality of sisters connecting personally and politically for the purpose of transformation and healing.

The program of regular meetings and retreats provides a place for women to be themselves with others. It seeks to be a safe space where women feel at home so that the fractured pieces of their lives can come back together. It provides a community of African American women who can make connections with other political activists, who are each involved in their own issues but need a way to form supportive networks and friendships. The program is a place of healing through the telling of stories and being heard into speech, so that there can be new naming of reality together with others. This sister circle has opened itself to a sister spirituality that is embodied in a community of faith and struggle, connected to our Christian faith traditions yet transforming those traditions through the connections to women's lives.[55]

If our feminist spirituality is a spirituality of connection to communities of faith and struggle, then we need to know not only how to make the choices that connect us to God, to ourselves, and to our neighbors in the margins of life but also how to recognize the grace-filled moments when we experience the coming together of the bits and pieces of our lives in a way that transcends the sum of the parts and nurtures the connections.

We call this experience of well-being and wholeness an *experience of spirituality* because in the Christian tradition it is the Spirit of God that moves us in this way, at once disturbing us and yet filling us with the power of God's love. We also recognize such short-lived moments as gifts of God's grace, free gifts of the power of love to move in and through the everyday moments to a deeper dimension of connectedness. All of our life is a gift of God and is sustained by the presence and power of God's Spirit, so that all of our life can be one of spirituality in which we practice the God connection in our lives. Yet the moments of overplus, to use Margaret Farley's word, where we experience joy and wholeness, help us to stay connected.

These moments may happen in prayer, in church worship, in retreat, at dinner, in bed, on quiet walks in the woods, or on marches to Washington. They happen wherever you find yourself most connected, and yet they happen in very unexpected ways. For those who practice spirituality of connection, the moments are most likely to happen when very different people come together in a surprising experience of community that supports and lifts us.

This has happened to me a couple of times recently in small group discussions on feminist theology, and I must say that I could only thank God for that gift. It also has happened in larger groups such as a conference of the Women's Theological Center in Boston on Whose World? What Order? It was not the speeches, or the ritual, or even lunch in a high school cafeteria that did it. It was connecting with a mixture of women of different races, classes, faiths, and sexual orientations who nevertheless (at least for those few hours) were willing to trust one another and to share their common struggles for transformation of this society's disorder.

Unfortunately for feminists, this experience seldom happens in institutional church structures, because churches seldom practice a spirituality of connection to the margin, and there is often not enough diversity to tempt the Spirit to make us all one. Yet many of us continue to participate in these structures in order to be part of the transformation of church life. And even here, occasionally, we are blessed by an outpouring of the Spirit, who always blows wherever she will!

How do we recognize this experience of spirituality of connection when it happens? What are some of the clues to this experience? In a way this is easy because we feel it as an experience of joy, and because we already know that the experience can be fostered by working on our connections. In another way it is difficult to describe such an experience of embodied spirituality. The best clues that I can give are that at such moments of grace there is synergy, serendipity, and sharing.[56]

Synergy refers to the overplus of the sum to the parts. In spirituality of connection we discover that the Spirit is at work when those who are gathered together experience a multiplication of energy, joy, and empowerment that is not equal to the amount of energy or gifts brought to the group by the participants. There we are with all the same difficult and different people and an ordinary agenda, but the Spirit multiplies that into an experience of wonderful people, including ourselves!

Serendipity comes from Serendip, an old word for Sri Lanka, and refers to a fairy story of a prince searching for his fortune who keeps finding other most marvelous things along the way. So, too, spirituality of connection goes on in its difficult struggling way of solidarity day by day, and yet at certain moments we are surprised by joy—joy in the midst of struggle that we know to be a pure gift of God's love.

Sharing is both the basis of the experience of spirituality of connection and the result of that experience. What happens is that we are suddenly connected and energized to share not only with our immediate community but with others who call out to us as our brothers and sisters in need (Matt. 25:31–46). For what we experience as "sister spirit" reaches out and overflows as all women, men, and children and all nature and creation are included in God's gift of partnership.

If we return once more to the story of Henna Han and her ministry with Korean-American women we can catch a glimpse of one moment in which the spirituality of connection was discovered in a coming together of synergy, serendipity, and sharing. It often happens that reaching out to women who are in difficulty because of moving to the United States as wives of G.I.s leads to new challenges. One of these was an appeal from

Koreans living in North Carolina who were struggling to free Chong Sun France from a twenty-seven year sentence in a maximum security prison in Raleigh. A New York Free France Committee was formed by Henna Han and four other women in response to the challenge.[57]

Chong Sun France had come to the United States with a G.I. but was divorced in 1982. Subsequently she had two children with another man but ran away to North Carolina to escape this man's violence toward her and the children. There a tragic accident occurred. She could only find work at night and couldn't afford a baby-sitter. Leaving the children at home in bed with the TV going she went to work, only to find on return that her son had smothered to death under the dresser when he had tried to climb up to adjust the TV. When the police arrived, Chong Sun said in very limited English, "I killed him. It is my fault." This is a Korean woman's typical and traditional response to any tragedy that befalls her children. The police mistook it for a confession of guilt. Without even the benefit of a translator she was tried and convicted of murder and sentenced to a prison term in an isolated cell, not allowed to receive newspapers, magazines, or letters written in Korean.[58]

Joining this national and international struggle to free Chong Sun France, the New York Committee traveled by car to North Carolina to interview the prisoner, to bring her news of her Korean relatives, and support the local committee in its appeal to the governor for a pardon. On the long trip they rehearsed what they had to do and why they were doing it and, very importantly, their recognition that Chong Sun is in prison because she is a poor foreign woman who could find no other means of support for herself and her children than working in bars at night. As one of us, Sook Min Mullinax, said, "I could be in her place, for I am the same age and I am married to a man of another race." As I helped work for her release I began to see what the violation of human rights and the oppression of poor women is all about.[59]

The process of this discovery both during and after the trip to North Carolina was a moment of spiritual awakening for the women who had sought to open the circle of their community to Chong Sun France. The call to action was itself unexpected and serendipitous, as were the unexpected gifts of the Spirit that gave them the courage needed for a campaign against great odds. They discovered a synergy in this and their many other gatherings that made them "almost like church," as the needed energy multiplied for the task of confronting the powerful prison officials and the governor and organizing a national and international campaign. The intimate circle of sharing in the car as partners around the task of restoring human rights to Chong Sun France formed a community of connection and care that was a gift of liberating spirituality in their lives.

Round table partnership

As we seek to discern the way that spirituality of connection is practiced by those who are in search of a round table church, it is not always easy to discern the way God may be at work in a community of faith and struggle. The difficulties are clearly underlined in the lives of any of us who have sought to live out a feminist ecclesiology of church in the round while our efforts are ignored, questioned, or rejected. These difficulties have been with the gathered Christian communities from their beginning. This is why Paul, while emphasizing our unity as partners in the resurrected body of Christ, also makes clear that not everything that happens in the church at Corinth is inspired by the empowering Spirit of the risen Christ. It would seem that the some of the church leaders, especially the women prophets, have "gotten out of hand" and do not respect his authority. For instance, they pray and prophesy without covering their heads because they understand themselves as a new creation in Christ, and not, as Paul tries to show in 1 Corinthians 11:1–16, subject to their husbands who are their head.[60]

In 1 Corinthians 12, Paul seeks to provide a few guidelines for what it might mean to be gathered in the round as partners in the Spirit. Even though we need to be critical of the text because of our suspicion that Paul is using his arguments for unity in order to suppress the authority of the women, we can be assisted by his description of the meaning of partnership. With his Trinitarian allusions in verses 4–6, Paul affirms that there is partnership among God, Christ, and the Holy Spirit. They work together for the common good and together provide the basis of new life.[61] This affirmation is echoed in 2 Corinthians with the blessing: "The grace of the Lord Jesus Christ, the love of God, and the communion [partnership; *koinonia*] of the Holy Spirit be with all of you" (2 Cor. 13:13).

Koinonia, participation in or with Christ, is the basis of Christian community, and it is the Spirit that connects us with Christ, making this partnership possible.

In the midst of division and chaos in the Corinthian church, the guidelines for sharing of the Spirit not only point toward the koinonia of a Trinitarian God but also to the koinonia of members of the church. Baptized into a new relationship in Jesus Christ, they share in his life, death, and resurrection and are set free for Christ's service. The community itself, as the place where Christ is Lord, becomes the firstfruits of the resurrection and is called to manifest that new life as partners with Christ in a life style of service and hospitality to others.

The first guideline of partnership is that *Jesus and the Spirit are one.* Ecstasy and supernatural gifts in worship are to be judged not by the manner of the experience but rather by their content. If the Spirit is the power of the risen Lord at work in the church and in the world, its actions are consistent with those of Jesus. Teachings that contradict his life and message are not inspired by the Spirit of Christ, according to verse 3.

The second guideline is that *the spiritual gift is for the common good* of the congregation and of its mission to witness to Christ's welcome by its word and work. If it destroys the partnership in the Spirit, it is not a gift that serves the common good. This does not mean that all will agree, or that all will have the same gifts, but rather that the different gifts of the Spirit contribute to partnership in worship and service. Thus in verses 8–10 the gifts seem to be in pairs so it is clear that they are not uniform and that one is able to correct and interpret the other.

In the discussion of unity in the church and partnership in the Spirit, Paul uses the metaphor of the body to indicate a third guideline: *Different gifts are not an occasion for pride.* The gifts are present because the entire church in all its members are partners in Christ's resurrected body, and all the riotous varieties of gifts and members are needed for its service and witness in the world. Spirituality is not something otherworldly but is connected to the ongoing life of the church as Christ's body, where true worship includes putting one's body on the line on behalf of the outsider as an offering to God.

Partnership without hierarchy is a key metaphor for the church which, unfortunately, is lost both here in 1 Corinthians 11:1–16 and in Ephesians 4:15–16, when Jesus is designated as the head rather than the whole body in which we are partners. In both cases it would seem that the language of headship is an attempt to return to the paradigm of authority as domination by male heads of households and subordination of females, slaves, and other less powerful groups. In Corinthians the situation in the church is very fluid and Paul's convictions about New Creation are often mixed with the patriarchal expedience of "old creation." For instance, as we saw in chapter 2, 1 Corinthians 12:27–31 describes gifts that seem to allude to offices in the church, such as apostle, prophet, teacher, but at the same time this possible hierarchy is undercut as Paul speaks of the final guideline, striving "for the greater gifts" of faith, hope, and love. All gifts ultimately have to be tested according to whether they convey the love of God to the world and to creation itself. In this way there is freedom, but only in terms of that which expresses love, care, hospitality, and partnership with others (Gal. 5:1–15).

Partnership in the Spirit makes it possible to "Welcome one another . . . just as Christ has welcomed you, for the glory of God" (Rom. 15:7). The Spirit creates a lively and vibrant community in the round where persons of different classes, nationalities, and genders are made welcome in the name of God's love. "For in the one Spirit we were all baptized into one body—Jews or Greeks, slaves or free—and we were all made to drink of one Spirit" (1 Cor. 12:13).

Hidden in this statement, however, is another ambiguity of Paul's welcoming of women and fear of women in his ministry. Antionette Wire has pointed out that it is probably because of his argument with the uppity women prophets in the Corinthian church that Paul leaves out the "no longer male and female" phrase that occurs in what appears to be a baptismal confession more fully stated in Galatians 3:27–28.[62] This confession is familiar to the churches as well as to Paul and alludes back to the creation of male and female in the image of God (Gen. 1:27–28; Gen. 5:1b–2). It affirms that through baptism in Christ there is a new creation in which the interpretation of Genesis as legitimizing separate roles and male privilege no longer has any authority in the life of the congregation.[63]

Paul works hard to make clear the meaning of partnership in Christ, and of the welcome that all receive as they gather at the round table in the community to share in the breaking of bread. Yet even here we see the way in which a particular dispute over his authority leads him to fall back on traditions of male domination and try to undercut the baptismal confession of the transforming power of the waters of baptism. It is no wonder that God has to keep on doing "a new thing" when the old passes away with such great difficulty (Isa. 43:19). Nevertheless, the tensions and alienations so visible in Corinth can serve to encourage us all as we also try to find our way beyond these divisions and join the Corinthian sisters in making "room for the Spirit" at the round table.

In our own time and place we keep discovering signs of this new thing of welcome and hospitality in the midst of former places of exclusion and keep rejoicing in these small signs in spite of their ambiguities. One small new sign occurred recently at Yale as the university tried to make some connection to the women whom it for so long refused to acknowledge or welcome. Across from its main library there is going to be a new monument. Of course, building monuments is nothing new, but this one was designed by Maya Lin, a graduate of the Yale Architectural School, who designed the Vietnam War Memorial in Washington, D.C., and the Civil Rights Memorial in Selma, Alabama. The new memorial, part of the celebration of the twentieth anniversary of women attending Yale College, is named Women's Table. The sculpture will be a large elliptical table of green granite on a blue stone base and will incorporate water bubbling from the top and flowing in sheets off the surface of the stone. It will be placed in the center of the campus so that students can gather round the table and be refreshed by its everflowing stream.

As the water wells up from the center it will spiral out across the names of representative Yale women in each class since 1870 (the university, though not Yale College, has admitted women since then) and, symbolically, will include those who have been marginal to the community in a sister circle of life, struggle, and tradition. There is no baptism and no eucharistic table here, but there is a welcome table with many connections to the waters of life and the sacrifices of lives that often received little more than crumbs from the patriarchal table. Although it is made of stone, perhaps the Women's Table can be a symbol of the round table for us, helping us to remember the spirituality that brings both trouble and beauty to our lives, a spirituality of connection to sister choice, sister outsider, and sister circle.

After all these many words, I hope to leave you with images of the sisters' choice quilt and sisters' welcome table as an encouragement to *stay well connected*. Stay well connected *to our embodied selves* and question the dualism of those who try to separate us from our own bodies and from our own kitchen table realities. Stay well connected *to your communities of faith and struggle* and question those who use dogma to prevent spiritual gifts of transformation from being shared at the round table. Stay connected as well *to the margins* and question those who perpetuate contradictions and structures of domination that deny the hospitality of God's welcome table to the "outsiders." For those who wish to open themselves and their churches to what new thing God might be doing in their lives, I can only say, "Stay well connected," and perhaps you will discover the gift of church in the round in and through the many table connections that disturb and nourish us day by day.

Notes

Full publishing information not presented here appears in the Bibliography.

Preface

1. See "Church and World: The Unity of the Church and the Renewal of Human Community." An example of this work in the National Council of Churches of Christ in the U.S.A. is Letty M. Russell, ed., *The Church with AIDS: Renewal in the Midst of Crisis.*
2. Letty M. Russell, *Household of Freedom: Authority in Feminist Theology*, pp. 25–26. This book will follow *Household of Freedom* in speaking of the kingdom of God as "household of God," the church as "household of faith," and the signs of God's household both within and outside the church as "household of freedom."
3. Letty M. Russell, *Christian Education in Mission* (Philadelphia: Westminster Press, 1967).
4. Paul Minear, *Images of the Church in the New Testament* (Philadelphia: Westminster Press, 1960). For a current discussion of the predominant images, see Peter C. Hodgson, *Revisioning the Church: Ecclesial Freedom in the New Paradigm*, pp. 28–35.
5. Minear, *Images*, pp. 67, 259. Minear uses "fellowship in faith" rather than "partnership in faith," but he is translating the same word: *koinonia*. See Letty M. Russell, *The Future of Partnership* (Philadelphia: Westminster Press, 1979), pp. 106–107.
6. Rosemary Radford Ruether, *Women-Church: Theology and Practice of Feminist Liturgical Communities;* Elisabeth Schüssler Fiorenza, *Bread Not Stone: The Challenge of Feminist Biblical Interpretation.*
7. See Letty M. Russell, ed., *Feminist Interpretation of the Bible.*
8. Paul D. Hanson, *The People Called: The Growth of Community in the Bible.*

Part One: Round Table Connection

1. Chuck Lathrop, "In Search of a Roundtable," in *A Gentle Presence*, p. 5. This

poem was first brought to my attention by Virginia Davidson, an elder at the Downtown United Presbyterian Church, Rochester, N.Y. See Virginia West Davidson, "Ministry: A Partnership Affair," unpublished dissertation, Colgate Rochester Divinity School/Bexley Hall/Crozer Theological Seminary, Aug. 1990, pp. 101–102.

2. See Kwok Pui-lan, ed., "Women, Church, China" in *In God's Image* 10:3 (Autumn, 1991). The entire volume includes essays by the participants on their experiences of gathering together with women and men in churches, seminaries, and YWCAs in China.

3. C. S. Song, *Jesus, The Crucified People* (Bloomington, Ind.: Meyer-Stone Books, 1989), pp. 191–203.

4. Paul Minear, *Images of the Church in the New Testament* (Philadelphia: Westminster Press, 1960), pp. 262.

5. The NRSV version of the Bible presents the Old and New Testaments and the Apocrypha as Hebrew Scriptures, Deuterocanonical Books, and New Testament. See "The Number and Sequence of the Books of the Bible," *The New Oxford Annotated Bible: New Revised Standard Version*, ed. Bruce M. Metzger and Roland E. Murphy (New York: Oxford University Press, 1991), pp. xxi–xxiii. Many scholars prefer to change the name of the Old Testament in order to recognize that the Hebrew Scriptures are the full scriptures for the Jewish people. The word "deuterocanonical" indicates that these books, which are part of the Roman Catholic, Greek Orthodox, and Slavonic Bibles, are not apocryphal, or "hidden," but rather books that were included after the closing of the Hebrew canon.

The Greek translation of the Hebrew Testament, or Septuagint, is often called the Greek Scriptures. Although Daniel 2:4b to 7:28 is written in Aramaic, most of the Old Testament is written in Hebrew, and it is part of the authoritative canon of all Christian faith traditions. The Deuterocanonical Books are written in Hebrew, Aramaic, and Greek, but the New Testament is entirely in Greek. There is no one adequate way to designate the scriptures that is acceptable to everyone. In this book I will use Hebrew Testament, Deuterocanonical Books, and Greek Testament. In doing so, I wish to symbolize that the scriptures belong to various faith traditions and the designation of the collections by reference to the language or sequence categories is an attempt to be neutral in describing those scriptures.

6. Minear, *Images*, pp. 66, 36–42.

7. Minear, *Images*, p. 37.

8. See Beverly Wildung Harrison, *Making the Connections: Essays in Feminist Social Ethics*, ed. Carol S. Robb (Boston: Beacon Press, 1985).

1: Round Table Talk

1. Paul S. Minear, *Commands of Christ* (Nashville: Abingdon Press, 1972), pp. 179–

180. See also John Koenig, *New Testament Hospitality: Partnership with Strangers as Promise and Mission*, pp. 85–123; David P. Moessner, *Lord of the Banquet: The Literary and Theological Significance of the Lukan Travel Narrative* (Minneapolis: Fortress Press, 1989), p. 2.

2. "The Ministry of All Christians—Mission and Ministry of the Church, Section VI: The Journey of a Connectional People," *The Book of Discipline of the United Methodist Church* (Nashville: United Methodist Publishing House, 1988), pp. 116–117. This material on connectionalism was provided by Ann Craig, Women's Division, The United Methodist Church.

3. Jon Sobrino, *Spirituality of Liberation: Toward Political Holiness*, p. 147.

4. Dorothy L. Sayers, *Are Women Human?* (Grand Rapids: Wm. B. Eerdmans Publishing Co., 1947), p. 47.

5. Heinrich Heppe, *Reformed Dogmatics*, ed. Ernst Bizer, trans. G. T. Thomson (London: George Allen & Unwin, 1950), pp. 530–534. See Letty M. Russell, *Human Liberation in a Feminist Perspective—A Theology* (Philadelphia: Westminster Press, 1974), p. 125.

6. See Emerito Nacpil, "The Critical Asian Principle," in *Asian Christian Theology*, ed. Douglas J. Elwood (Philadelphia: Westminster Press, 1980), pp. 56–59. Quoted in Virginia Fabella, ed., *Asia's Struggle for Full Humanity: Towards a Relevant Theology* (Maryknoll, N.Y.: Orbis Books, 1980), p. 5. The same term is sometimes used in mainstream male Eurocentric theology as well. For instance, it is employed by Gordon D. Kaufman in *The Theological Imagination*, where he speaks of a principle that is "the criterion of humanization" (Philadelphia: Westminster Press, 1981), p. 168.

7. "Toward an Asian Principle of Interpretation: A Filipino Woman's Experience," EATWOT Asian Feminist Theology Meeting, Madras, India, Dec. 15–20, 1990; mimeographed, p. 18.

8. On hospitality to those who are the "least" as a mark of holiness, see Marjorie Suchocki, "Holiness and a Renewed Community," in *The Church with AIDS: Renewal in the Midst of Crisis*, ed. Letty M. Russell, p. 116.

9. Luise Schottroff, "Women as Followers of Jesus," in *The Bible and Liberation: Political and Social Hermeneutics*, ed. Norman K. Gottwald (Maryknoll, N.Y.: Orbis Books, 1983), p. 423.

10. Dietrich Bonhoeffer, *Letters and Papers from Prison*, ed. Eberhard Bethge (New York: Macmillan Publishing Co., 1972), p. 17.

11. Gustavo Gutiérrez, *The Power of the Poor in History: Selected Writings*, trans. Robert R. Barr (Maryknoll, N.Y.: Orbis Books, 1983), p. 178.

12. Gutiérrez, *The Power of the Poor*, p. 193.

13. bell hooks, *Feminist Theory: From Margin to Center*, p. 15. bell hooks is the pen name of Gloria Watkins and is written with all lower-case letters.

14. Marilyn Frye, *The Politics of Reality: Essays in Feminist Theory*, pp. 148–150.

15. bell hooks, *Talking Back: Thinking Feminist, Thinking Black* (Boston: South End Press, 1989), p. 16.

16. Both the dangers of using the image of center and margin as well as the dynamic

aspect of the moving margin were pointed out to me by Henna Han and Nancy Martell in my class on Liberation Ecclesiology at Yale Divinity School, January 23, 1991.

17. Phyllis Trible, *Texts of Terror* (Philadelphia: Fortress Press, 1984), pp. 8–29; Elsa Tamez, "The Woman Who Complicated the History of Salvation," in *New Eyes for Reading: Biblical and Theological Reflections by Women from the Third World*, ed. John S. Pobee and Bärbel Von Wartenberg-Potter (Geneva: WCC Publications, 1986), pp. 5–17.

18. Delores S. Williams, "The Analogous Relation Between Hagar's Experience and African-American Women's Experience: A Challenge Posed to Black Liberation Theology," unpublished Ph.D. dissertation, Union Theological Seminary, New York, 1990. Williams contends that the metaphor of wilderness is more central to African American women's experience than the exodus and seeks to use Hagar's story as a basis for developing womanist theology.

19. Alice Walker, *In Search of Our Mothers' Gardens* (New York: Harcourt Brace Jovanovich, 1983), pp. xi–xii. Cited in Delores Williams, "The Analogous Relation," pp. i–ii. See Katie Geneva Cannon, *Womanist Ethics* (Atlanta: Scholars Press, 1988); Jacqueline Grant, *White Women's Christ, Black Women's Jesus* (Atlanta: Scholars Press, 1989); Delores S. Williams, "Womanist Theology: Black Women's Voices," in *Weaving the Visions*, ed. Judith Plaskow and Carol P. Christ (San Francisco: Harper & Row, 1989), pp. 178–186. In her dissertation, p. ii, Williams says other scholars who are developing womanist theology are Cheryl Townsend Gilkes, Toinette M. Eugene, Kelly Brown, Renita Weems, Clarise Martin, Marcia Riggs, Emilie M. Townes, Jacqueline Carr-Hamilton, and Joan Speaks.

20. The terms "difference and connection" were used by Williams in lecturing on the relationship of Hagar and Sarah as a "Paradigm of Difference and Connection," Yale Divinity School, April 7, 1988, in a class on Feminist Theology and Ethics taught by Margaret Farley and Letty Russell. See Delores S. Williams, "Black Women's Surrogacy Experience and the Christian Notion of Redemption," in *After Patriarchy: Feminist Transformations of the World Religions*, ed. Paula M. Cooey, William R. Eakin, and Jay B. McDaniel (Maryknoll, N.Y.: Orbis Books, 1991), pp. 1–14.

21. Williams's dissertation, pp. 72–73.

22. See forthcoming manuscript by Phyllis Trible on "The Sacrifice of Sarah," available on tape from the 1991 Caldwell Lectures, Louisville Presbyterian Theological Seminary, 1044 Alta Vista Road, Louisville, KY 40205. This story of sacrifice points to the necessity of rereading it from the perspective of abused children and those who have been sacrificed by their parents, although there is little in the story to help us with that particular task except the indication that one of the sources for the tradition was the Hebrew belief that God does not desire human sacrifice.

23. Trible, *Texts of Terror*, p. 18. See Elsa Tamez, "The Woman Who Complicated the History of Salvation," *New Eyes for Reading*, pp. 5–17.

24. Delores Williams's dissertation, pp. 373–375.

25. "Come Out de Wilderness," in *Songs of Zion* (Nashville: Abingdon Press, 1981), No. 136. For the significance of the wilderness see D. Williams's dissertation, "The Analogous Relation," pp. 114–119.

26. Mercy Amba Oduyoye, "Reflections from a Third World Woman's Perspective," in *Irruption of the Third World: Challenge to Theology*, Papers from the Fifth International Conference of the Ecumenical Association of Third World Theologians, August 17–19, 1981, New Delhi, India, ed. Virginia Fabella and Sergio Torres (Maryknoll, N.Y.: Orbis Books, 1983), p. 247.

In using the term "Third World" in my book I concur with the description given by the editors of this EATWOT volume, p. xii: "The term 'Third World,' which first came into use two decades ago, is still in popular usage. Unlike faddish expressions destined to fade away after a brief passage of time, 'Third World' has acquired instead layers of meaning which vary from the purely geographic ('the South') to the socioeconomic ('poor,' 'underdeveloped') to the political ('nonaligned') and even the theological ('from the underside of history'). To those who met in Delhi, Third Worldness is characterized by massive poverty and oppression."

Not all of the people who live in the Two Thirds World (outside the Euro-American First World and what used to be the Eastern block Second World) are marginal, but the majority are marginal and live in poverty. Many of those in the First and Second worlds are also marginal to the social and economic privileges of their own societies, but they dwell in modern nations that have controlled political, military, and economic forces. Although not synonymous, the terms "marginal" and "Third World" are both indicators of those who are searching for empowerment as full participants in decisions that affect their lives and the world in which they live.

27. Beverly Wildung Harrison, ed., *Making the Connections: Essays in Social Ethics* (Boston: Beacon Press, 1985), pp. 249–263; Katie Geneva Cannon, unpublished lectures in a course titled "Feminist Theology in Third World Perspective," Yale Divinity School, January 1987.

28. See Letty M. Russell, "A Model for Bible Study in Context," in *Changing Contexts of Our Faith*, ed. Letty M. Russell (Philadelphia: Fortress Press, 1985), pp. 102–108.

29. Global Women of Faith in Dialogue/Asian and Asian-American Women in Theology and Ministry, Stony Point Center, N.Y., March 21–23, 1991.

30. Chung Hyun Kyung, "Welcome the Spirit; Hear Her Cries: The Holy Spirit, Creation, and the Culture of Life," *Christianity and Crisis*, 51:10/11 (July 15, 1991), pp. 220–223; Chung Hyun Kyung, "Following Naked Dancing and Long Dreaming," in *Inheriting Our Mothers' Gardens*, ed. Letty M. Russell, Kwok Pui-lan, Ada María Isasi-Díaz, and Katie Geneva Cannon (Philadelphia: Westminster Press, 1988), pp. 54–72.

31. For a discussion of *han* see Chung Hyun Kyung, *Struggle to Be the Sun Again: Introducing Asian Women's Theology*, p. 42.

32. Robert McAfee Brown, "What Is Contextual Theology?" in *Changing Contexts of Our Faith*, ed. Letty M. Russell, pp. 89–94.

33. Frye, *The Politics of Reality*, p. 155.

34. Michael Kinnamon, *Truth and Community: Diversity and Its Limits in the Ecumenical Movement*, pp. 15–18, 111–115.

35. "Church and World: The Unity of the Church and the Renewal of Human Community," pp. 3–4.

36. Bert Hoedemaker, "Comments on the Relation Between Situational Analysis and Ecclesiological Discussion," unpublished paper (Groningen, Netherlands, Christmas 1985), p. 7.

37. Deotis Roberts, informal remarks presented at a panel on Taking Stock of Theology in America Today, American Theological Society, Princeton Theological Seminary, April 24, 1987. See also J. Deotis Roberts, *Black Theology in Dialogue* (Philadelphia: Westminster Press, 1987).

38. "Simple Gifts," in *Sisters and Brothers, Sing!* 2nd ed., ed. Sharon Neufer Emswiler and Tom Neufer Emswiler (The Wesley Foundation Campus Ministry, 211 North School Street, Normal, IL 61761, 1977), p. 17. The similarity of this hymn and the theological spiral was pointed out by David O'Malley, a former student at Yale Divinity School.

39. hooks, *Talking Back*, pp. 10–18.

40. Elisabeth Schüssler Fiorenza, *Bread Not Stone: The Challenge of Feminist Biblical Interpretation*, p. xiv. In her article in *The Christian Century* titled, "Changing the Paradigms," Fiorenza cites Susan Moller Okin, *Women in Political Thought*, as helping her understand the roots of patriarchy, ". . . a sociopolitical graduated male pyramid of systemic dominations and subordinations [that] found its classical articulation in Aristotelian philosophy, which restricts full citizenship to Greek propertied, freeborn, male heads of households. The order of the patriarchal household becomes the model for the order of the state. It excludes freeborn women, slaves, and barbarians—women and men—from citizenship and public leadership because their 'natures' do not make them fit to 'rule.'" *Christian Century* 107:25 (Sept. 5–12, 1990), p. 799. See also Elisabeth Schüssler Fiorenza, "The Politics of Otherness: Biblical Interpretation as a Critical Praxis of Liberation," in *The Future of Liberation Theology*, ed. Marc H. Ellis and Otto Maduro (Maryknoll, N.Y.: Orbis Books, 1988), pp. 311–325.

41. Audre Lorde, "The Transformation of Silence Into Language and Action," in her *Sister Outsider*, pp. 40–44.

42. Rosemary Radford Ruether, "Sexism as Ideology and Social System: Can Christianity Be Liberated from Patriarchy?" in *With Both Eyes: Seeing Beyond Gender*, ed. Patricia Johnson and Janet Kalven (New York: Pilgrim Press, 1988), pp. 162–163.

43. Judith Plaskow and Carol P. Christ, eds., *Weaving the Visions: New Patterns in Feminist Spirituality* (San Francisco: Harper & Row, 1989), pp. 1, 9.

44. See Letty M. Russell, *Human Liberation in a Feminist Perspective—A Theology* (Philadelphia: Westminster Press, 1974), pp. 74–80.

45. Paul S. Minear, ed., *Faith and Order Findings* (London: SCM Press, 1963), pp. 16–18. See Yves Congar, *Tradition and Traditions*, trans. A. N. Woodrow (London: Burns & Oates, 1966).

46. Congar, *Tradition*, pp. 287–288.

47. Russell, *Human Liberation*, p. 75.

48. Rita Nakashima Brock, unpublished speech at a meeting of the Asian and Asian-American Women in Theology and Ministry, Princeton Theological Seminary, May 30, 1990.

49. See Ruether, *Sexism and God-Talk*; Fiorenza, *Bread Not Stone*; Letty M. Russell, *Household of Freedom: Authority in Feminist Theology*; as well as the expansion of this discussion in Susan Brooks Thistlethwaite and Mary Potter Engel, eds., *Lift Every Voice: Constructing Christian Theologies from the Underside*, pp. 259–291.

50. See Russell, *Household of Freedom*; Richard Sennett, *Authority* (New York: Vintage Books, 1981).

51. David H. Kelsey, *The Uses of Scripture in Recent Theology* (Philadelphia: Fortress Press, 1975), pp. 167–175, 194.

52. Carol P. Christ, "Why Women Need the Goddess: Phenomenological, Psychological, and Political Reflections," in *Womanspirit Rising: A Feminist Reader in Religion*, ed. Carol P. Christ and Judith Plaskow (San Francisco: Harper & Row, 1979), pp. 273–286.

53. Robert J. Schreiter, *Constructing Local Theologies*, pp. 113–121.

54. Ibid., p. 115.

55. The analogy between theological "grammar" and "round table manners" was pointed out to me in conversation by Serene Jones, June 1992.

56. Schreiter, *Constructing Local Theologies*, p. 117. For the emphasis on Bible as a historical *prototype* that can be critically evaluated by the church of women rather than as an eternal *archetype* that must be accepted or rejected see Fiorenza, *Bread Not Stone*, pp. 9–10.

57. Paul D. Hanson, *The People Called: The Growth of Community in the Bible*, p. 467.

58. Raymond E. Brown, *Biblical Exegesis and Church Doctrine* (New York: Paulist Press, 1985), pp. 114–119.

59. Peter C. Hodgson, *Revisioning the Church: Ecclesial Freedom in the New Paradigm*, p. 25.

60. Paul S. Minear, "Church: Idea of," *The Interpreter's Dictionary of the Bible*, ed. George A. Buttrick (Nashville: Abingdon Press, 1962), vol. 1, p. 608.

61. Gutiérrez, *The Power of the Poor*, pp. 210–211.

62. Hans Küng, *The Church*, p. 13.

63. James Viterbo, *De Regimine Christiano*. Cited in "Church," by Marie-Joseph le Guillou, in *Sacramentum Mundi*, ed. Karl Rahner (New York: Herder & Herder, 1968), vol. 1, p. 317.

64. Küng, *The Church*, pp. 30–35. See also Karl Barth, *The Faith of the Church: A Commentary on the Apostles' Creed according to Calvin's Catechism*, ed. Jean-Louis Leuba, trans. Gabriel Vahanian (New York: Meridian Books, 1958), pp. 148–149; also "Confessing the One Faith," p. 16.

65. Dorothee Sölle, *Thinking About God: An Introduction to Theology* (Philadelphia: Trinity Press International, 1990), pp. 137–138.

2: Leadership in the Round

1. Henry Frith, *King Arthur and His Knights* (Garden City, N.Y.: Garden City Publishing Co., 1932), p. 69. See also the contemporary feminist version of this tale by Marion Zimmer Bradley, *The Mists of Avalon* (New York: Ballantine Books, 1982).

2. The idea about "courtly advisers, castle help, and peasants" was suggested to me by Joan Martin, June 17, 1992.

3. "To the Knights in the Days of Old," or "Follow the Gleam," words copyright by the National Board of the YWCA and music copyright by Sallie Hume Douglas, 1920. See "Follow the Gleam," *Premier Hymns*, ed. R. E. Magill and B. D. Ackley (Richmond: John Knox Press, 1926), p. 133.

4. Karl Rahner, "Supernatural Order," in *Sacramentum Mundi: An Encyclopedia of Theology*, ed. Karl Rahner (New York: Herder & Herder, 1969), vol. 4, pp. 297–300.

5. Gerhard Ebeling, *Word and Faith*, trans. James W. Leitch (Philadelphia: Fortress Press, 1963), pp. 363–364.

6. "Baptism, Eucharist, and Ministry," pp. 20–32.

7. Letty M. Russell, *Human Liberation in a Feminist Perspective—A Theology* (Philadelphia: Westminster Press, 1974), p. 176.

8. Jürgen Moltmann, *The Church in the Power of the Spirit*, p. 292.

9. See "Flight from Ministry," in Letty M. Russell, *The Future of Partnership* (Philadelphia: Westminster Press, 1979), p. 133.

10. Lynn N. Rhodes, *Co-Creating: A Feminist Vision of Ministry*, pp. 11–24.

11. Musimbi R. A. Kanyoro, "A Lutheran Pilgrimage: My Dilemma," unpublished manuscript of a lecture given at the Lutheran Theological Seminary, Saskatoon, Saskatchewan, Canada, May 8–10, 1991, p. 4 (mimeographed). See other examples in Ella P. Mitchell, ed., *Those Preachin' Women: Sermons by Black Women* (Valley Forge, Pa.: Judson Press, 1985), and the illustration in this chapter of Henna Han's ministry in the Rainbow Church.

12. For instance, "Ordination: A Questionable Goal for Women," *The Ecumenist* 11:5 (July–Aug. 1973), p. 84; Rosemary Radford Ruether, *Women-Church: Theology and Practice of Feminist Liturgical Communities*. On page 283 Ruether says that the term "Woman Church" was first used at a conference of Roman Catholic women in November 1983 but was later changed to Women-Church to signify that there are many types of such churches, not just one. Since 1985 the Woman of the Church Coalition has adopted "the term 'women-church' when speaking of the idea and reality of the *ecclesia* of women throughout history, and 'Women-Church' when speaking about the particular historical movement and organization today." Of women-church, Elisabeth Schüssler Fiorenza says in *Bread Not Stone*, p. xiv, that it is

not exclusionary of men but a "political-oppositional term to patriarchy." She describes it as "the movement of self-identified women and women-identified men in biblical religion." For further discussion of these feminist Christian communities see chapter 3 in this book.

13. Rhodes, *Co-Creating*, pp. 17–18.

14. Barbara Brown Zikmund, "Changing Understandings of Ordination," in *The Presbyterian Predicament: Six Perspectives*, ed. Milton J Coalter, John M. Mulder, and Louis B. Weeks (Louisville, Ky.: Westminster/John Knox Press, 1990), pp. 149–158.

15. Ibid., pp. 178–179, n. 31. Zikmund is citing Jean Baker Miller, *Toward a New Psychology of Women* (Boston: Beacon Press, 1976); Carol Gilligan, *In a Different Voice: Psychological Theory and Women's Development* (Cambridge, Mass.: Harvard University Press, 1982), and other such studies.

16. See Edward Schillebeeckx, *The Church with a Human Face: A New and Expanded Theology of Ministry* (New York: Crossroad, 1985), p. 119.

17. Zikmund, "Changing Understandings," pp. 153–156.

18. Ruether, *Women-Church*, pp. 87–91.

19. See Jeanette Shannon Clarkson, "In the Beginning Was the Word: Implications of Inclusive Language for Religious Education," unpublished doctoral dissertation, Teachers College, Columbia University, 1989, p. 126.

20. Letty M. Russell, *Household of Freedom: Authority in Feminist Theology*, pp. 21–23. See Richard Sennett, *Authority* (New York: Vintage Books, 1981), pp. 16–21.

21. Fiorenza, *Bread Not Stone*, p. xiv.

22. Russell, *Household of Freedom*, p. 33.

23. Rosemary Radford Ruether, *Sexism and God-Talk: Toward a Feminist Theology*, p. 18.

24. Barbara Smith, "Racism and Women's Studies," in *All the Women Are White, All the Blacks Are Men, but Some of Us Are Brave: Black Women's Studies*, ed. Gloria T. Hull, Patricia Bell Scott, and Barbara Smith (Old Westbury, N.Y.: Feminist Press, 1982), p. 49. See bell hooks, *Feminist Theory: From Margin to Center*, p. 8.

25. Sally Helgesen, *The Female Advantage: Women's Ways of Leadership*, pp. 44–47.

26. Bernice Johnson Reagon, "Ella's Song," Songtalk Publishing Company.

27. George V. Pixley, *God's Kingdom: A Guide for Bible Study* (Maryknoll, N.Y.: Orbis Books, 1981), p. 75. See Russell, *Household of Freedom*, pp. 62–64; Audre Lorde, "The Master's Tools Will Never Dismantle the Master's House," *Sister Outsider*, pp. 110–113.

28. Elisabeth Schüssler Fiorenza, *In Memory of Her: A Feminist Theological Reconstruction of Christian Origins*, pp. 150–151.

29. Ruether, *Sexism and God-Talk*, pp. 1–11, 134–138.

30. Mary Rose D'Angelo, "Images of Jesus and the Christian Call in the Gospels of Luke and John," *Spirituality Today* 37:3 (Fall 1985), pp. 197–212. See also D'Angelo, "Images of Jesus and the Christian Vocation in the Gospels of Mark and Matthew," *Spirituality Today* 36:3 (Fall 1984), pp. 220–235.

31. The pictures of Jesus at the end of each Gospel are taken from the two articles

in *Spirituality Today* just cited. The following quotations are from vol. 36:3, pp. 220–221 and vol. 37:3, pp. 196–197.

32. Fiorenza, *In Memory of Her*, pp. 130–140. See Susan Cady, Marian Roman, and Hal Taussig, *Wisdom's Feast: Sophia in Study and Celebration* (San Francisco: Harper & Row, 1989).

33. See Letty M. Russell, "Ordination of Women," in *A New Dictionary of Liturgy and Worship*, ed. J. G. Davies (London: SCM Press, pp. 417–419).

34. Fiorenza, *In Memory of Her*, pp. 315–334.

35. Hans Küng, *The Church.*, p. 418.

36. Ibid., pp. 402–407.

37. Antionette Clark Wire, *The Corinthian Women Prophets: A Reconstruction Through Paul's Rhetoric*, pp. 135–158.

38. Fiorenza, *In Memory of Her*, pp. 300–302.

39. Elisabeth Schüssler Fiorenza, "Word, Spirit, and Power: Women in Early Christian Communities," in *Women of Spirit: Female Leadership in the Jewish and Christian Traditions*, ed. Rosemary Ruether and Eleanor McLaughlin (New York: Simon & Schuster, 1979), pp. 39–44. See also Bonnie Bowman Thurston, *The Widows: A Women's Ministry in the Early Church* (Minneapolis: Fortress Press, 1989).

40. For this history see Rosemary Ruether, "Mothers of the Church: Ascetic Women in the Late Patristic Age," and Eleanor McLaughlin, "Women, Power, and the Pursuit of Holiness in Medieval Christianity," in *Women of Spirit*, pp. 71–130.

41. Personal interview with my former student Henna Han, pastor of the Rainbow Church at Washington and Waverly Avenues, Seaford, N.Y., November 14, 1991.

42. This image of Sarah's Circle was created by Carole Ann Etzler, the singer and songwriter, who was working in the church bureaucracy at that time. See *Sometimes I Wish*, Sisters Unlimited, Atlanta, Georgia, 1976. Cited by Matthew Fox, *A Spirituality Named Compassion, and the Healing of the Global Village, Humpty Dumpty and Us* (Minneapolis: Winston Press, 1979), p. 275, n. 18.

43. *Talitha, qumi: Proceedings of the Convocation of African Women Theologians, 1989*, story told by Mercy Amba Oduyoye and Musimbi Kanyoro (Ibadan, Nigeria: Daystar Press, 1990).

44. *In God's Image*, ed. Rev. Sun Ai Lee Park, Room 802, Christian Building, 136–46 Yonchi-Dong, Chongro-Ku, Seoul, Korea.

45. Virginia Fabella and Mercy Amba Oduyoye, eds., *With Passion and Compassion: Third World Women Doing Theology*.

46. Mercy Amba Oduyoye, *Who Will Roll the Stone Away? The Ecumenical Decade of the Churches in Solidarity with Women* (Geneva: WCC Publications, 1990), p. 68.

47. Ibid., pp. 44, 50–51.

48. "Confessing the One Faith," p. 81.

49. Ernst Käsemann, *Essays on New Testament Themes*, p. 63.

50. Schillebeeckx, *The Church with a Human Face*, p. 35.

51. Käsemann, *Essays on New Testament Themes*, pp. 65–67; Schillebeeckx, *The Church with a Human Face*, p. 119.

52. Fiorenza, *In Memory of Her*, pp. 208–213.

53. Moltmann, *The Church in the Power of the Spirit*, pp. 296–300.

54. Käsemann, *Essays on New Testament Themes*, p. 69. The word "cybernetic" refers to steering or governing and is an English form of the Greek word *kubernesis*, which is translated as "leadership" in 1 Corinthians 12:28.

55. Ibid., pp. 65, 80.

56. "Co-Ministry: Some Starting Points," June 1987, p. 1 (mimeographed). Available from Virginia W. Davidson, Downtown United Presbyterian Church, 121 North Fitzhugh Street, Rochester, NY 14614. See also "Ministry: A Partnership Affair," by Virginia West Davidson, unpublished dissertation, Colgate Rochester Divinity School/Bexley Hall/Crozer Theological Seminary, August 1990.

57. For extensive discussion of authority, power, and the possibilities of exercising leadership through partnering others, see Russell, *Household of Freedom.*

58. Joan Brown Campbell, "Toward a Renewed Community of Women and Men," in *Women and Church: The Challenge of Ecumenical Solidarity in an Age of Alienation,* ed. Melanie A. May, pp. 85–87.

59. Phyllis Trible, "Bringing Miriam Out of the Shadows," *Bible Review* 5:1 (Feb. 1989), pp. 14–25, 34.

60. Leonardo Boff, *Ecclesiogenesis: The Base Communities Reinvent the Church*, p. 24.

61. Küng, *The Church*, p. 363.

62. Randall C. Bailey, "Beyond Identification: The Use of Africans in Old Testament Poetry and Narratives," in *Stony the Road We Trod: African American Biblical Interpretation*, ed. Cain Hope Felder (Minneapolis: Fortress Press, 1991), p. 179.

63. Jean Caffey Lyles, "Moves of the Spirit: Diversity or Syncretism?" *Christian Century* 108:9 (March 13, 1991), pp. 284–286.

64. "What Is the Peace and Justice Center Anyway?" Brochure from St. George Church, Guilford, Conn. See also "Ruling a Parish Divided; New Priest Seeks to Quell Instability, Independent Laity," *Hartford Courant*, Feb. 9, 1991, section A, p. 1.

65. Trible, "Bringing Miriam Out of the Shadows," pp. 19, 25.

66. Ibid., p. 19.

67. See Charlotte Bunch, "Making Common Cause: Diversity and Coalitions," in *Bridges of Power: Women's Multicultural Alliances*, ed. Lisa Albrecht and Rose M. Brewer (Philadelphia: New Society Publishers, 1990), pp. 49–57.

68. Name withheld for confidentiality. Reflection paper, Feminist Theology in Third World Perspective, Feb. 14, 1991, Yale Divinity School (unpublished), p. 5.

69. Pat Boozer, reflection paper, Feminist Theology in Third World Perspective, Feb. 14, 1991, Yale Divinity School (unpublished).

70. Doris Ellzey Blesoff, "We Are Gathered," in *Everflowing Streams*, ed. Ruth C. Duck and Michael G. Bausch (New York: Pilgrim Press, 1981), pp. 2–3.

71. Many of these ideas were tested out and challenged by my class on Liberation Theology, Yale Divinity School, Spring 1991.

72. Judy Chicago, *The Dinner Party: A Symbol of Our Heritage* (Garden City, N.Y.: Doubleday & Co., Anchor Books, 1979), p. 22.

73. See Alice Walker, "One Child of One's Own," in *In Search of Our Mothers' Gardens: Womanist Prose* (New York: Harcourt Brace Jovanovich, 1983), pp. 372–374.

74. Chicago, *The Dinner Party*, p. 56.

75. Judy Chicago, *Embroidering Our Heritage: The Dinner Party Needlework* (Garden City, N.Y.: Doubleday & Co., Anchor Books, 1980), p. 265.

76. Ibid.

Part Two: Kitchen Table Solidarity

1. *Bartlett's Familiar Quotations*, 15th ed. (New York: Little, Brown & Co., 1980), p. 788. This aphorism was used in a variety of versions by President Harry S Truman in his speeches and writings.

2. Joan Martin pointed this out to me in an informal conversation on June 17, 1992.

3. Chuck Lathrop, "In Search of a Roundtable," in *A Gentle Presence*, p. 5.

4. Elisabeth Schüssler Fiorenza, *In Memory of Her: A Feminist Reconstruction of Christian Origins*, p. 165.

5. Mary Rose D'Angelo, "Women Partners in the New Testament," *Journal of Feminist Studies in Religion* 6:1 (Spring 1990), pp. 78–79.

6. Fiorenza, *In Memory of Her*, pp. 164–167.

7. D'Angelo, "Women Partners," p. 80.

8. Fiorenza, *In Memory of Her*, pp. 169–170; D'Angelo, "Women Partners," p. 75.

3: Communities of Faith and Struggle

1. *Against Machismo*, interviews by Elsa Tamez (Oak Park, Ill.: Meyer Stone Books, 1987), p. 135. The reference to Vidales is to her interview with Raul Vidales, who says, "The conception of ordinary, everyday life as fundamental helps us understand the Last Judgment in Matthew 25, where everything is related to everyday life [p. 119]."

2. Leonardo Boff, *Ecclesiogenesis: The Base Communities Reinvent the Church*, p. 5.

3. "Introduction: The Recovery of Kairos," in *Kairos: Three Prophetic Challenges to the Church*, ed. by Robert McAfee Brown (Grand Rapids: Wm. B. Eerdmans Publishing Co., 1990), pp. 2–4.

4. Brown, *Kairos*, p. 26.

5. For an earlier version of this section on Luke 4 see Letty M. Russell, "Prophet Without Welcome," *Christian Century* 109:1 (Jan. 1–8, 1992), p. 10.

6. Sharon Ringe, *Jesus, Liberation, and the Biblical Jubilee: Images for Ethics and Christology* (Philadelphia: Fortress Press, 1985), p. 36.

7. Elsa Tamez, *The Bible and the Oppressed* (Maryknoll, N.Y.: Orbis Books, 1979).

8. Tom Hoyt, "Bible Study (Luke 6:16–30)," in *The Kairos Covenant: Standing with South African Christians*, ed. Willis H. Logan (Oak Park, Ill. and New York: Meyer Stone Books and Friendship Press, 1988), pp. 135–143. See "The Kairos Document," Section 4:5, pp. 33–34, in Brown, *Kairos*.

9. African American spiritual, "Rise, Shine, for Thy Light Is A-comin'," *Alleluia! Hymnbook for Inner-City Parishes* (Delaware, Ohio: Cooperative Recreation Service, 1962), p. 86.

10. Brown, *Kairos*, pp. 9–12.

11. Charles Villa-Vicencio, "Towards a Post-Exilic Theology: Anticipating Theology Beyond Liberation." Paper delivered at the American Academy of Religion meeting in Chicago, Nov. 1990. Parts of the paper appear in "Towards a Theology of Nation Building: Church and State in Africa Today," *Journal of Church and State*, Spring 1990. The numbers in brackets in this section represent numbers in "The Kairos Document."

12. Wade Clark Roof and William McKinney, *American Mainline Religion: Its Changing Shape and Future*, p. 6.

13. Ibid., pp. 236–237. See William McKinney, "Of Centers and Margins," *Witness* 72:1 (Jan. 1989), p. 21.

14. Rosemary Radford Ruether, "New Friends, Old Enemies," *Christianity and Crisis* 49:9 (June 12, 1989), p. 181.

15. Roof and McKinney, *American Mainline Religion*, pp. 186–187.

16. Ibid., p. 242. See Robert Wuthnow, "The Restructuring of American Presbyterianism: Turmoil in One Denomination," *The Presbyterian Predicament: Six Perspectives*, ed. Milton J Coalter, John M. Mulder, and Louis B. Weeks (Louisville, Ky.: Westminster/John Knox Press, 1990), pp. 27–46.

17. For a discussion of both the "New Paradigm" and its agenda for a new ecclesiology in contrast to the "Classic Paradigm" and its style of ecclesiology see Peter C. Hodgson, *Revisioning the Church: Ecclesial Freedom in the New Paradigm*. On paradigms of authority see Letty M. Russell, *Household of Freedom: Authority in Feminist Theology*, p. 33.

18. "Keeping Body and Soul Together: Sexuality, Spirituality, and Social Justice," p. 34. See John J. Carey, "Sexuality: What We Couldn't Say," *Christianity and Crisis* 51:12 (Aug. 19, 1991), pp. 258–259.

19. "Keeping Body and Soul Together," p. 10.

20. "The Kairos Document," Section 1.1.

21. Audrey R. Chapman, *Faith, Power, and Politics: Political Ministry in Mainline Churches* (New York: Pilgrim Press, 1991), p. 159.

22. Mary McClintock Fulkerson, "Contesting Feminist Canons: Discourse and the Problem of Sexist Texts," *Journal of Feminist Studies in Religion* 7:2 (Fall 1991), pp. 72–73.

23. Tex Sample, *U.S. Lifestyles and Mainline Churches: A Key to Reaching People in the 90's*, pp. 64–67.

24. Ibid., pp. 9–11.

25. Anthony B. Robinson, "Learning from Willow Creek Church," *Christian Century* 108:3 (Jan. 23, 1991), pp. 70–71; Cathy Lynn Grossman, "Houston's Second Baptist Pursues a King-size Mission," *USA Today*, Aug. 6, 1991, p. 4D.

26. Roof and McKinney, *American Mainline Religion*, p. 229.

27. Hodgson, *Revisioning the Church*, p. 12.

28. Ibid., p. 17.

29. In contemporary missiology and in this book, "Mission" is used to indicate God's Mission or *missio Dei*, while "mission" indicates the missionary work of the church as a participation in God's sending action.

30. Karl Barth, "Die Theologie und die Mission in der Gegenwart" [1932], *Theologische Fragen und Antworten* 5:3 (Zollikon: Evangelischer Verlag, 1957), pp. 100–126; Emil Brunner, *The Word and the World* (New York: Charles Scribner's Sons, 1931), p. 108. For a discussion of this concept of *missio Dei* see Letty M. Russell, "Tradition as Mission: Study of a New Current in Theology and Its Implications for Theological Education," unpublished dissertation, Union Theological Seminary, New York, March 1969.

31. See Hans J. Margull, *Hope in Action*, trans. Eugene Peters (Philadelphia: Muhlenberg Press, 1962).

32. *The Church for Others and the Church for the World*, Department of Studies in Evangelism (Geneva: World Council of Churches, 1967), pp. 69–71, 75–77.

33. Walter M. Abbott and Joseph Gallagher, eds., *The Documents of Vatican II* (New York: Guild Press, 1966), p. 17.

34. Leonardo Boff, *Church, Charism, and Power: Liberation Theology and the Institutional Church* (New York: Crossroad, 1985), p. 2.

35. Boff, *Ecclesiogenesis*, pp. 3–4.

36. Gustavo Gutiérrez, *The Power of the Poor in History: Selected Readings* (Maryknoll, N.Y.: Orbis Books, 1983), pp. 169–221. See also his *A Theology of Liberation* (Maryknoll, N.Y.: Orbis Books, 1971 [Spanish], 1973 [English, 1st ed.], 1988 [English, 2nd. ed.]).

37. See Johannes Christiaan Hoekendijk, *The Church Inside Out*, trans. Isaac C. Rottenberg (Philadelphia: Westminster Press, 1966).

38. Informal conversation with Barbara Anne Keely at Union Theological Seminary, Richmond, Va., April 13, 1991; cf. her "Partnership and Christian Education in the Work of Letty M. Russell," unpublished dissertation, Presbyterian School of Christian Education, Richmond, Va., May 1991. See Hoekendijk, *The Church Inside Out*, pp. 42–46.

39. Johannes Christiaan Hoekendijk, *The Church for Others*, pp. 83–86. See Letty M. Russell, *Christian Education in Mission* (Philadelphia: Westminster Press, 1967), and "Forms of the Confessing Church Today," *Journal of Presbyterian History*, Spring 1983, pp. 99–109.

40. Boff, *Ecclesiogenesis*, pp. 5–9.

41. Ibid., p. 5. See Avery Dulles, *A Church to Believe In* (New York: Crossroad, 1985), p. 22, for a position that sees these two ecclesial types as far more distinct and seeks to identify institutional structures that are constitutive of Church as such: doctrine, worship, government, regulations for behavior.

42. Robert J. Schreiter, *Constructing Local Theologies*, pp. 117–121.

43. See Jack Nelson Pallmeyer, *War Against the Poor: Low-Intensity Conflict and Christian Faith* (Maryknoll, N.Y.: Orbis Books, 1989), p. 17; Pablo Galdamez, *Faith of a People: The Story of Christian Community in El Salvador, 1970–1980* (Maryknoll, N.Y.: Orbis Books, 1983).

44. Gustavo Gutiérrez, *We Drink from Our Own Wells: The Spiritual Journey of a People* (Maryknoll, N.Y.: Orbis Books, 1984), pp. 20–21.

45. Virginia West Davidson, "Ministry: A Partnership Affair," unpublished dissertation, Colgate Rochester Divinity School/Bexley Hall/Crozer Theological Seminary, 1988 (rev. 1990), pp. 122–140.

46. Seven members of the Session and staff of the church met with Virginia Davidson to record this oral history at my request on behalf of a Task Force on Catholicity and the Global Mission of the Church of the General Assembly of the United Presbyterian Church in 1987. Mimeographed document.

47. "Lesbian Minister Called," *Christian Century* 109:2 (Jan. 15, 1992), p. 39. This call to the Rev. Jane Spahr was later set aside by the church courts. "PCUSA Rules Against Lesbian Pastor," *Christian Century* 109:34 (Nov. 18–25, 1992): 1057.

48. Preston Robert Washington, *God's Transforming Spirit: Black Church Renewal* (Valley Forge, Pa.: Judson Press, 1988), p. 13; see pp. 93–114.

49. See Eleanor Scott Meyers, ed., *Envisioning the New City: A Reader on Urban Ministry* (Louisville, Ky.: Westminster/John Knox Press, 1992).

50. Kittredge Cherry and James Mitulski, "We Are the Church Alive," in *The Church with AIDS: Renewal in the Midst of Crisis*, ed. Letty M. Russell, p. 165. The entire chapter, pp. 163–174, is a description of the church and its ministry with AIDS.

51. Ibid., p. 167.

52. Janet Crawford, "Non-Patriarchal Models of Community," in *The Search for New Community*, ed. Thomas F. Best (Geneva: WCC Publications, 1989), pp. 16–31.

53. Sherry Wu Dunn, "China Cracks Down Harder on Christian Activities Outside Official Church," *New York Times International*, Jan. 13, 1992, p. A3.

54. See K. H. Ting, *No Longer Strangers: Selected Writings of Bishop K. H. Ting* (Maryknoll, N.Y.: Orbis Books, 1989); Philip L. Wickeri, *Seeking Common Ground* (Maryknoll, N.Y.: Orbis Books, 1988).

55. For an account of my participation in a dialogue of Asian and U.S. women theologians in China in 1990 see Kwok Pui-lan, ed., "Women, Church, China," *In God's Image* 10:3 (Autumn 1991), pp. 52–58.

56. James O'Halloran, *Signs of Hope: Developing Small Christian Communities* (Maryknoll, N.Y.: Orbis Books, 1991), pp. 55–95. See Margaret and Ian Fraser, *From Wind and Fire: The Spirit Reshapes the Church in Basic Christian Communities*

(Dunblane, Scotland: Basic Communities Resource Centre, Scottish Churches' Council, 1986).

57. Rosemary Radford Ruether, "'Basic Communities': Renewal at the Roots," *Christianity and Crisis* 41:14 (Sept. 21, 1981), p. 234. See the detailed account of a parish in Campos Elíseos in the state of Rio de Janeiro, Brazil, for the weaving together of theological praxis, people's struggles, and the ministry of Frei David, a Franciscan priest, in Jane Kramer, "Letter from the Elysian Fields," *New Yorker*, March 2, 1987, pp. 40–75.

58. João Evangelista Martins Terra, "The Ecclesiological Significance of the Churches' Involvement in Issues of Justice in Brazil," unpublished report (Geneva: WCC Commission on Faith and Order, Study on Unity of the Church and Renewal of Human Community, Porto Alegre, Brazil, Nov. 12–20, 1987), pp. 1–3.

59. Ibid., p. 1. Material on the Philippines from lectures by Bishop Fortich and Father Rolex Nueva at Yale Divinity School, November 24, 1990. See also Dorothy Friesen, *Critical Choices: A Journey with the Filipino People* (Grand Rapids: Wm. B. Eerdmans Publishing Co., 1988), pp. 79–92.

60. Gustavo Gutiérrez, "The Poor and the Christian Communities," in *The Challenge of Basic Christian Communities*, ed. Sergio Torres and John Eagleson (Maryknoll, N.Y.: Orbis Books, 1981), p. 116.

61. Gutiérrez, "The Poor and the Christian Communities," p. 118.

62. Visit to Lima as part of the Faith and Order Commission of the WCC, 1982.

63. Speech by Father Rolex at Yale Divinity School, November 24, 1990. See Report of the Yale Divinity School Third World Travel Seminar, "Encountering God's Liberating Power in the Philippines," Dec. 30, 1990, to Jan. 12, 1991.

64. O'Halloran, *Signs of Hope*, pp. 55–73.

65. Commission on Theological Concerns of the CCA, ed. *Minjung Theology: People as the Subjects of History* (Maryknoll, N.Y.: Orbis Books, 1983).

66. Sun Ai Lee Park, "A New Phase in the Ecumenical Movement: One Woman's Perspective on Asian Activities," in Melanie A. May, ed., *Women and Church*, pp. 152–162.

67. Rosemary Radford Ruether, *Women-Church: Theology and Practice of Feminist Liturgical Communities*, pp. 25–31.

68. "Julio de Santa Ana," *Against Machismo*, interviews by Elsa Tamez, p. 18.

69. Cora Ferro, "The Latin American Woman: The Praxis and Theology of Liberation" (Final Document of the EATWOT Women's Seminar, Oct. 2–5, 1979, Mexico), in *The Challenge of Basic Christian Communities*, ed. Torres and Eagleson, p. 33. See *And She Said No! Human Rights, Women's Identities and Struggles*, ed. Liberato Bautista and Elizabeth Rifareal, Program Unit on Human Rights, NCCP, Quezon City, Philippines, 1990.

70. Adair Lummis, Allison Stokes, and Miriam Therese Winter, "Grant Proposal: Effects of Women's Base Communities of Support and Inspiration on Participants and Congregations in Catholic and Protestant Traditions," unpub-

lished document, p. 1. This study is funded by the Lilly Foundation and is being conducted in 1991–92 in coordination with Hartford Seminary. It will provide significant statistical data concerning those communities that are related to the white mainline churches. See also Robert Wuthnow, *The Restructuring of American Religion* (Princeton, N.J.: Princeton University Press, 1988), p. 229, quoted in the "Grant Proposal."

71. Mary E. Hunt, "Ecumenism Begins at Home," *WATERwheel: A Quarterly Newsletter of the Women's Alliance for Theology, Ethics, and Ritual* 4:1 (Spring 1991), pp. 1–3. Available from WATER, 8035 13th Street, Silver Spring, MD 20910.

72. Ruether, *Women-Church*, pp. 283, 57.

73. Fiorenza, *Bread Not Stone*, p. xiv. See chapter 1, "Women-Church: The Hermeneutical Center of Feminist Biblical Interpretation," pp. 1–22.

74. Pointed out by Sr. Rachelle Harper in an oral report on "Women-Church" for my class on Liberation Ecclesiology, Yale Divinity School, April 1991. The report was based in part on Gretchen E. Ziegenhals, "Meeting the Women of Women-Church," *Christian Century* 106:16 (May 10, 1989), pp. 492–494; and Miriam Therese Winter, "The Women-Church Movement," *Christian Century* 106:8 (March 8, 1989), pp. 258–260. See also the data in "Final Report: Planning Grant Activities, Findings, and Dilemmas in Regard to the Study of Woman-Church and Similar Spiritual Support Groups in the Mainline Protestant and Roman Catholic Traditions," by Adair Lummis, Allison Stokes, and Miriam Therese Winter of WomanCircle, a program emphasis at Hartford Seminary, June 30, 1990.

75. Letty M. Russell, "Human Liberation in a Feminine Perspective," *Study Encounter/20* 7:1 (Geneva: World Council of Churches, 1972), pp. 1–12. For a more detailed analysis of how this group functioned, see Letty M. Russell, *Growth in Partnership* (Philadelphia: Westminster Press, 1981), pp. 151–161.

76. *WATERwheel*, Spring 1991, p. 2.

77. Nancy Richardson, "Feminist Theology/Feminist Pedagogy: An Experimental Program of the Women's Theological Center," *Journal of Feminist Studies in Religion* 1:2 (Fall 1985), pp. 115–122.

78. Beverly D. Johnson, "Loves Herself . . . Regardless: A Journey Toward Self-Discovery/Rediscovery," *WTC Newsletter*, Sept. 1991, p. 3. Available from the Women's Theological Center, P.O. Box 1200, Boston, MA 02117.

79. Edward H. Schroeder, "Korean Women Search for the Silver Coin," *Christian Century* 107:15 (May 2, 1990), pp. 252–454.

80. Lieve Troch, "The Feminist Movement in and on the Edge of the Churches in the Netherlands: From Consciousness-raising to Womenchurch," *Journal of Feminist Studies in Religion* 5:2 (Fall 1989), p. 116.

81. Ruether, *Women-Church*, pp. 91–94.

82. Schroeder, "Korean Women Search," p. 253.

83. Julia Esquivel, *Threatened with Resurrection: Prayers and Poems from an Exiled Guatemalan* (Elgin, Ill.: Bethany Press, 1982), pp. 58–63.

84. Robert Adolfs, *Grave of God: Has the Church a Future?* trans. N. D. Smith (New York: Harper & Row, 1966), p. 151.

4: Justice and the Church

1. A "love feast" is an agape meal that is celebrated without a formal eucharist, or prior to eucharist, in memory of the early church practice of eating a meal as part of the eucharist (1 Cor. 11:17–22). For the story of this worship service see Beryl Ingram-Ward, "Space for Hospitality and Hope," in *The Church with AIDS*, ed. Letty M. Russell, pp. 69–78, hereafter cited as Russell, *AIDS*.

2. Mary Catherine Bateson and Richard Goldsby say that "the imagination of AIDS is the imagination of human unity, intimately held in the interdependent web of life," in *Thinking AIDS* (Reading, Mass.: Addison-Wesley Publishing Co., 1988), p. 10.

3. Susan E. Davies, "Oppression and Resurrection Faith," in Russell, *AIDS*, pp. 90–104.

4. Ingram-Ward, "Space for Hospitality," in Russell, *AIDS*, p. 72.

5. The pastor of the Metropolitan Community Church of San Francisco is James Mitulski. For a description of the ministry of the church see "We Are the Church Alive" by Kittredge Cherry and James Mitulski, in Russell, *AIDS*, pp. 163–174.

6. Paul D. Hanson, *The People Called: The Growth of Community in the Bible*, p. 426.

7. Ron Russell-Coons, "Letter to Connie," in Russell, *AIDS*, p. 48.

8. Ron Russell-Coons, "We Have AIDS," in Russell, *AIDS*, p. 38.

9. "Keeping Body and Soul Together: Sexuality, Spirituality and Social Justice," p. 34.

10. J. Verkuyl, *The Message of Liberation in Our Age* (Grand Rapids: Wm. B. Eerdmans Publishing Co., 1970), pp. 17–21. See Letty M. Russell, *Human Liberation in a Feminist Perspective—A Theology* (Philadelphia: Westminster Press, 1974), pp. 106–109.

11. Claus Westermann, "Der Friede (schalom) im Alten Testament," *Zeichen der Zeit* 10 (1970), pp. 361–375; Verkuyl, *Message*, p. 18. See also Claus Westermann, *What Does the Old Testament Say About God?* ed. Friedemann W. Golka (Atlanta: John Knox Press, 1979), pp. 32–34.

12. Russell, *Human Liberation*, pp. 107–108.

13. A. Richardson, "Salvation, Savior," *The Interpreter's Dictionary of the Bible*, ed. George A. Buttrick (Nashville: Abingdon Press, 1962), vol. 4, pp. 177–181.

14. Karl Rahner and Herbert Vorgrimler, "Extra Ecclesiam Nulla Salus," *Theological Dictionary* (New York: Herder & Herder, 1965), pp. 162–163.

15. Gustavo Gutiérrez, *A Theology of Liberation: History, Politics, and Salvation*, 2nd ed., ed. and trans. Sister Caridad Inda and John Eagleson (Maryknoll, N.Y.: Orbis Books, 1988), p. 85.

16. Gutiérrez, *Theology of Liberation*, p. 90.

17. Walter Brueggemann says: "In a *shalom* community the king listens to the prophet and cares for the poor, because that is his office; the prophet speaks boldly and constructively, because he knows the king intends to rule well; the powerless are coming to power." *Living Toward a Vision: Biblical Reflections on Shalom* (Philadelphia: United Church Press, 1976), p. 100. Cited

in Katharine Doob Sakenfeld, *Faithfulness in Action: Loyalty in Biblical Perspective* (Philadelphia: Fortress Press, 1985), pp. 127–128.

18. Gerhard von Rad, *Old Testament Theology*, vol. I, trans. D.M.G. Stalker (San Francisco: Harper & Row, 1962), p. 370.

19. In *Faithfulness in Action*, Sakenfeld refers to the translation of "humility" as "considered attention to another," from James L. Mays, *Micah* (Philadelphia: Westminster Press, 1976), pp. 101–103, 142.

20. Krister Stendahl, *Paul Among Jews and Gentiles* (Philadelphia: Fortress Press, 1976), pp. 30–31. See also Von Rad, *Theology*, p. 372.

21. Nestor Miguez, "The Witness to Justice and the Renewal of the Church: A Biblical Approach." Unpublished paper presented at the Consultation of the Faith and Order Commission, WCC, at Porto Alegre, Brazil, November 13–20, 1987, on the Ecclesiological Significance of the Churches' Involvement in Issues of Justice, FO/87:33, p. 4. See also "Church and World: The Unity of the Church and the Renewal of Human Community" pp. 38–49.

22. Ernst Käsemann, *Essays on New Testament Themes* (London: SCM Press, 1964), p. 75.

23. Elsa Tamez, *The Scandalous Message of James: Faith Without Works Is Dead*, p. 65.

24. Ibid., pp. 65–66, 89–90.

25. Hugh T. Kerr, ed., *A Compend of the Institutes of the Christian Religion by John Calvin* (Philadelphia: Westminster Press, 1964), p. 115.

26. Origen, *In Jesu Nave, 3, 5.* Quoted by Hans Küng, *The Church*, pp. 313–314.

27. David Kelsey, *The Uses of Scripture in Recent Theology* (Philadelphia: Fortress Press, 1975), pp. 170–175.

28. Küng, *The Church*, pp. 315–316.

29. Robert McAfee Brown, "The 'Preferential Option for the Poor' and the Renewal of Faith," in *Churches in Struggle: Liberation Theologies and Social Change in North America*, ed. William K. Tabb (New York: Monthly Review Press, 1986), p. 10.

30. Gustavo Gutiérrez, *The Power of the Poor in History: Selected Writings*, trans. Robert R. Barr (Maryknoll, N.Y.: Orbis Books, 1983), p. 140.

31. Jürgen Moltmann and M. Douglas Meeks, "The Liberation of Oppressors," *Christianity and Crisis* 38:20 (Dec. 25, 1978), pp. 310–317.

32. Edward Schillebeeckx, *Church: The Human Story of God*, pp. 5–13.

33. Carter Heyward, *Our Passion for Justice: Images of Power, Sexuality, and Liberation* (New York: Pilgrim Press, 1984).

34. Sallie McFague, *Models of God: Theology for an Ecological Nuclear Age*, p. 183.

35. James H. Cone, *Speaking the Truth: Ecumenism, Liberation, and Black Theology*, p. 112.

36. Adrienne Rich, "Split at the Root: An Essay on Jewish Identity (1982)," *Blood, Bread, and Poetry: Selected Prose, 1979–1985* (New York: W. W. Norton & Co., 1986), pp. 100–123.

37. Lillian Smith, *Killers of the Dream*, rev. ed. (New York: W. W. Norton & Co., 1978), p. 29.

38. Piet Schoonenberg, "Sin," *Sacramentum Mundi*, vol. 6, pp. 87–92. See also Russell, *Human Liberation*, pp. 109–113.

39. S. J. De Vries, "Sin, Sinners," *The Interpreter's Dictionary of the Bible*, ed. George A. Buttrick (Nashville: Abingdon Press, 1962), vol. 4, pp. 361–373.

40. For an excellent analysis of sin from the perspective of victims of rape and domestic violence see Mary Potter Engel, "Evil, Sin, and Violation of the 'Vulnerable,'" in *Lift Every Voice: Constructing Christian Theologies from the Underside*, ed. Susan Brooks Thistlethwaite and Mary Potter Engel (San Francisco: Harper & Row, 1990), pp. 152–164.

41. See Letty M. Russell, "Searching for a Round Table in Church and World," *Women and Church: The Challenge of Ecumenical Solidarity in an Age of Alienation* (Grand Rapids: Wm. B. Eerdmans Publishing Co., 1991), p. 177.

42. Robin Scroggs, *Paul for a New Day*, p. 52. See also Michael Kinnamon, *Truth and Community*, p. 37.

43. "Keeping Body and Soul Together," p. 34.

44. Robert McAfee Brown, ed., *Kairos: Three Prophetic Challenges to the Church*, pp. 45–47.

45. These oral examples were told to me by Tony Smith, Susan Meredith, and Serene Jones.

46. Anthony B. Robinson, "Learning from Willow Creek Church," *Christian Century* 108:3 (Jan. 23, 1991), pp. 70–71. See Tex Sample, *U.S. Lifestyles and Mainline Churches*, pp. 64–67.

47. Robert N. Bellah et al., *Habits of the Heart: Individualism and Commitment in American Life* (San Francisco: Harper & Row, 1985), pp. 71–72.

48. Translation by Hans Hoekendijk, in an unpublished lecture at Union Theological Seminary, 1975.

49. Rich, *Blood, Bread, and Poetry*, p. 176.

50. Sister Marie Augusta Neal, informal remarks at the Hartford Consultation on Women Church, Lakeville, Conn., Feb. 28–March 1, 1992.

51. Anna Case-Winters, "Salvation," *Encyclopedia of the Reformed Faith*, ed. Donald K. McKim (Louisville, Ky.: Westminster/John Knox Press, 1992), p. 335. Calvin's use of "double grace" was first pointed out to me by Sheila Gustafson in a D. Min. seminar of McCormick Theological Seminary for students in Minneapolis/St. Paul, Oct. 15–19, 1990.

52. See Letty M. Russell, *Becoming Human* (Philadelphia: Westminster Press, 1982), pp. 88–91.

53. Karl Barth, *Church Dogmatics*, vol. II, part 2, ed. G. W. Bromiley and T. F. Torrance (Edinburgh: T. & T. Clark, 1957), pp. 115–118, 351–353.

54. Letty M. Russell, *Household of Freedom: Authority in Feminist Theology*, pp. 25–26, 82–85.

55. Rosemary Radford Ruether, *To Change the World: Christology and Cultural Criticism* (New York: Crossroad, 1981), pp. 42–43.

56. Marjorie Hewitt Suchocki, "In Search of Justice: Religious Pluralism from a Feminist Perspective," in *The Myth of Christian Uniqueness: Toward a Pluralistic Theology of Religions*, ed. John Hick and Paul F. Knitter (Maryknoll, N.Y.: Orbis Books, 1987), p. 149.

57. Ruether, *To Change the World*, pp. 38–39. See also her "Feminism and Jewish-

Christian Dialogue: Particularism and Universalism in the Search for Religious Truth," in *The Myth of Christian Uniqueness*, ed. Hick and Knitter, pp. 137–148.

58. Jürgen Moltmann, *The Church in the Power of the Spirit*, pp. 121–132.

59. Russell, *Household of Freedom*, pp. 74–76.

60. Moltmann, *The Church*, p. 132.

61. Robert J. Schreiter, "Marks of the Church in Times of Transformation," in Russell, *AIDS*, p. 122.

62. "Confessing the One Faith: An Ecumenical Explication of the Apostolic Faith as It Is Confessed in the Nicene-Constantinopolitan Creed" (381).

63. Küng, *The Church*, pp. 268–269.

64. Schreiter, "Marks of the Church," in Russell, *AIDS*, pp. 122–132.

65. Mary Tanner, "Toward a Common Confession of the Apostolic Faith Today," in *Women and Church*, ed. Melanie A. May, pp. 179–180.

66. Hanson, *The People Called*, p. 426.

67. Suchocki, "Holiness and a Renewed Church," in Russell, *AIDS*, p. 117.

68. Schreiter, "Marks of the Church," in Russell, *AIDS*, pp. 131–132.

69. David T. Shannon and Gayraud S. Wilmore, eds., *Black Witness to the Apostolic Faith* (Grand Rapids: Wm. B. Eerdmans Publishing Co., 1985), p. 67.

70. Schreiter, "Marks of the Church," in Russell, *AIDS*, p. 124.

71. Leonardo Boff, "Theological Characteristics of a Grassroots Church," in *The Challenge of Basic Christian Communities*, ed. Sergio Torres and John Eagleson, pp. 124–144.

72. Colin W. Williams, *New Directions in Theology Today: The Church*, vol. 4 (Philadelphia: Westminster Press, 1968), p. 15. See also Johannes Christiaan Hoekendijk, *The Church Inside Out*, trans. Isaac C. Rottenberg (Philadelphia: Westminster Press, 1966), p. 42.

73. Moltmann, *The Church*, pp. 340–341. Suchocki and Schreiter spell out their positions in Russell, *AIDS*, pp. 109–132.

74. James H. Cone, *For My People* (Maryknoll, N.Y.: Orbis Books, 1984), p. 123. See also Jacqueline Grant, "Black Christology: Interpreting Aspects of the Apostolic Faith," in *Black Witness*, ed. Shannon and Wilmore, pp. 26–27.

75. Russell-Coons, "Letters," in Russell, *AIDS*, pp. 49–51.

76. Ingram-Ward, "Space for Hospitality," in Russell, *AIDS*, pp. 77–78.

77. Letty M. Russell, "A Church for Troubled Waters," in Russell, *AIDS*, pp. 136–141.

78. Calvin, *A Compend*, IV.i.9.

79. Küng, *The Church*, p. 267.

80. Moltmann, *The Church*, p. 341.

81. For the discussion of discipline as a third mark I am indebted to Mary Marple Thies in her unpublished STM thesis at Yale Divinity School, "A Woman Looks at the Church: A Feminist Critique of the Presbyterian Church," May 1, 1992.

82. John Calvin, "Preface," 1559 edition. Quoted in *A Compend*, p. vi.

83. Sallie McFague, *Metaphorical Theology* (Philadelphia: Fortress Press, 1982), p. 9.

84. McFague, *Models of God,* pp. 97–99.

85. Russell, *Household of Freedom,* pp. 43–57.

86. "The Scripture and Homosexuality," John J. McNeill, *The Church and the Homosexual,* 3rd ed. (Boston: Beacon Press, 1988), pp. 36–66.

87. "Baptism, Eucharist, and Ministry," p. 2.

88. Ibid., p. 10.

89. Marjorie Procter-Smith, *In Her Own Rite: Constructing Feminist Liturgical Tradition,* pp. 152–153.

90. Rosemary Radford Ruether, *Women-Church: Theology and Practice of Feminist Liturgical Communities;* Elisabeth Schüssler Fiorenza, *Bread Not Stone: The Challenge of Feminist Biblical Interpretation.*

91. Ruth C. Duck, *Gender and the Name of God: The Trinitarian Baptismal Formula;* Procter-Smith, *Rite.*

92. *Book of Worship: United Church of Christ* (New York: United Church of Christ, Office for Church Life and Leadership, 1986), p. 141.

93. Duck, *Gender,* pp. 127–137.

94. Ibid., pp. 163–166.

95. Ibid., p. 170; Fiorenza, *In Memory of Her,* p. 208.

96. The inclusion of "heterosexual and homosexual" was suggested to me by Paul Patton in his unpublished term paper, "All One in Christ Jesus! A Theology of Gay and Lesbian Liberation," Yale Divinity School, May 1992.

97. Procter-Smith, *Rite,* pp. 149–151.

98. Ibid., p. 160. Procter-Smith is citing James F. White, *Sacraments as God's Self Giving* (Nashville: Abingdon Press, 1983), pp. 54–61.

99. Nancy Jay, "Sacrifice as Remedy for Having Been Born of Woman," in *Immaculate and Powerful: The Female in Sacred Image and Social Reality,* ed. Clarissa W. Atkinson, Constance H. Buchanan, and Margaret R. Miles (Boston: Beacon Press, 1985), p. 283. See also Carol P. Christ, "Mircea Eliade and the Feminist Paradigm Shift," *Journal of Feminist Studies in Religion* 7:2 (Fall 1991), pp. 75–94.

100. Robert Bly, *Iron John: A Book About Men* (Reading, Mass.: Addison-Wesley Publishing Co., 1990), pp. 14–21.

101. Jay, "Sacrifice," pp. 285, 297.

102. Ibid., p. 300.

103. The description of the Aladura churches is from an unpublished STM thesis by Caleb O. Oladipo, Yale Divinity School, 1988.

104. Ada María Isasi-Díaz, unpublished lecture at a consultation on Women in Religious Communities, American Academy of Religion, Nov. 1989. Also reported in a newsletter of the Women's Coalition to Stop U.S. Intervention in Central America and the Caribbean, 475 Riverside Drive, Room 812, New York, NY 10115, July 8, 1986.

105. Antionette Clark Wire, *The Corinthian Women Prophets: A Reconstruction Through Paul's Rhetoric,* pp. 41, 174–175. See also her "Economics and Early Christian Voices," *Pacific Theological Review* 19:1 (Fall 1985), pp. 21–22.

106. C. K. Barrett, *A Commentary on the First Epistle to the Corinthians* (New York: Harper & Row, 1968), p. 273.
107. Hans Ruedi Weber, *Power: Focus for Biblical Theology* (Geneva: WCC Publications, 1989), pp. 131–137.
108. See James H. Cone, *Speaking the Truth*, p. 128.
109. See Alice Walker, "The Welcome Table," in *In Love and in Trouble: Stories of Black Women* (New York: Harcourt Brace Jovanovich, 1967), pp. 81–87.

Part Three: Welcome Table Partnership

1. Sam Keen, *Fire in the Belly: On Being a Man* (New York: Bantam Books, 1991), p. 63.
2. Chuck Lathrop, "In Search of a Roundtable," in *A Gentle Presence*, p. 7.
3. "Welcome Table," Afro-American spiritual, in *An Advent Sourcebook*, ed. Thomas O'Gorman (Chicago: Liturgy Training Publications, 1988), p. 50. Cf. Letty M. Russell, "Searching for a Round Table in Church and World," in *Women and Church*, ed. Melanie A. May, pp. 177–178.
4. Clarice J. Martin, "The *Haustafeln* (Household Codes) in African American Biblical Interpretation: 'Free Slaves' and 'Subordinate Women,'" in *Stony the Road We Trod*, ed. Cain Hope Felder, pp. 206–231. Ironically, the German *Haustafeln* is sometimes translated as "house tables" in English. Such lists or "tables" are the opposite of the tables in *Church in the Round*.
5. Letty M. Russell, *Becoming Human* (Philadelphia: Westminster Press, 1982), pp. 23–26.
6. Barbara Brown Zikmund, " . . . God Shows No Partiality," *Praxis: News from Hartford Seminary*, Spring 1992, p. 1.

5: Community of Hospitality

1. Henri Nouwen, *Reaching Out* (Garden City, N.Y.: Doubleday & Co., 1975), p. 51; John Koenig, *New Testament Hospitality*, p. 8.
2. Michael Kinnamon, *Truth and Community*, p. 64.
3. Gayraud S. Wilmore and James H. Cone, eds., *Black Theology: A Documentary History, 1966–1979* (Maryknoll, N.Y.: Orbis Books, 1979), p. 6; "Keeping Body and Soul Together: Sexuality, Spirituality, and Social Justice."
4. See "Owning the Spirit: The Pluralism-Unity Debate After Canberra," *Christianity and Crisis* 51:10/11 (July 15, 1991), pp. 220–232. These reflections on the meeting by a number of authors include Dr. Chung's speech on "The Holy Spirit, Creation, and the Culture of Life."
5. "A Case Study by Gladys Moore," Jan. 1991, mimeographed. This study is available from the Working Group on Faith and Order, NCCCUSA, Room 868, 475 Riverside Drive, New York, NY 10115-0050.
6. Page numbers in parentheses refer to the mimeographed copy of the case study, listed in the Faith and Order files as WOFO, U/R, 3/91, Moore.

7. Adrienne Rich, "Notes Toward a Politics of Location," *Blood, Bread, and Poetry: Selected Prose 1979–1985* (New York: W. W. Norton & Co., 1986), p. 218. Rich is reflecting on a description of oppressions "experienced simultaneously" from the 1977 Combahee River Collective statement of black feminists. See Barbara Smith, ed., *Home Girls: A Black Feminist Anthology* (New York: Kitchen Table/Women of Color Press, 1983), pp. 272–283.

8. John W. de Gruchy, "Towards a Confessing Church," in *Apartheid Is a Heresy*, ed. John W. de Gruchy and Charles Villa-Vicencio (Grand Rapids: Wm. B. Eerdmans Publishing Co., 1983), p. 80; quoted by Michael Kinnamon, in *Truth and Community*, p. 68.

9. Parker J. Palmer, *The Company of Strangers: Christians and the Renewal of America's Public Life*, p. 130.

10. Doreen Potter, "The Wall Is Down," No. 18 in *Break Not the Circle: Twenty Hymns*, by Fred Kaan and Doreen Potter (Agape, 1975). This is the logo of the Stony Point Center in Stony Point, N.Y. Quoted in Letty M. Russell, *Household of Freedom: Authority in Feminist Theology*, p. 28.

11. Audre Lorde, *Sister Outsider: Essays and Speeches*, p. 115.

12. Ibid.

13. This phrase comes from Joan Martin of Temple University. Joan Martin and Judith Mintier were very helpful to me in a discussion of my paper during its preparation in August 1991.

14. Peggy McIntosh, "White Privilege and Male Privilege: A Personal Account of Coming to See Correspondences Through Work in Women's Studies," Working Paper No. 189 (mimeographed), pp. 5–6, 9, Wellesley College, Center for Research on Women, Wellesley, MA 02181.

15. Ibid., p. 10.

16. Ibid., p. 14.

17. Elisabeth Schüssler Fiorenza, *In Memory of Her*, p. 29. See Fiorenza, *Bread Not Stone*, p. xiv; Russell, *Household of Freedom*, pp. 29–42.

18. This comprehensive critique of patriarchal structures urged by Elisabeth Fiorenza is also taken up by Renita Weems as a womanist "hermeneutical approach [to the Bible] that is able to include as many people as there are disenfranchised." Renita J. Weems, "The State of Biblical Interpretation: An African-American Womanist Critique," unpublished manuscript of a lecture at Princeton Theological Seminary, May 17, 1988, at a conference entitled Gender, Race, Class: Implications for Interpreting Religions. Cf. Renita J. Weems, *Just a Sister Away: A Womanist Vision of Women's Relationships in the Bible* (San Diego: LuraMedia, 1988); and Ada María Isasi-Díaz, "The Bible and *Mujerista* Theology," Kwok Pui-lan, "Discovering the Bible in the Non-Biblical World," and Sharon H. Ringe, "Reading from Context to Context: Contributions of a Feminist Hermeneutic to Theologies of Liberation," in *Lift Every Voice: Constructing Christian Theologies from the Underside*, ed. Susan Brooks Thistlethwaite and Mary Potter Engel, pp. 261–291.

19. Elisabeth Schüssler Fiorenza, "Changing the Paradigms," *Christian Century*

107:25 (Sept. 5–12, 1990), pp. 799–800. Fiorenza cites the research of Susan Moller Okin in *Women in Political Thought* in her discussion of oppression and patriarchy.

20. Russell, *Household of Freedom*, pp. 25–26.

21. Letty M. Russell, *The Future of Partnership* (Philadelphia: Westminster Press, 1979), pp. 17–20.

22. In this paper God's household or household of God is understood as a description of the kingdom or reign of God. See Russell, *Household of Freedom*, pp. 83–85.

23. Mary John Mananzan (Philippines) and Sun Ai Park (Korea), "Emerging Spirituality of Asian Women," in *With Passion and Compassion: Third World Women Doing Theology*, ed. Virginia Fabella and Mercy Amba Oduyoye (Maryknoll, N.Y.: Orbis Books, 1988), pp. 83–84.

24. Sharon H. Ringe, "A Gentile Woman's Story," in *Feminist Interpretation of the Bible*, ed. Letty M. Russell, p. 67.

25. Weems, "The State of Biblical Interpretation." See also Cain Hope Felder, *Troubling Biblical Waters: Race, Class, and Family* (Maryknoll, N.Y.: Orbis Books, 1989); Paul D. Hanson, *The People Called: The Growth of Community in the Bible.*

26. Weems, "The State of Biblical Interpretation," pp. 31–32. Tapes of this lecture are available from Princeton Theological Seminary, along with the responses of Mary Ann Tolbert, Pheme Perkins, and Cain Felder.

27. Judith Plaskow, *Standing Again at Sinai: Judaism from a Feminist Perspective* (San Francisco: Harper & Row, 1990), pp. 116–117.

28. Felder, *Troubling Biblical Waters*, pp. 43–46; Felder is quoting Gerhard von Rad, *Old Testament Theology* (New York: Harper & Row, 1962), vol. 1, p. 7. See also von Rad, pp. 223–226.

29. Norman K. Gottwald, *The Tribes of Yahweh: A Sociology of the Religion of Liberated Israel, 1250–1050 B.C.E.* (Maryknoll, N.Y.: Orbis Books, 1979), p. 693.

30. Ibid., p. 692.

31. Weems, "The State of Biblical Interpretation," p. 38.

32. Horst Seebass, "*bachar*," *Theological Dictionary of the Old Testament*, vol. 2, ed. Johannes Botterweck and Helmer Ringgren, trans. John T. Willis (Grand Rapids: Wm. B. Eerdmans Publishing Co., 1975), pp. 84–85.

33. Phyllis Trible, "Journey with Jonah," the Caldwell Lectures, Louisville Presbyterian Theological Seminary, Spring 1991. Taped lecture available from Louisville Presbyterian Theological Seminary, 1044 Alta Vista Road, Louisville, KY 40205.

34. Hanson, *The People Called*, p. 539.

35. Pheme Perkins, response to Weems's paper, "The State of Biblical Interpretation," on the tape of the conference.

36. Hanson, *The People Called*, p. 425.

37. Ibid., pp. 400, 403.

38. This idea of Jesus as the chosen one is also in Mark 1:11 and 9:7, where Jesus is

called "Beloved." See F. F. Bruce, "Election, NT," *Interpreter's Dictionary of the Bible: Supplementary Volume*, ed. Keith Crim et al. (Nashville: Abingdon Press, 1976), pp. 258–259.

39. Mary Rose D'Angelo, "Images of Jesus: Christian Calling in the Gospels of Luke and John," *Spirituality Today* 37:3 (Fall 1985), pp. 210–211.

40. Elsa Tamez, *The Scandalous Message of James: Faith Without Works Is Dead*, p. 24. See John H. Elliott, *A Home for the Homeless: A Sociological Exegesis of I Peter, Its Situation and Strategy* (Philadelphia: Fortress Press, 1981), pp. 21–58. Cain Felder, *Troubling Biblical Waters*, pp. 118–120, concurs with Tamez that James is an important book for the oppressed and excluded.

41. Phyllis Trible, "Journey with Jonah."

42. In *In Memory of Her*, Elisabeth Fiorenza has reconstructed the community gathered around Jesus as a "discipleship of equals" and has pointed to the important role of women as leaders in Pauline churches, but this still constitutes a small glimpse of a vision that was soon swallowed up as churches accommodated to the patriarchal structures of domination in the surrounding society. On women in Pauline churches see pp. 205–236. On racism see Cain Felder, *Troubling Biblical Waters*, esp. chapters 6–9; Delores Williams, "The Analogous Relation Between Hagar's Experience and African-American Women's Experience: A Challenge Posed to Black Liberation Theology," unpublished dissertation, Union Theological Seminary, New York, 1990.

43. Van A. Harvey, *A Handbook of Theological Terms* (New York: Macmillan Co., 1964), pp. 76–77, 187–189.

44. Dewey D. Wallace, "Predestination," in *Encyclopedia of the Reformed Faith*, ed. Donald K. McKim (Louisville, Ky.: Westminster/John Knox Press, 1992), pp. 291–293.

45. Benjamin A. Reist, *A Reading of Calvin's Institutes* (Louisville, Ky.: Westminster/John Knox Press, 1991), p. 74. Reist is using the 1559 edition of *Calvin: Institutes of the Christian Religion*, ed. John T. McNeill (Philadelphia: Westminster Press, 1960), III:xxi–xxiv.

46. Wilhelm Niesel, *The Theology of John Calvin* (Philadelphia: Westminster Press, 1956), p. 160. See Calvin's *Institutes of the Christian Religion*, 1559 edition, III:21.

47. William H. Logan, ed., *The Kairos Covenant* (New York: Friendship Press, 1988), p. 9.

48. Harvey, *Handbook*, p. 188.

49. Karl Barth, *Church Dogmatics*, vol. II, part 2, ed. G. W. Bromiley and T. F. Torrance (Edinburgh: T. & T. Clark, 1957), pp. 115–118.

50. Ibid., pp. 351–353.

51. Hanson, *The People Called*, p. 426.

52. Thomas W. Ogletree, *Hospitality to the Stranger: Dimensions of Moral Understanding* (Philadelphia: Fortress Press, 1985), pp. 1–2.

53. Koenig, *New Testament Hospitality*, p. 8.

54. Ibid., p. 10.

55. See Russell, *The Future of Partnership*, pp. 17–20.

56. Nouwen, *Reaching Out*, p. 51. Quoted by Palmer, *Company of Strangers*, p. 68.

57. Palmer, *Company of Strangers*, pp. 87–88.

58. In "Ella's Song," Bernice Johnson Reagon sings of "Not needing to clutch for power, not needing the light just to shine on me. I need to be one in the number as we stand against tyranny" [B. Johnson Reagon/Songtalk Pub. Co.] *We All . . . Everyone of Us,* sung by Sweet Honey in the Rock, @ Flying Fish Records, Inc., 1304 W. Schubert, Chicago, IL 60614.

59. Plaskow, *Standing Again at Sinai*, p. 105.

60. Ibid., p. 107.

61. Letty M. Russell, "A Christian Movement: Yes or No?" *YWCA Magazine*, Nov. 1973.

62. The Purpose Statement is available from the National Board of the YWCA, 726 Broadway, New York, NY 10003.

63. bell hooks, *Feminist Theory: From Margin to Center*, p. 15.

64. Kinnamon, *Truth and Community*, pp. 108–111.

65. Jamie T. Phelps, "Choose Life: Reflections of a Black African-American Roman Catholic Woman Religious Theologian," in *Women and the Church*, ed. Melanie A. May, p. 47.

66. Bonhoeffer, *Letters and Papers from Prison*, pp. 282, 312, 337.

67. Ibid., p. 282.

68. Nancy Richardson, "The Women's Theological Center: Learning and Acting for Justice," *Study/Action, 1991–1992* (Women's Theological Center, 140 Clarendon Street, Boston, MA 02117), pp. 7–9; this article first appeared in the Feb. 1–8, 1989, issue of *Christian Century.* See also Nancy Richardson, "Feminist Theology/Feminist Pedagogy: An Experimental Program of the Women's Theological Center," *Journal of Feminist Studies in Religion* 1:2 (Fall 1985), pp. 115–122.

69. Kinnamon, *Truth and Community*, pp. 112–115.

70. "Keeping Body and Soul Together," p. 27.

71. Kinnamon, *Truth and Community*, p. 113.

72. In the discussion of unacceptable diversity, Kinnamon cites James D. G. Dunn, *Unity and Diversity in the New Testament: An Inquiry Into the Character of Earliest Christianity* (Philadelphia: Westminster Press, 1977), pp. 373, 386–387.

73. Kinnamon, *Truth and Community*, p. 110.

74. "Owning the Spirit: The Pluralism-Unity Debate After Canberra," pp. 219–232. See also Jeffrey Gros, "Christian Confession in a Pluralistic World," *Christian Century* 108:20 (June 26–July 3, 1991), pp. 644–646.

75. John Deschner, "Legitimating, Limiting, Pluralism," *Christianity and Crisis* 50: 10/11 (July 15, 1991), pp. 230–232. The two-page text passed at Canberra is available from Faith and Order, World Council of Churches, Box 2100, CH-1211, Geneva 2, Switzerland.

76. Russell, "Searching for a Round Table in Church and World," in *Women and Church*, ed. by Melanie A. May, pp. 177–178.

6: Spirituality of Connection

1. The inscription on the quilt reads: "This quilt was designed by and crafted by: Michele Basche, Sarah Taylor and Alison Heston. With the help of: Dineen Dowling, Diana Varela, Kathy Haga and Marjorie Conine. Through the encouragement and appreciation of: The many generations of women and students with whom Letty has shared her life, knowledge and insights.

   "And because of the inspiration and courage of: Our mothers, sisters, aunts, grandmothers, cousins and role models who taught us to stitch the many colored and richly lived remnants of herstories, lives and dreams into brightly patterned quilts of sisterhood which empower us and give us courage to warm, comfort and sustain one another.

   "It is with great love, admiration and joy that all the women from all the years at Yale Divinity School give this quilt, The Sister's Choice, to Letty Russell. February 15, 1990."

2. Quoted by Delores Williams, "Feminist/Womanist Dialogue: Problems and Possibilities." Unpublished lecture delivered at Yale Divinity School on March 2, 1992. This need to bear witness by remembering the story of your people is highlighted in the Introduction of *Bearing Witness: Selections from African-American Autobiography in the Twentieth Century,* ed. Henry Lewis Gates, Jr. (New York: Pantheon Books, 1991), p. 6. Toni Morrison talks about "rememory" in *Beloved* (New York: Alfred A. Knopf, 1987), p. 215.

3. Walter Kendrick, "A Quilt, Not a Tapestry," review of *Sister's Choice: Tradition and Change in American Women's Writings* by Elaine Showalter, *New York Times Book Review,* Dec. 29, 1991, p. 10. In 1992 the AIDS Memorial Quilt had close to two hundred thousand names and more than twenty thousand panels when it was displayed at the steps of the capitol in Washington, D.C. The NAMES Project that coordinates the quilt was founded in 1987 "to illustrate the enormity of the epidemic by showing the humanity behind the statistics." Publicity from the NAMES Project, 2362 Market Street, San Francisco, CA 94114-9926.

4. See Alice Walker, *The Color Purple* (New York: Harcourt Brace Jovanovich, 1982), p. 53.

5. This chapter is developed out of the Spring Lectures on Spirituality of Connection, delivered by Letty M. Russell at Garrett Evangelical Theological Seminary on April 21–22, 1992.

6. Nelle Morton, *The Journey Is Home* (Boston: Beacon Press, 1985).

7. In regard to meeting the need for "Reclaiming Spirituality and Community as Gay Men and Lesbians," see Chris Glaser, *Come Home!*

8. See Robert Bly, *Iron John: A Book About Men* (New York: Addison-Wesley Publishing Co., 1990); Sam Keen, *Fire in the Belly: On Being a Man* (New York: Bantam Books, 1991); James B. Nelson, *The Intimate Connection: Male Sexuality, Masculine Spirituality.*

9. For a critique of Robert Bly and the men's liberation movement see Jill Johnston, "Why Iron John Is No Gift to Women," *New York Times Book Review,*

Feb. 23, 1992, pp. 1, 28–33; Susan Brooks Thistlethwaite, "Great White Fathers"; and Garth Baker-Fletcher, "Escape Artists," *Christianity and Crisis* 51:19 (Jan. 13, 1992), pp. 416–420.

10. Zora Neale Hurston, *Their Eyes Were Watching God* (Urbana, Ill.: University of Illinois Press, 1978 [originally published in 1937]), p. 9.

11. Paula Giddings, unpublished speech at a convocation at Riverside Church, New York City, Oct. 1986, "When and Where I Enter: Soul Power of Black Women." The idea of a black woman having to "invent herself" because she has nothing to fall back on, "not maleness, not whiteness, not ladyhood, not anything," is from Toni Morrison and is quoted in Paula Giddings, *When and Where I Enter . . . The Impact of Black Women on Race and Sex in America* (New York: William Morrow & Co., 1984), p. 15.

12. Nelson, *The Intimate Connection*, p. 14.

13. Conversation with the Rev. Henna Han at Yale Divinity School on April 10, 1992.

14. Francine Cardman, "Liberating Compassion: Spirituality for a New Millennium," *The Way,* Jan. 1992, p. 3.

15. Mary Hunt, "Spirituality for Creative Survival," Tape #A 1795 from Credence Cassettes (National Catholic Reporter Publishing Co.), 1983.

16. "Keeping Body and Soul Together: Sexuality, Spirituality, and Social Justice," pp. 28–31.

17. This comment was frequently attributed to Bonhoeffer by my late husband, Hans Hoekendijk, but I do not know the written source. See Dietrich Bonhoeffer, *Letters and Papers from Prison* (New York: Macmillan Company, 1972), enlarged ed.

18. bell hooks, *Yearning* (Boston: South End Press, 1990), pp. 206–207.

19. Morton, *The Journey Is Home*, p. 164.

20. Nelson, *The Intimate Connection*, p. 127.

21. Unpublished lecture by Margaret Farley in a class on Feminist Theology and Ethics, Yale Divinity School, April 16, 1992.

22. Audre Lorde, *Sister Outsider*, p. 54.

23. Ibid., p. 55.

24. See Sally McFague's description of "The Love of God as Lover: Eros" in *Models of God*, pp. 130–131.

25. Carter Heyward, *Touching Our Strength: The Erotic as Power and the Love of God*, p. 99.

26. Joanna Dewey, "An End to Sacrifice," *Christianity and Crisis* 51; 10/11 (July 15, 1991), p. 213.

27. Chuck Lathrop, *A Gentle Presence*, p. 7.

28. Virginia Fabella, "Christology from an Asian Woman's Perspective," in *We Dare to Dream: Doing Theology as Asian Women*, ed. Virginia Fabella and Sun Ai Lee Park (Maryknoll, N.Y.: Orbis Books, 1990), pp. 7–8. Delores Williams and other womanist theologians also make the same point. See Delores Williams, "Black Women's Surrogacy Experiences," in *After Patriarchy: Feminist Transformations of the World Religions*, ed. Paula M. Cooey et al. (Maryknoll, N.Y.: Orbis Books, 1991), pp. 12–13.

29. Ernst Käsemann, *Essays on New Testament Themes*, p. 68.

30. Lorde, *Sister Outsider;* bell hooks, *Feminist Theory: From Margin to Center.* "Sister Outsider" comes from a poem by Audre Lorde entitled "Black Unicorn," about two sisters who are still outsiders to each other, in Audre Lorde, *Black Unicorn* (New York: W. W. Norton & Co., 1978), p. 106.

31. Lorde, "Age, Race, Class, and Sex: Women Defining Difference," *Sister Outsider*, pp. 114–123.

32. Lorde, *Sister Outsider*, pp. 110–113.

33. The idea of using the tools to saw off the corners of the table was shared with me by Joan Martin, June 17, 1992.

34. hooks, *Yearning*, p. 153.

35. Bernice Johnson Reagon, "Coalition Politics: Turning the Century," in *Home Girls: A Black Feminist Anthology*, ed. Barbara Smith (New York: Kitchen Table/Women of Color Press, 1983), pp. 356–357.

36. Susan Brooks Thistlethwaite, *Sex, Race, and God; Christian Feminism in Black and White* (New York: Crossroad, 1989), p. 141.

37. Lorde, *Sister Outsider*, p. 115.

38. "The Rainbow Connection," lyrics and music by Paul Williams and Kenny Ascher, Welbeck Music Corporation, c/o ATV Music Group, 6255 Sunset Boulevard, Los Angeles, CA 90028. The music was first shared with me by Julie Elaine Fitzpatrick of Guilford, Conn.

39. Carolyn McDade, "Trouble and Beauty," *This Tough-Spun Web: Songs of Global Struggle and Solidarity, Songs of Carolyn McDade*, Womancenter at Plainville, 76 Everett Skinner Road, Plainville, MA 02762.

40. The discussion of "worrying with God" is a revision and development of my "Living by the Word: Worrying with God," *Christian Century* 109:3 (Jan. 22, 1992), p. 65.

41. In the summer of 1979, Stendahl and I gave lectures at the Shalom Center, Augustana College, North Dakota. See Krister Stendahl, "God Worries About Every Ounce of Creation," *Harvard Divinity Bulletin* 9:5 (June/July 1979), p. 5.

42. James Forbes, "Is There a Word From the Lord—About Class?" unpublished sermon, Riverside Church, New York, July 28, 1991.

43. Paul D. Hanson, *The People Called: The Growth of Community in the Bible*, p. 403.

44. "Welcome Table," in *An Advent Sourcebook*, ed. Thomas O'Gorman (Chicago: Liturgy Training Publications, 1988), p. 50.

45. John Koenig, *New Testament Hospitality*, p. 111.

46. Beverly Wildung Harrison, ed., *Making the Connections: Essays in Feminist Social Ethics* (Boston: Beacon Press, 1985), p. 231.

47. Robert McAfee Brown, *Saying Yes and Saying No: Rendering to God and Caesar* (Philadelphia: Westminster Press, 1986), p. 11. See also his *Spirituality and Liberation: Overcoming the Great Fallacy.*

48. bell hooks, *Talking Back: Thinking Feminist/Thinking Black* (Boston: South End Press, 1989), pp. 10–18.

49. Walker, *The Color Purple*, pp. 164–168.

50. Carol Christ and Judith Plaskow, eds., *Weaving the Visions: New Patterns in Feminist Spirituality* (San Francisco: Harper & Row, 1989), pp. 1, 9.

51. Rosemary Radford Ruether, *Women-Church*, pp. 3–4. See also her *Womanguides: Readings Toward a Feminist Theology* (Boston: Beacon Press, 1985).

52. Nancy Richardson, "Feminist Theology/Feminist Pedagogy: An Experimental Program of the Women's Theological Center," *Journal of Feminist Studies in Religion* 1:2 (Fall 1985), pp. 115–122.

53. See Alice Walker, *In Search of Our Mothers' Gardens* (New York: Harcourt Brace Jovanovich, 1983), pp. xi–xii.

54. Beverly D. Johnson, "Loves Herself . . . Regardless: A Journey Toward Self-Discovery/Rediscovery," *WTC Newsletter*, Sept. 1991, p. 3. Available from the Women's Theological Center, P.O. Box 1200, Boston, MA 02117.

55. Conversation with Donna Bivens, Renae Scott, Joan Martin, Beverly Smith, and others at the board meeting of the Women's Theological Center, February 7, 1992, in Boston.

56. Letty M. Russell, *Growth in Partnership*, p. 33.

57. The other three women were Faye Moon, Sook Min Mullinax, and Hye Jung Park.

58. "Statement on Behalf of Chong Sun France: New York Free France Committee," 1992, c/o United Methodist Church, Washington and Waverly Avenues, Seaford, NY 11783.

   Chong Sun France was released from prison into the care of the Rainbow Church on December 30, 1992.

59. From an oral presentation on Liberation Spirituality, by Faye Moon and Sook Min Mullinax at the Ad Hoc Committee on Racism, Sexism, and Classism, Guilford, Conn., May 30, 1992.

60. Antionette Clark Wire, *The Corinthian Women Prophets*, p. 126.

61. The discussion of the guidelines for partnership of the Spirit is a revision and development of my "Living by the Word: Partnership of the Holy Spirit," *Christian Century* 108:37 (Dec. 18–25, 1991), p. 1193.

62. Wire, *The Corinthian Women Prophets*, pp. 122–128.

63. Ibid., pp. 126–128; Fiorenza, *In Memory of Her*, pp. 205–214.

Bibliography

"Baptism, Eucharist, and Ministry." Faith and Order Paper No. 111. Geneva: World Council of Churches, 1982.

Barreiro, Alvaro. *Basic Ecclesial Communities: The Evangelization of the Poor.* Maryknoll, N.Y.: Orbis Books, 1982.

Boff, Leonardo. *Ecclesiogenesis: The Base Communities Reinvent the Church.* Trans. Robert R. Barr. Maryknoll, N.Y.: Orbis Books, 1986.

Brown, Robert McAfee. *Spirituality and Liberation: Overcoming the Great Fallacy.* Philadelphia: Westminster Press, 1988.

————, ed., *Kairos: Three Prophetic Challenges to the Church.* Grand Rapids: Wm. B. Eerdmans Publishing Co., 1990.

Chung Hyun Kyung. *Struggle to Be the Sun Again: Introducing Asian Women's Theology.* Maryknoll, N.Y.: Orbis Books, 1990.

"Church and World: The Unity of the Church and the Renewal of Human Community." Faith and Order Paper No. 151. Geneva: World Council of Churches, 1990.

Commission on Theological Concerns of the Christian Conference of Asia. *Minjung Theology: People as the Subjects of History.* Maryknoll, N.Y.: Orbis Books, 1983.

Cone, James H. *Speaking the Truth: Ecumenism, Liberation, and Black Theology.* Grand Rapids: Wm. B. Eerdmans Publishing Co., 1986.

"Confessing the One Faith: An Ecumenical Explication of the Apostolic Faith as It Is Confessed in the Nicene-Constantinopolitan Creed." Faith and Order Paper No. 153. Geneva: World Council of Churches, 1991.

Duck, Ruth C. *Gender and the Name of God: The Trinitarian Baptismal Formula.* New York: Pilgrim Press, 1991.

Dulles, Avery. *A Church to Believe In: Discipleship and the Dynamics of Freedom.* New York: Crossroad, 1987.

Fabella, Virginia, and Mercy Amba Oduyoye, eds. *With Passion and Compassion: Third World Women Doing Theology.* Maryknoll, N.Y.: Orbis Books, 1988.

Felder, Cain Hope, ed. *Stony the Road We Trod: African American Biblical Interpretation.* Minneapolis: Fortress Press, 1991.

Fiorenza, Elisabeth Schüssler. *Bread Not Stone: The Challenge of Feminist Biblical Interpretation.* Boston: Beacon Press, 1984.

————. *In Memory of Her: A Feminist Reconstruction of Christian Origins.* New York: Crossroad, 1983.

Frye, Marilyn. *The Politics of Reality: Essays in Feminist Theory.* Freedom, Calif.: Crossing Press, 1983.

Glaser, Chris. *Come Home! Reclaiming Spirituality and Community as Gay Men and Lesbians.* San Francisco: Harper & Row, 1990.

Hanson, Paul D. *The People Called: The Growth of Community in the Bible.* San Francisco: Harper & Row, 1986.

Helgesen, Sally, *The Female Advantage: Women's Ways of Leadership.* Garden City, N.Y.: Doubleday & Co./Currency, 1990.

Heyward, Carter. *Touching Our Strength: The Erotic as Power and the Love of God.* San Francisco: Harper & Row, 1989.

Hodgson, Peter C. *Revisioning the Church: Ecclesial Freedom in the New Paradigm.* Philadelphia: Fortress Press, 1988.

hooks, bell. *Feminist Theory: From Margin to Center.* Boston: South End Press, 1984.

Käsemann, Ernst. *Essays on New Testament Themes.* Studies in Biblical Theology No. 41. London: SCM Press, 1964.

"Keeping Body and Soul Together: Sexuality, Spirituality, and Social Justice." Louisville, Ky.: General Assembly of the Presbyterian Church (U.S.A.), 1991.

Kinnamon, Michael. *Truth and Community: Diversity and Its Limits in the Ecumenical Movement.* Grand Rapids: Wm. B. Eerdmans Publishing Co., 1988.

Koenig, John. *New Testament Hospitality: Partnership with Strangers as Promise and Mission.* Philadelphia: Fortress Press, 1985.

Küng, Hans. *The Church.* New York: Sheed & Ward, 1967.

Lathrop, Chuck. "In Search of a Roundtable," in *A Gentle Presence.* Washington, D.C.: Appalachian Documentation (ADOC), 1977, pp. 5–8. Reprinted in Janet Schaffran and Pat Kozak, *More than Words: Prayer and Ritual for Inclusive Communities.* New York: Meyer Stone Books, 1988, pp. 159–162.

Loades, Ann, ed. *Feminist Theology: A Reader.* Louisville, Ky.: Westminster/John Knox Press, 1990.

Lorde, Audre. *Sister Outsider: Essays and Speeches.* Trumansburg, N.Y.: Crossing Press, 1984.

May, Melanie A., ed. *Women and Church: The Challenge of Ecumenical Solidarity in an Age of Alienation.* Grand Rapids: Wm. B. Eerdmans Publishing Co., 1991.

McFague, Sallie. *Models of God: Theology for an Ecological Nuclear Age.* Philadelphia: Fortress Press, 1987.

McNeill, John J. *The Church and the Homosexual.* 3rd ed. Boston: Beacon Press, 1988.

Moltmann, Jürgen, *The Church in the Power of the Spirit: A Contribution to Messianic Ecclesiology.* San Francisco: Harper & Row, 1977.

Neal, Marie Augusta. *The Just Demands of the Poor.* New York: Paulist Press, 1987.

Nelson, James B. *The Intimate Connection: Male Sexuality, Masculine Spirituality.* Philadelphia: Westminster Press, 1988.

Oduyoye, Mercy Amba, and Musimbi R. A. Kanyoro. *The Will to Arise: Women, Tradition, and the Church in Africa.* Maryknoll, N.Y.: Orbis Books, 1992.

Palmer, Parker J. *The Company of Strangers: Christians and the Renewal of America's Public Life.* New York: Crossroad, 1983.

Procter-Smith, Marjorie. *In Her Own Rite: Constructing Feminist Liturgical Tradition.* Nashville: Abingdon Press, 1990.

Rhodes, Lynn N. *Co-Creating: A Feminist Vision of Ministry.* Philadelphia: Westminster Press, 1987.

Roof, Wade Clark, and William McKinney. *American Mainline Religion: Its Changing Shape and Future.* New Brunswick, N.J.: Rutgers University Press, 1987.

Ruether, Rosemary Radford. *Sexism and God-Talk: Toward a Feminist Theology.* Boston: Beacon Press, 1983.

———. *Women-Church: Theology and Practice of Feminist Liturgical Communities.* San Francisco: Harper & Row, 1985.

Russell, Letty M. *Household of Freedom: Authority in Feminist Theology.* Philadelphia: Westminster Press, 1987.

———. *Growth in Partnership.* Philadelphia: Westminster Press, 1981.

———, ed. *The Church with AIDS: Renewal in the Midst of Crisis.* Louisville, Ky.: Westminster/John Knox Press, 1990.

———. *Feminist Interpretation of the Bible.* Philadelphia: Westminster Press, 1985.

Russell, Letty M., et al., eds. *Inheriting Our Mothers' Gardens.* Philadelphia: Westminster Press, 1988.

Sample, Tex. *U.S. Lifestyles and Mainline Churches: A Key to Reaching People in the '90s.* Louisville, Ky.: Westminster/John Knox Press, 1990.

Schillebeeckx, Edward. *Church: The Human Story of God.* New York: Crossroad, 1990.

Schreiter, Robert J. *Constructing Local Theologies.* Maryknoll, N.Y.: Orbis Books, 1985.

Scroggs, Robin. *Paul for a New Day.* Philadelphia: Fortress Press, 1977.

Smith, Christine M. *Weaving the Sermon: Preaching in a Feminist Perspective.* Louisville, Ky.: Westminster/John Knox Press, 1989.

Sobrino, Jon. *Spirituality of Liberation: Toward Political Holiness.* Maryknoll, N.Y.: Orbis Books, 1988.

Stendahl, Krister. *Paul Among Jews and Gentiles.* Philadelphia: Fortress Press, 1976.

Tamez, Elsa. *The Scandalous Message of James: Faith Without Works Is Dead.* Maryknoll, N.Y.: Orbis Books, 1990.

Thistlethwaite, Susan Brooks, and Mary Potter Engel, eds. *Lift Every Voice: Constructing Christian Theologies from the Underside.* San Francisco: Harper & Row, 1990.

Torres, Sergio, and John Eagleson, eds. *The Challenge of Basic Christian Communities.* Maryknoll, N.Y.: Orbis Books, 1981.

Wire, Antionette Clark. *The Corinthian Women Prophets: A Reconstruction Through Paul's Rhetoric.* Philadelphia: Fortress Press, 1990.

Zikmund, Barbara Brown. *Discovering the Church.* Philadelphia: Westminster Press, 1983.

Index of Scripture References

Index of Subjects

Index of Names

Printed in the United States
16701LVS00005B/1-24